# Think Big! Become Big!!

## Fulfil Your Dreams!



Tarun Engineer

DIAMOND BOOKS

**Publisher** : **Diamond Pocket Books (P) Ltd.**
X-30, Okhla Industrial Area, Phase-II
New Delhi-110020
Phone : 011-40712200
E-mail : wecare@diamondbooks.in
Website : www.diamondbooks.in
Edition : 2025

---

Think Big! Become Big!! Fulfil Your Dreams!
by: *Tarun Engineer*

# Dedicated

in memory of my

**mother**

(Late Urmila Rastogi)

who taught me to write,

**My father**

(Shree Ram Nath Rastogi)

who sent me to study at

Nainital

and

**My wife**

(Shreemati Preeti Rastogi)

who influenced me

to write

**THINK BIG, BECOME BIG!**

Fulfil Your Dreams!

Everybody wishes to become

**Dhirubhai Ambani,**

but doesn't
think like him.

**The book**
**is written for those**
**who merely dream to become**
**the richest person but don't**
**become so in reality. So, it is**
**advised to you that keep this**
**book intact from those**
**who want to be opulent**
**before you.**

**Dream**
does not come
during sleeping hours.
Dreams are those
that don't allow you to sleep
but perplex you to
fulfil those dreams.

# THINK BIG! BECOME BIG!

## Fulfil Your Dreams!

I have queried my six-year old daughter Vilsha, when she qualified through UKG, '*What is your ambition when you grow old?*'

She answered after thinking upon wry smile, '*I wish to become some heroine like Aishwarya Rai.*'

I told after gazing her, on being taken aback over her swift answer, '*Why do you wish to become heroine?*

She went on thinking for a while, and said, '*I am deeply interested in dance. It is pretty good for me to copy others' acts. So, I wish to become the heroine. I believe I shall have utmost happiness on working in films. It shall remain the cause for my becoming bigger, which could make me realize about the spiritual bliss.*'

I went on wondering how bigger ambition the young girl had in her life. Could she justify her ambition? My conscience replied, '*Yes, why not? It might be so.*' '*How could we become bigger when stop dreaming over such thoughts?* So, think for a while, do so in hurry. Think always big.' For, some lyricist has claimed,

*Each difficulty being carved out in our destiny*
*Any response could make enjoy celestial bliss*
*Your frequent gaze towards the horizon!*
*Shall fetch impetus to align with such horizon!*

It is true that seldom shall any invisible force trod in to mobilize you to think big. You should make yourself self-confident. You need not proclaim about your ambition. You could become that big shot on your sustained efforts. However, you need to chalk out some objective and hold yourself till you attain such objective. The book could become some effective guide on that ground.

*However, how should one chalk out an objective? How should he become successful in materializing such objective? The book could transform your life and make you some big shot through its formulae.* Give some thought to read unless you feel yourself confident.

**–Tarun Engineer**

# AN ENTREATY

*Think always something anew,*
*Have some big spirit from within.*
*The job in which you get involved*
*You'll have overall progress in that.*
*Neither been you worthless nor unjust*
*Your dreams shall have superior spirit.*
*Stoop unto your work*
*You shall get your path.*
*Lit back your extinguished lamp*
*The goddess of wealth shall reach your bode*
*Have confidence on yourself,*
*Your entreaty shall get fulfilled*
*Dream through eyes wide open,*
*You shall have strength from bigger thought*
*It will browse through your characters,*
*The volume shall trod you the path.*
*Get your mind involved in bigger thought,*
*Your fortune shall blossom some day ahead.*

The entreaty could be the most splendid one. The treatise could be an appropriate response. For, the volume would make you struggle and work accordingly. It would compel you to become some big shot. It would mobilize you to become so.

*The Sermon of the Lord* (Bhagavad-Gita) would make you venturesome. Epics such as the *Ramayana* would make you work-oriented; *Mahabharata* could make you acquainted with the strategies of war. A thinker has claimed an entreaty owes to confidence and the confidence remains the wheels of such chariot. It shall have proportionally deeper impact on earth, the more it becomes burdensome.

You could say something about such entreaty. For, the lines of entreaty shall gallop towards the objective. It shall have deeper impact of success on enlivened earth.

# HOW COULD THIS VOLUME TRANSFORM YOUR FUTURE?

*"He alone could get things unless his spirit is at stake,*
*He would loose things to tread by saving everything."*

The above statement applies on us. For, the uppermost porch of our body remains like some complex riddle. However, a few believe that our brain thinks more. The guys with such bigger brain have the stamina to think big. Such guys would be extremely intelligent.

You will get into serious thinking on my vetoing about this statement. An elephant among the fauna could have survived as the most intelligent mammal unless the statement holds the truth. Lion is smaller in size to an elephant. It has appreciably smaller brain but proves to be extremely intelligent.

The same analogy applies on homosapiens. The more the size of human brain, the more he could prove to be intelligent. Examples of Indian heads of government such as Lal Bahadur Shastri and Manmohan Singh have justified their intelligence in reigning over the Indian mass. So, think not about your insignificance. Can't you think big? You could do everything, which you desire often.

For, you've the latent desire to become big. You could influence history. You could become an influential personality. You need to be bold by moving forward with firmness sparing from obstinacy. For, you have to become superior with respect to others. You need to think big, making such objective and fulfill your dreams. But how come! The volume will tell about some techniques. It is enough you emulate the under mentioned formulae in your practical life:

A question arises in us to think whether
we can become opulent on observing big personalities.

—TARUN ENGINEER

The book
is replete with formulae
in becoming
the richest person
in the world analogous to
the large hadron collider
used for solving knotty issues
irretrievable from
the cosmos.

# CONTENTS

# PRAYER FOR SURVIVAL

*I do survive without any objective*
*Is this any mode of survival?*
*Seldom there be glimpse of happiness!*
*Is this any mode of survival?*

*The cart of my physical age*
*I do drag that pretty farther*
*The burden of affliction and humiliation*
*Why should I drag that everyday?*

*The umbrella casts severe darkness*
*I do get rather frightened*
*Seldom could I get happiness*
*I shall get annihilated in my dreams.*

*I do survive without any objective*
*Is this any mode of survival?*
*Seldom there be glimpse of happiness*
*Is this any mode of survival?*

*Laughter subjects itself under vigil*
*What shall happen for the agony?*
*Could I become something in my career?*
*My heart was taken aback over frequent thinking.*

*How long should I get burnt?*
*I have the will to become something*
*Hi lord, the Almighty, open the gates*
*My life has-been cherished for Thee!*

*I do survive without any objective*
*Is this any mode of survival?*
*Seldom there be glimpse of happiness!*
*Is this any mode of survival?*

# WHY THE NEED FOR ANOTHER VOLUME?

Why have I scripted the volume *Think Big! Become Big?* The market has been flooded with thousands of titles on this subject. I have targeted three points in devising the formulae.

- *Most of the titles brought in the market were enlightening you of the dream journey, far from reality.*
- *The enshrined facts were seldom found feasible for Indian economy, without influencing you at all.*
- *Most of the titles were written by those writers who were treading through miserable life.*

However, I have been the professional businessman, adapting the concept of industrialist Dhirubhai Ambani—*Think Big! Become Big!* I have been subjected to slew of trials and tribulations in making my business outstretch across the continents. So, the volume was not scripted by any writer, other than the experience of a successful businessman hailing from an ordinary family. I have made utmost efforts through my vocabulary so that you could become some big shot thereby fulfilling your dreams. Anybody has the will to become successful in life. It doesn't mean that mere thinking could make you successful. Your dreams shall flourish as long as your failure to emulate the efficacious means to become successful in real life. You need to practice those means of efficacy unless you wish to bring back into reality.

- The first means of efficacy is to stay put on your decision. Confidence is the sine qua non. For, it could put you undeterred in life proportional to the decision you have undertaken.

*It has been justified from the research that about seventy per cent of paradise seekers swerve from their objective on being frightened of their maiden failures. The guys could seldom reach the horizons of success in their lives. However, the twenty per cent of those left over shall stay firm in their decisions despite initial failures. Certainly, they would become successful in their lives irrespective of them being delayed in definite approach.*

- *Everybody looks well prepared irrespective of its gainsaying when the issue of taking suitable advice comes into picture. It could lead to sheer difficulties on whom should one rely upon.*

*It could have been better for them with least possible expertise in specific field so that they accept suitable advice from successful paradise seekers. Moreover, you could learn more from such guys who have suffered failures. Generally speaking, they could make out better plans, but remain unsuccessful in executing them. You could learn lessons from their failures.*

- *You need to evaluate how far your plan had been successful while executing such plans in real life. You had to find out whether you're getting the desired success in life? You need to change such options in the time available, if not. It would save you from those hardships arising from swerving off the objectives.*
- *Successful paradise seekers shall remain aloof from worthless lot. For, their thoughts get neutralized on aligning with them. Avoid from mingling with such guys on your desire of becoming splendidly successful. Keep your thoughts positive for ever. Lose not your self-confidence under any circumstance.*
- *The probability of your success becomes more had your friend in specific field been successful. Obviously, such guys would get motivated and would influence you to become successful.*

*You would tread the path of success on aligning with such guys, when you get induced from their positive thoughts.*

- *Lord, the Almighty has bestowed any human being with certain pluses. You need to identify those pluses. Identify such happiness latent within you through introspection and stabilize your forte. Nobody will object you from becoming successful.*
- *Knowledge, of course, is the key to success. Go on updating such knowledge through periodic harnessing. Have an attitude to learn constantly. Such bits of knowledge would make you tread afar and enhance your desire to become successful.*
- *People often think themselves to live in reality rather upon fantasies. It doesn't mean you should stop dreaming. You need to visualize such dreams so that you've the motive to fulfill such dreams.*

*Focus on your mental catharsis on finding self-drifting apart from your objective. Think frequently about your objective. Shut your eyes and realize within you on reaching the destination. Accustom such practice at least thrice a day. See to yourself how far the self-confidence in you propels up.*

- *Hard work alone could lead you straight in transforming your plan. Bear in mind your dreams could seldom be fulfilled so long as you wouldn't work hard.*

The adage claims—*One who apperceives the importance of Time could find oneself being glorified by the monster. Appreciate the importance of Time and always be prepared to tread ahead in the path of success.*

The formula of efficacy will always help but how will you enjoy? Certainly, the treatise shall help you in achieving such success. For, the hypothesis of *Think Big! Become Big* has been incorporated and analyzed on the specimens of thinking adapted by industrial giants in their practical lives. The giants have not only stabilized Indian economy at each stage but also have successfully fathomed the path from ground level to the zenith.

Your desires in browsing through this page warrant us believe of you becoming damn impatient in reaching the destination and becoming successful giant proportional to the quantum of your desire. For, this volume shall help you in acquiring success at each stage. How to become some giant through perseverance thereby fulfilling your dreams?

For, Prashant Yogi, an Indian philosopher advises you to read this treatise without fail in order to fulfill your ambition in your life as desired earlier.

For, this volume could transform you in becoming some giant. It doesn't warrant you to have unbelievable bank balance other than mere thinking with firm will in your mind. It could be tantamount to the famous billionaire Henry Ford, who has designed and develop his model *'Ford'* of four-wheeler.

Henry Ford was born to some poor family. He couldn't even get two square meals a day. He wore rags without even possessing any new wear during Christmas. However, he dreamt of becoming

> Reject the idea of becoming – **laity.**
> Oppose the idea of being – **the medium**
> Plan to become the giant for, an idea is necessary for becoming **big personality.**

the billionaire some day in life. He made up his mind to become elite-some day, with such dream without any penny to eke out his livelihood.

However, he had the will to do so, which made him get the loan of some five dollars from his friend. He went on repairing punctured bicycle tubes on pavement from early morning to late night.

Ford stuck to his routine after returning the money he had to owe within a fortnight. He went on lending two used bicycles for the needy following their buy. He opened a shop repairing the bicycles. Meanwhile, he began buying and selling bicycles when his business was through. The development transformed him into big trader dealing with two-wheeler bicycles. He bought an old car after sometime. He went on overhauling the four-wheeler, on appreciating the mystery of dismantling. He laid the foundation stone for manufacturing the four-wheeler Ford. He became the richest persona on earth on his nearing death.

So, Henry Ford, born and brought up in a poor family has justified in the world of someone becoming giant through strong will. Now, it is enough of you emulating his principles of working hard. For, the strong will have some hidden force. This treatise will enlighten you through such formulae of stabilizing one's hidden will power. You need to stabilize the thoughts leading to strong will power through browsing and imbibing in your practical life through utter seriousness. You need to repeat the performances of those millions of readers.

Don't make delay. Go ahead. For, less time is available to unlock your sealed destiny.

> **The giants in the universe become so owing to their sustained efforts and struggles rather from destinies.**
>
> —Tarun Engineer

# A PRAYER FOR AN OBJECTIVE

Oh lord, the Almighty, shower mercy on me,
Let me offer my salutations unto Thee.
Enlivening Thy image in my heart,
Let me tread ahead towards my objective.

Vices galore have permeated in this universe,
Keep me isolated from the influence of vices.
Vouch me with such boon forever
Let my dreams get fulfilled at the earliest.

I have the ambition of becoming much more,
Guide me forever in Thy desired path.
My life appears like some rosy flower
But, I wish to tread on its thorns....

Bestow me with Thy immense power,
Let me glorify about my acts and deeds.
My eyes were replete with scores of dreams,
Let me fulfill those unaccomplished dreams.

Oh lord, the Almighty, shower mercy on me,
Let me offer my salutations unto Thee.
Enlivening Thy image in my heart.
Let me tread ahead towards my objective.

# DO YOU WISH TO BECOME BILLIONAIRE?

Do you dream of becoming a billionaire? My dear! Please browse through this treatise on your endorsement. Man dreaming about paradises alone could fulfill them. You need to self-evaluate how far your dreams are true? Disallow anyone coveting of your dreams. Hear what your conscience addresses you irrespective of its outcome ahead.

Let me recollect some small story, which my mother used to share quite frequently. A tiny tot belonged to some poor family, whose father was a clerk in local hospital.

The boy went on changing schools from this fact. He was asked to write an essay when he reached in higher class, whose title was—*What would you do on becoming an adult?*

The pupil (boy) wrote an essay of seven pages. He mentioned about raising some private hospital equipped with ultra equipments of treatment available around the world, on qualifying as some specialist. He mentioned comprehensively about his dream, and drew the portrait of 200-acre land sporting various buildings, operation theatre and emergency wards.

He drew also the image of staff quarters, which he desired to raise as an annexure to the private hospital.

He handed the essay to his class teacher on explaining about his prospective project. The teacher asked the boy to meet him after the recess, returning the specimen, graded with F *(failed)*.

The dreaming pupil sought the teacher during recess, '*Why have you disqualified me?*'

The teacher replied irresponsibly, '*You have written the essay as some figment of imagination. For, the raising of such hospital needs appreciable funds. You belong to some poor family without any resources. You couldn't complete the project under any circumstances. I am well prepared to reevaluate your performance on some achievable objective within your means.'*

The boy went on pondering over the thought seriously on returning home. He told the teacher, *'Earmark with your grading forever. I shall keep my dream forever,'* reproducing the same essay after weeklong deliberation.

The teacher got the invitation after nearly two decades inauguration of that hospital. Someone touched the feet of the teacher after the inaugural ceremony. He has already fulfilled his dreams of achieving the superiority status in the field of physicians.

I believe the materialization of his dreams on the counts of positive thinking. You also need to fulfill your dreams in letter and spirit, because the term positive attributes practically something else.

It will describe–

P–O–S–I–T–I–V–E

P : Patience
O : Optimistic
S : Satisfaction
I : Inspiration
T : Target
I : Ideal
V : Victor
E : Easy

**Patience:** Patience is the most eligible key to success. It is quite obvious of your patient approach disallowing any negative thoughts. 'I couldn't avail this opportunity.' 'Alas, my ward could have been extraordinary.' 'What will happen now following my spouse losing his job?'

Such comments would seldom achieve any objective. You could be swerved from such worry had you enliven the confidence and explore every possibility over some solution under such crisis.

**Optimistic**: Always remain optimistic in approach. For, your hopes galore alone could make you reach the staircase of destination. *'Disappointment often finds me relieved from scores of riddles. I shall avail the opportunity now. Always stay on such thoughts.' 'Curse not about your destiny as shattered. Everybody in the world is pretty insecure from my deeds.'* Give a trial for such optimism, when all the riddles will perish without any ado.

**Satisfaction**: Always remain contented and happy forever. You would go on thinking about positive thoughts the moment you appear satisfied. Always remain happy on whatever and how far you have had. Scriptures eulogize that *Santosham paramasukham.*

The world doesn't have anything other than happiness. The psychiatrist Prabhakar Pande claims about *happiness as the only available recourse during depression.*

**Inspiration**: Take some inspiration. It is obvious someone gets inspired from some other person or object. Get inspired from those who remains always happy in his (her) life. Everybody has some plus points in his (her) life. Someone might be organized; somebody else might be venturesome or other thinking about positive thoughts and yet another flaring up with positive sentiments.

**Target**: Keep your objective alive forever. Seldom could you find disappointed or penniless without any fixed objective. *What should you do? When should you do? Where should you do?* Ascertaining about such agenda is optional. You should be prepared with alternative option. *You need not think of becoming an engineer or doctor or go for becoming a musician, or remain vapid throughout life.*

**Ideal**: Always remain an ideal for others. You should orient your personality in such manner making others emulate your ideals forever. *Ascertain whether you emulate the ideals of your parents or teacher.* Certainly, someone might have specific traits that could influence your career. Why don't you become such ideal for others?

**Victor**: Always remain triumphant. Make it an objective. Get not disheartened on frequent failures but go ahead with renewed vigour. Always believe that success and failure alternate frequently in life. Don't lose your confidence on failure. *Persuade yourself frequently that someday you would be successful.*

**Easy**: Let your mission be real and easier. For, the people enjoying real life seldom entertain negative thoughts. Let them live the real life to that of artificial one! You would never encounter any difficulty. Such reality should be the part of your domestic and professional life.

It could create some obstacle in your success, but others will also sideline on being disturbed about your behaviour.

So, this is the secret of the term *positive*, working wonders like some panacea during the intrinsic thought process. Only those will become the giants in life who emulate such principles in letter and spirits.

Your browsing of this page could endorse you to become an eligible giant. You might fulfill the ambition in your life. You wish to accomplish that objective for which you have dreamt. You have held the book to sustain your burning ambition and exploring tools to accomplish the objectives.

This is an intrinsic trait latent in you, which availed you of this wonderful treatise. The treatise is an armoury capable of overhauling your personality by awakening your skills.

It could make you over-confident compelling you to think big, asunder—

*A car mechanic produces new model through the debris of an old.*

*A carpenter assembles new lattice through the worthless pieces of wood.*

*A mason would build new building through debris of dilapidated home.*

*A draper would produce new ready-to-wear garments through rags.*

*An electrician could produce fluorescent lamp anew from fused tube.*

Perhaps, you might be thinking why not every citizen become billionaire provided the book is made available across the country.

The reason being everyone would seldom think alike. S/he could have been billionaire had s/he thought so.

*You have to think of becoming a billionaire in the world like Dhirubhai Ambani, hailing from poor background.*

*You need to think of being a super celluloid star like Amitabh Bachchan despite being raised through non-celluloid environment.*

**The interest in your objective is dependent on your thirst. For, you will work for the objective with deep attachment proportional to the intensity of your thirst.**

*You need to think of becoming an astronaut like Kalpana Chawla who became the first woman astronaut in the world despite being born in Karnal (Haryana).*

*You have to think of becoming Kiran Bedi, the maiden Indian Police Service woman officer in the country despite being born in middle class lineage.*

*You have to think of becoming Dilip Singh Rana, despite being born in a poor family, joined the ranks of oiled cakes in the W. W. F. toiling day and night.*

You need to think about such persons, who have dreamt of becoming the giants in their own spheres. Upanishads, which deify the creator Brahma, claims—

*Manaevar Manushyaanaam Kaaranam bandhamokshyo*
*Bandhasya vishayaasaktam muktye nirvisham smritam.*

It signifies that mind alone owes to man's attachment and salvation. Mind attracted to worldly pleasures becomes the cause of detachment through issueless identity. For, mind remains infinite, to say, it has immense power.

**Your brain has hundreds of acres of fertile land but what you sow on it depends on your self-confidence.**

Mind functions through conscious, unconscious and semi-conscious planes. It carries the activities such as determining, or finding out alternative options or sustained thinking and deliberation. Successful people vanquish the spate of difficulties regulating their mind.

They flee across the space without leaving the plane by believing the phase of failure as some unbelievable incident. For, they knew that success could be gained through hard work and perseverance rather from destiny. It happens to be the principal hypothesis to get success in their lives.

So, you need to think big from this very day. You could become so proportional to the mode of thinking. For, mind has its own control panel, regulating the cell structure of the entire body. So, you could ascertain the outcome of your destiny changing you altogether at the cost of your directives.

*You will realize about giant course of happiness.*
*You shall have inflated revenue.*
*Your friend will become influential.*
*You shall have enhanced stature in the world.*

Do you want *'yes,'* delay not anymore through swift endorsement. Commence immediately and realize how you are directing your brain to think. Everybody seeks such stature from you. For, Dhirubhai Ambani said sometime back, *'Think Big,*

*Think swiftly. Transform such thought into reality. You could become some giant like me.'*

You could learn from this treatise on *earning more money or improving the status of your business or get some plum job or transform altogether your thoughts or fulfill your dreams into reality, or live happily forever.*

However, you need to expel the fear, which is putting you unstable. You might have dreamt about bigger paradises. You need to transform your body to work extremely hard. You need to think like political leaders.

Go ahead in browsing through the data provided you're interested in undertaking the job. For, the treatise has explained how to amplify your thoughts and reach the zenith of success in the pages ahead.

–TARUN ENGINEER
301 3rd Floor, Raj Kamal Sadan
Community Centre, Preet Vihar
NEW DELHI-110 092 (INDIA)

Mobile : (O)9899153952
e-mail : tarunengineer2003@yahoo.com

# IMAGINE YOURSELF TO BE SUCCESSFUL

I used to dream of such positions of eminence, when I was pretty young. I used to dream of becoming a celluloid hero, or a lyricist or an engineer, or a writer of eminence or a businessman or a playback singer.

However, the sole ambition behind such dreams was something else, which I wish to let you know.

Imagine about my sole ambition. I wish to know from you what sort of dream you fantasize to brighten your future and change altogether accordingly.

Everybody is bound to dream in life. *Perhaps, you too could dream so. It might be so, you might have dreamt of becoming the splendid fortune seeker in the world. You might have dreamt of becoming a famous hero or singer or writer, or politician or a radical thinker, not the least, an athlete or civil service officer.*

You might have fulfilled dreams of least or mediocre levels. However, you might have had some dream, for which, your heart might be yawning continuously to fulfill the unprecedented and biggest dream.

I shall let you know about the technique of fulfilling such dream, which is virtually based on psychological facts or truth. I am enclosing the list of most influential universal giants, who've established their identity in various fields. You had to evaluate the common ambition through the techniques of reasoning-reflex-conditioning. *The giants include, Indians such as Dhirubhai Ambani, Sonia Gandhi, Gulshan Nanda, Sachin Tendulkar, Amitabh Bachchan, Anil Moolchandani, M.F. Hussain, Hema Malini, Surinder Kapur, Kiran Bedi, Pankaj Advani, Sheila Dixit, Lakshmi Mittal, K.P. Singh and an American such as Henry Ford.*

Have you ever thought of such common feature amongst these giants, where their fields of eminence are pretty different?

Dhirubhai Ambani was a business magnate. He established Reliance Industries at meagre investment of 15,000 Indian rupees. Today, his sons Mukesh and Anil Ambani have been recognized as financial 'barons' across the continents.

Sonia Gandhi is the widow of slain Indian premier Rajiv Gandhi. She was hardly connected to the Indian political scenario. Today, she regulates the political arena through gestures. Millions of Indian brethren acknowledge her address as damn influential parameter.

> **Becoming big person does not depend on age or education but depends on how far you visualize biggest dreams.**

Gulshan Nanda underwent hardship during childhood. He penned many novels under the influence of invisible force. Many of his novels got filmed glorifying him as the emperor of literary society.

Amitabh Bachchan was born to the family of an ordinary poet. However, he carved a niche on the celluloid screen through the blend of roles, glorifying him to be the emperor of Indian celluloid screen—Bollywood.

Anil Moolchandani was selling saris in Delhi's Kamla Nagar market. Today, he is the managing director of departmental and stationary store—Archies.

M.F. Hussain was a small-time painter from Bangalore meandering through acute hardships. Today, his paintings fetch millions of dollars in the international museums including London's Sotheby art gallery.

Hema Malini was a Bharatanatyam (temple dance) dancer during her childhood. Indian celluloid screen has glorified her as a famous heroine. She has won and enthralled millions of fellow Indians as their *dream girl*, despite entering sixty of her age.

Surinder Kapur was some small-scale jeweller in Delhi's bullion market. Today, he is the chairman of Sona Group of Industries, which produces steering wheel of Maruti-Suzuki's car models.

Kiran Bedi became India's maiden police service officer despite being born to a middle class family. Delhites recollect her even today as "Crane Bedi," for her role as the traffic cop in lynching vehicles parked without any permission on Delhi roads. She has not spared in lynching the official car of former premier Indira Gandhi.

Pankaj Advani started playing billiards at the age of 21. He became the successful snooker player. Former president APJ Abdul Kalam felicitated him with 'Khel Ratna' award.

Sheila Dixit had her formal education from Jesus and Mary College in Delhi, though born at Punjab's Kapurthala. She is the chief minister of Delhi.

Lakshmi Mittal was born across Churu district of Rajasthan belonging to an ordinary lineage. He got into the business after qualifying for commerce degree from Saint Xavier's loluge of Calcutta. He is the steel giant of the world under the logo Arcelor Mittal Inc.

**Society ushers what you are, but this book lets how you become some giant.**

K.P. Singh hailing from Bulandshahar (Uttar Pradesh) controls the real estate through DLF Estates incorporated, as the chairman and managing director after resigning from the Indian Army.

Henry Ford, an American, had his formal education despite being born in a poor family. He had been acknowledged as the *"father of automobile industry"* across the continents for establishing some plant manufacturing Ford model cars.

Most of the personalities found in the list were rated as influential giants in their own specific fields. Could you evaluate the specific characteristic appearing as common amongst them?

We shall let you know for they have emulated the concept of 'Big Thinking', which helped them transform into giants in their respective fields, with no equivalents elsewhere for grand success.

The zenith of success means becoming the richest in the world. Such life often incorporates their stay in luxurious apartments with cozy comfort inaccessible to laity, holiday making, buying of new gadgets, regulating stable economy, relieved off the slew of worries and getting felicitated from time to time from the society of establishment.

I believe you ought to achieve success in life for enjoying life replete with happiness. Success would remain the hallmark of slew of achievements in life. Perhaps, you might be interested in achieving everything in life. Find out whether you're interested in achieving such success in life. George Bernard Shaw, the great philosopher believed, *'Books work like logistic support in the battlefront of ideas. People should read such books which influence them in transforming their lives altogether.'*

**Law of attraction claims like objects attracting similar objects. So, those who think of opulence, the richness get attracted to them.**

Hindi poet Dadu Dayal reinforces that idea into Indian society as,

*Dheev Doodh se rami rahya,*
*vyapak sab hee thaur*
*Dadu kahe jeevan ka satya,*
*mathi kaadhe te aur.*

Dadu describes man sporting such biggest thought just like milk possessing ghee. The biggest thought could be arrived at by sustained deliberation just like ghee extracted from similar churning.

Man goes on deliberating over negative aspect of such thinking for the future on being deprived of such capacity to ponder over the present state of development. *'Do deeds without expecting fruits either.'* They know very well of such initiation could mean completing the task to certain level. You need to recapitulate over the verse from the *Sermon of the Lord* (Shri Madbhagavadgeeta) to become versed with the technique of such deliberation.

*Uddharedatmanaatmanam Naatmanaamavasaadayet*
*Aatmaiava Hathaatmano Bandhuraatmaiva ripuraatmanaha.*

The interpretation goes as—lighten your spirit for achieving success in life. Keep yourself in power. Have confidence in your lineage deity of choice. Shun the slew of negative thoughts. Nobody else could do for your salvation other than thyself.

Accuse not anyone for your success or failure. For, you have been squarely responsible for thy acts and deeds. Your count down shall begin the moment you went on blowing your own trumpet for slew of successes.

The analogy has been reflected even in the Sermon of the Lord. The interpretation substantiates the state of development even today despite the verse scripted some eons before. One needs to deliberate over the significance of this verse before initiating any task anew.

***Karmanyevaadhyikaraste Maa phaleshu Kadachan!***

It describes *man to function without expecting any fruits for his acts and deeds.* Let him keep everything at stake. Shun from thinking anything while doing some task. For, it will have its impact on your future through overpowering thereby subjecting you over stress.

*Expect not the fruits won't mean you disclaim enjoy them.* Certainly, you'll reach the portals while doing such task.

However, the situation warrants you to chalk out some objective. It would bring confidence for anyone over such objective. The confidence would automatically influence the central nervous system to explore available options, techniques and plans in achieving such goal.

**I ought to become the giant..........**

**..............................**

**..........................**

**(Example, to become the giant like Dheerubhai Ambani)**

Perhaps, you have arrived at such plan endorsing about your future. Think of some giant who has inspired your thought system amongst the above list of giants. Write down the name of such giant in the box below.

## IMPETUS

Why hath thy investment burdensome?
Thou became an important entity.
Thou have charted out an objective.
The world shall laugh at thee.
Trod ahead rejecting the defeat ahead!
Thy destination is only four steps afar.
Acquaint something from this book.
The destiny could change thee altogether.
Always remain noble and worth thy salt.

You have pondered over such giant. He became the object of your impetus. You ought to become such and such giant at some stage in life. You need to ponder over the level of success for your fixing up of objective had been through at the moment.

This happens to be the formulae of efficacy of success. You need to constantly remember over this formula. Your future course would be ushered through this book. You had to emulate the techniques brought in the book. You have already the laboratory of choice as explained earlier.

Enlist some fifteen folks who're about to get successful. Incorporate only those whose objectives resemble the successful giants enlisted above. Explore the slew of positive thoughts; objectives and ideals that have lynched the giants to reach zenith in respective fields.

English poet Ralf W Emerson cites, *'Anybody with certain objective in life would certainly reach the point at some stage in life.'*

You shall find the shortlist of fifteen folks resemble your objectives of explained giants in respective fields. The folks were optimistic, firm in belief; possessed elevated thoughts, honest, perseverant, had faith in what they opt for, good orators, relieved of stress and remained euphoric in the field of their choice.

Believe me, some day your deliberation could certainly lynch you to the portals of success. *You ought to harness such virtues and vouchsafe honestly with firm belief in fulfilling your dreams with hard work and courage.*

❑

The giants in the world so far were so from their efforts and struggle but not from destiny.

–Tarun Engineer

# ANY TIME COULD SHAKE EVEN THE VALLEY

The analogy applies only for the courageous people. For, such guys could shake even the toughest valley on earth through positive, constructive and creative ideas. You shall find umpteen hypothesis, techniques and corresponding thoughts through this treatise.

It could transform your imagined personality altogether through variable thought process, *when you could stoop to earth from heavens.* The treatise has many examples through which you could reach the zenith of success, equating with one's real life, making you to assimilate with such techniques in letter and spirit.

It has ushered you to emulate such path through appropriate techniques for reaching the zenith of success.

Let me know how strong is your thought? It is very essential to know about its strength to ascertain the mode of assessing your life. A questionnaire of some 36 questions seeks your opinion. Tick the appropriate answer with 'Yes', or 'No'.

01. Do you ever dream? Yes ☐ No ☐
02. Have you any objective in life? Yes ☐ No ☐
03. Have you any set target? Yes ☐ No ☐
04. Do you believe in yourself? Yes ☐ No ☐
05. Are you capable of determining yourself? Yes ☐ No ☐
06. Do you have the forte to achieve something? Yes ☐ No ☐
07. Could you think alone? Yes ☐ No ☐
08. Do you have the ambition to explore? Yes ☐ No ☐
09. Do you venture in assimilating something? Yes ☐ No ☐
10. Do you desire to gift something for others? Yes ☐ No ☐
11. Are you optimistic about thoughts? Yes ☐ No ☐
12. Could you imagine something unbelievable? Yes ☐ No ☐
13. Do you discard unwanted objects? Yes ☐ No ☐

14. Could you underestimate the training skills? Yes ☐ No ☐
15. Are you frightened of staying in solitude? Yes ☐ No ☐
16. Are you physically weak? Yes ☐ No ☐
17. Are you capable of shoving somebody? Yes ☐ No ☐
18. Do you have awful dreams? Yes ☐ No ☐
19. Could you laugh at your way of life? Yes ☐ No ☐
20. Could you change yourself voluntarily? Yes ☐ No ☐
21. Could you persuade yourself? Yes ☐ No ☐
22. Do you believe in compromising? Yes ☐ No ☐
23. Could you downcast about others? Yes ☐ No ☐
24. Do you venture in hanging around? Yes ☐ No ☐
25. Could you give up complaining? Yes ☐ No ☐
26. Could you realign about yourself? Yes ☐ No ☐
27. Could you disseminate your knowledge to others? Yes ☐ No ☐
28. Do you hear what others comment? Yes ☐ No ☐
29. Do you share your secrecy with others? Yes ☐ No ☐
30. Are you afraid of working hard? Yes ☐ No ☐
31. Do you feel bored during serious work? Yes ☐ No ☐
32. Could you rethink on some topic? Yes ☐ No ☐
33. Could you hand self to somebody? Yes ☐ No ☐
34. Are you peeved quite frequently? Yes ☐ No ☐
35. Do you have faith in fortune? Yes ☐ No ☐
36. Do you feel euphoric on any issue? Yes ☐ No ☐

**Evaluate the scores of your answers.**

☑ You have been subjected to stressful life and drool around negative thoughts, when you score less than fifteen *Yes (s)*. You need to read the book in between lines, and work extremely hard to reach at the zenith of success.

☑ Your thought process hangs in balance when you score less than 25 *Yes (s)*. You neither could affiliate to negative nor positive thoughts. However, you brace ahead in assimilating to the changed circumstances voluntarily. Seldom have you any swiftness, or enthusiasm or motivation to tread ahead in life. You couldn't ascertain about your capability. You also need to read the book seriously to find yourself in the prospective path of success.

☑ You have positive thinking on scoring beyond 30 *Yes (s)*. You could fulfill your dreams in the least possible time at meagre reading. This could be the scientific technique ascertaining your thought process voluntarily from this book. So, read the under mentioned notes before going through the next chapter.

A hermit found a cub in a jungle. He went on rearing up the cub at his cottage with utmost love. The cub went on mingling with calves of sheep without ado in a couple of weeks. The cubs encountered a roaring adult lion on some day. The cub and calves tried to save their lives moving at random.

The adult lion wondered why the cub of lion was frightened of his roar. He persuaded the cub while taking near some pond, '*Why are you frightened? Are you a lion cub or a calf of sheep? See your shadow amidst the ripples of water. Repeat the roaring for yourself with gusto when I roar.*' The lion cub found its shadow resembling adult lion. It was overconfident of itself as the cub of lion but not the calf of some sheep.

The cub roared gently, whose roar resembled the adult lion. It was absolutely confident about the derived identity, which has hitherto failed to do so. Similarly, you've forgotten about your identity. Certainly, the treatise would glorify your talents in no time, compelling you to think seriously about your instincts and motivate to undertake serious risks in life. Prepare yourself to read this book ahead. For, the treatise could altogether change your life.

❑

**Go ahead if you become rich from other folks, but don't let them know that you're extremely rich beyond them.**

**—Tarun Engineer**

# Life

- Life is a challenge–**Face that with might.**
- Life is an adventure–**Mobilize the spirit from within.**
- Life is a sorrow–**Admit it wholeheartedly.**
- Life is a duty–**Accomplish it completely.**
- Life is a play–**Play it with delight.**
- Life is a mystery– **Unravel through your mind.**
- Life is music–**Enjoy its soothing effect.**
- Life is bliss–**Relish it with an urge.**
- Life is an opportunity– **Avail it to best mode.**
- Life is a dream–**Transform it into reality.**
- Life is a journey–**Enjoy it fully well.**
- Life is a promise– **Meet it with utmost dedication.**
- Life is a beauty– **Worship that with dedication.**
- Life is a struggle–**Fight it at every occasion.**
- Life is a target–**Acquire it with certainty.**

He couldn't have become **Jesus**
without being crucified.
He couldn't have become **Socrates**
without consuming poison.
He couldn't have become **Buddha**
without renunciation.
He couldn't have **qualified** without studies.
He couldn't have become
**great without struggles.**

# CULTIVATE TO REACH THE PINNACLE

An English term *vision* could be interpreted as—some foresight, imagination, power, or glimpse. However, the term could be interpreted beyond its significance. For, vision incorporates foreseeing of certain future under present state of developments. How come the future of the world simulates your apperception? It could have been adjudged as some specific science.

Generally, vision is nothing but the foreseeing of one's future. It looks pretty simple in sharing with facts, which is practically not feasible. How far your mind could abide by such independent thinking process? However, it remains proportional to ambitious and glorious warps and woofs of such future.

Everybody believes him to be an independent thinker empowered to think of his/her future. Hardly could you respond ascertaining about your position in the developed society after some twenty years.

It doesn't mean that you are wise or least lettered hog. For, you don't have any dreams about such future. You believe life as some torrent whereupon you could swam ahead unmotivated.

Carving out a niche for one's future and fulfilling unseen dreams is not an easy job. It needs some perseverance, faith and sustained hardship. However, you will shield the self from such contemporary developments, despite such fear over failure to success.

Sunil Mittal, the industrial giant of Airtel's India operation claimed on launching CDMA operations, *'Who shall believe that we could end up in success, others believe us in failure. Either of them was correct in their apprehension. Your mind deliberates on influential thoughts, which reflects their decision.'*

Have you ever perceived about such positive thinkers? The guys were rather dissatisfied lot on apperceiving over present state of developments. It was unfortunate of their swing to the tides when they proceeded after conceiving utopian thought. Imagine the vision of Wright Brothers making humans fly simulating birds. The duo flew aloft through glider subjected to modification and appropriate hardware through hard work and perseverance.

Modern psychoanalytic studies have evaluated of the gestation period of our thoughts to be 21 days under present state of developments. The thoughts could transform into reality steadily subjected to various forces in nature.

A French physician Doctor Emily Cue advised the ailing to think of normal health rather upon the morbid condition. He asked them recapitulate within selves, *'I am getting healthier every day.'* His technique has worked wonders for over two decades. However, anyone inferring about his decision as sheer dream would squarely forget about the reality that every thought could fructify from the stage of latency. The Sermon of the Lord interprets this as,

**People follow the leader just as blueprint guides building Construction.**

***Man ke haar-e-haar hai aur man ke jeet-e-jeet.***

You could be successful in life proportional to the magnitude of desire. The analogy applies equally well to our athletes. The budding boxers in recent Beijing Olympics have brought laurels to our country. A coach Jagdish has trained them, hailing from Bhiwani, in the northern Indian state of Haryana. Imagine how the solitary coach has made them excel lynching the image of our country.

This is the cue from positive thinking, fulfilling dreams of such positive thinker reaching the maiden step. Any negative thinker could disqualify such proposition ignoring the very blueprint of building before construction.

Similarly, your life shall advance on the present blueprint, conditioned by the mariners' compass and some navigational map.

Perhaps, you're aware of *Backward Integration* under the curricula of management studies, calling for the plan procedure to achieve the target. One had to draft the future plan, whereas your procedure remains extremely opposite.

For, you wallow over the present state of developments in anticipation of some bright-unseen future. How could one find such utopia? It could be some phased development to reach the preset target.

You believe that dreamers are pretty sloth bearers. However, every successful dreamer treads ahead in that particular direction through several phases. Any dreamless could find self in alibi like some football ground sans goalpost. Dream alone could be the conditioner of such progress.

A vision could be that perceiving through dreams such as an engine zooming on an array of wheels through steam, or finding some aircraft through wings of birds, or self-determination for the poor masses from imperialist forces.

Nowadays, you will find steady improvements in rendering the quality-oriented leadership proportional to reforms in such vision. For, you ought to shortlist desired path of convenience amongst host of such shoddy paths, capable of dragging you to the destined journey.

Imagine yourself running short of funds. What could you do under such conditions when you're damn confident of becoming successful?

An in-depth analysis could emerge as your vision. You ought to have realized about the potential of such vision to reach the portals of success. For, it functions as some driving force. What could have been the vision behind certain achievements of humankind? What do you wish to achieve in life? Indeed, it is quite apparent that many objectives shall get fructified when the beneficiary treads ahead after making such blueprints of vision.

**Call up certainly your friends who knows about your business and get advice regularly. For, t.v.programme KBC (Kaun Banega Karorepati or Becoming a Billionaire) has justified that phone-a-friend option could work as lifeline for your success.**

However, your confidence could condition such vision. Anyone fixing up some target through confidence attracts such probable circumstances of fructification. Disbelief could wreck any of such probabilities. The Sermon of the Lord has substantiated about the perishing of such disbelievers.

**The 21st century wonder remains who could become giant at any time by changing his stream of thoughts.**

The Holy Bible warns about *'the battalion of disbelievers as weaker oceanic tides, splitting apart through gusting steady wind. The steady wind gaze could favour upon mobilized confidence through spiritual power. Success shall be inevitable for you have stronger faith in self-confidence frequently subjected to the stimuli of invisible force.'* The verses interpret the significance, as

*You'll end up in failure, for you seldom seek success*
*You won't be successful despite making entreaties*
*Your iota of confidence could make many wonders*
*Calling for any mountain to drift apart without ado*
*Could certainly relocate that entity on the plains—*

The verses got justified through some recent title, *'Believe and Success'* reflecting the importance of confidence in shaping one's success. The Holy Bible interprets such confidence as *faith*, reflecting nothing as impossible for the Supreme Absolute Consciousness, as

*Lord, the Almighty never worries*
*Neither he gets separated nor leaves you*
*Such is the specialty of Him, supporting the devout*
*Seldom transforms the faithful into lose confidence.*

It explains the consummation of desires galore of any devout. The Sermon of the Lord has interpreted that as the triumph for him who equates with Arjuna, the charioteer of lord Krishna or lord, the Almighty, ever active in positive actions.

Arjuna is the symbol of all, who has been tied up with power, and remains his confidante.

Nobel laureate Rabindranath Tagore had absolute faith on lord, the Almighty. His magnum opus, *Geetanjali* focused virtually on lord, the Almighty, whose verses

**Daub my forehead with dust from Thy feet**
**Let my ego be replete with Thy love**
**Let my tears soak in Thy Ocean**
**Fructify desires through my life medium.**

Please swear on firm faith to let any evil thought disappear voluntarily. Any word or sentence uttered often through firm faith could surface voluntarily from sub-conscious sheath.

> Success is derived from impetus. For, you shall find awakening of that power when you get influenced from somebody.

My mind often pops up with the images of prince Harischandra, Gandhi, or any seeker of Truth, thereby mobilizing brain cells in that direction to hone my personality with specific characteristics on frequent swearing to utter truth. The gestation period for such adiabatic transformation could be proportional to the very intensity of our thoughts and ambition.

Jose Silva comments in his title- *'You the healer'—human mind as the conditioner of the brain, whereas the brain does so on the physique. The duo badly needs some positive vibrations for ascending at the top. He became some Hercules amongst fellow beings when he brings absolute change within himself.*

Psychoanalyst Richard Fox claims, *'Any positive change would certainly bring vibrations of virtues, not only transforming thy life but also influencing those swarming around, modifying your overall persona.'*

Indian actor Anupam Kher believes, 'Everybody seeks some change, especially someone finds self in abyss on being unsuccessful. The change under such circumstances could make way for positive actions.

It could be wonderful and unnatural at the premature level at the cost of immense potential on proceeding ahead. For, transformation certainly resembles some clod of flesh developed to make the guy enjoy life.'

Dr. Fox observes ahead, 'The change is inevitable when one finds discontented. Try to change your personality, for any difficulty hardly arises unless the situation warrants.'

Dr. Fox believes, 'It subsists on our resistance, but some people accomplish unbelievable feats when they wonder for such change. It could be the cause why people yearn to eat pizza or pasta despite getting good homely menu.'

The psychoanalyst stresses, 'They dream about some movie anew alive on pay channels. They wish to buy new automobiles. They explore possible options to find new relations from old friends. Such could be the level of change fanning your personality out and stabilize with the fundamentals of your progress.'

**Felicitate virtuous people. For, they could reciprocate you. But felicitate man of vices for such purpose so that they could insult you.**

For, Dr Fox has addressed some congregation, 'The people yearning for the transformed persona do connote their advancement through alternatives to chime with the change in times. Could we have ever accessed your retina through Internet and mobile phones, unless the situation has changed?'

Erstwhile Indian actress Waheeda Rehman believes, '*Change pops up when the desire for separation ferments for something anew following discontentment. It shoves us becoming the supreme persona. Change pertains to those talents anew. Such change could impart beings with new techniques and shake them completely.*'

Waheeda Rehman continues, '*Success could touch your feet when you realize of such transformation from within. Often you believe celestial beauties across continents might desire to befriend you. Most of the multinational firms might yearn to deal with you.*'

The Creator has not gifted less.
**It is the matter of your destiny, what have you got?**
Mother Nature has bestowed every individual with equal intellect. It entirely depends on you how far you have made use of it.

The actress believes, '*Similarly, the immense power across the universe might be eager to prostrate before your feet.*'

Indian industrial giant Dhirubhai Ambani has advised, 'Life manifests as a shaking pond. It gets replete completely with volume of water relocating sand particles beneath.

Our life does manifest accordingly. It finds some inhibition when negative thoughts get shoved. You could find the stage as successful when you encounter with the cleansed target.

❑

Sleep less to become a giant.
For, sleeping more could ruin your
moments of creative potential.

—Tarun Engineer

# ACQUAINT WITH THE FORMULAE OF BECOMING SUCCESSFUL

My three decade-long struggled life has taught me innumerable lessons in accomplishing unbelievable feats, as under

*Success = Strategy + discipline + hard work*

You need to inscribe this experimented formula unless you yearn for success. I don't know how many giants have been successful from this formula. Now, it is your turn, but one who adopts correct strategy alone could reach the destination.

It is true that every being is extremely busy in the present world. He works like a robot in his attempt to outperform others. The Y-generation, as such, had been extremely perplexed, what s(he) ought to do.

I wonder whether you have subjected your ship of objective to such uncertainty. For, one couldn't spare for such parameters—*if, however,* and *but* other than focusing on your destined objective with the determination that I shall accomplish this.

The former U.S. president Abraham Lincoln in his Gettysburg address spelt out, *'I shall swear before lord, the Almighty that I shall do this.'* The outcome of his determination was that he was utterly successful along with the declaration of independence.

A few people realize of any decision arrived at on firm determination has had immense power, which we claim as some wonders by virtue.

Perhaps, you might have witnessed the steam engine. The water in its chamber was made to boil at 212° C, when it began emitting steam. Neither it was able to chug the wheels ahead nor shaking the very engine itself. The situation warranted for storing the horsepower generated from such steam at 212° C. *Experience alone could usher one to accomplish such objective.*

A firm determination is the sine qua non for anybody becoming successful. The objective could be through had there been such determination. Dheerubhai Ambani, the industrial giant believed of harnessing the overall physical and mental powers after fixing up an objective. How come one achieves such concentration without harnessing such potential in any work? For, the vacillating mind disallows the accomplishment of any task.

Lord Buddha, the enlightened got self-realization on the basis of accumulated power. I shall recollect an incident related to lord's experiment with Truth that has altogether transformed his life subjected to pleasures of royal lineage. He underwent rigorous penance after renouncing the worldly pleasures and made up his mind to relocate to humankind after being immortalized.

**The folks living without objective shall die at earliest, but those folks dreaming to become something get glorified in the universe.**

Lord Buddha wondered how come some small squirrel could empty the pond of water through its determination. The squirrel insisted to accomplish its will power, whether the pond gets evacuated or not. He underwent Sadhana on finding some new direction about its firm conviction and loyalty. His experiment substantiated the fact any being could accomplish the task provided he has the will power.

Every sports fan had been aware of their hysterics, when some debutant gets into the arena of the WWF crying, *'I am the champion, and I am the champion.'* Indeed, the debutant emerges as the champion, the moment he comes out of the arena. For, he had been overconfident of his will-power, which has made him out with such success.

So, will power has hidden wonders. It rests on your confidence whether you end up in success or failure. Destiny backs up those relying on personal feats. Indian star Dev Anand believes *'Most of the folks end up in failure with disbelief, for they don't have the merits to reach the portals of success.'*

Lord, the Almighty supports him who has been confident on self. So, you need to believe upon yourself that you're quite capable of emerging successful.

As you proceed, that *I can do it*, then you're mobilizing such impetus, loyalty, self-confidence, determination and concentration within you. On the contrary, if you insist that *I can't do it*, you shall find trapped within some web of illusion, fear, impatience and negative sentiments. It would discourage you in becoming successful performer.

Let me share about the delegates of a seminar displaying self-confidence. Often, people inquire how to develop such self-confidence. What is the formula for making someone self-confident? I believe making appropriate preparations for such ordeal could make anybody overconfident.

> **A confused man resembles an ocean tide, who gets destroyed from swift wind. The self-confident man shall ruin such ocean tides.**

Anybody could become overconfident provided s(he) decides to brace ahead. You could become certainly successful with sustained experiments and self-confidence.

It would be quite natural anyone feels insecure over disbelief. One should discourage such attitudes for positive thoughts alone could steer one ahead. *Nothing is impossible in this world* provided you prepare for such encounter tooth and nail. You had to believe that iota of spiritual power. Imagine what French revolutionary Napoleon Bonaparte said the term *impossible finds slot amongst idiots jargon*, in response to his lieutenants' remarks of their inability to access atop Alps.

Confidence remains the forte in our Scriptures and preaching of spiritual missionaries. The missionaries would emulate that with diligence, when it comes pretty feasible. The truth could relate to any mode of thoughts. For, it has the guts to transform any positive or negative thought into reality, irrespective of any influence.

Your life is replete with incidents galore. Your brain often dictates you or recurring of any incident on preset thought. Such thought alone is inevitable which your brain endorses swiftly. You could attain only such things in life as you have decided earlier.

It is compulsory for you to train the stream of thoughts with positive vibrations. For, the world belongs to the believers hogging to the limelight on achieving the objectives in true spirit.

George Bernard Shaw was pretty confident of his success. In his memoirs, he cited, 'I was pretty confident while penning my literature that I would emerge as celebrity. However, at the outset, nobody was ready to bring my specimens of literature. I had earned some seven-pound sterling in two years, but kept adamant that some day I would join the list of celebrities.'

**One who is confident shall get one's desire fulfilled. For so long as, you're not confident upon yourself, you won't get success in your life.**

Man becomes serious when he convalesces upon firm faith. He prepares himself to live with seriousness by some formula, which we label as determination.

Swami Rama Teertha had immense will power. Some night, he decided to end up life unless he solves a ticklish arithmetic riddle. He arrived at the solution through that will power, for which he remained impatient for over a month.

Such was the model of firm will power, which made him pretty successful. Accomplishment of any task pivots on firm will power rather upon immense resource.

The experiment put him on the mettle. He became successful in answering the riddles with firm will power, qualifying him with merit in the university examination.

You couldn't become focused unless your mind is poised. You couldn't do any work without such concentration. Any finished task couldn't be so out of your unstable mind. For, you could reach the objective of choice through poised mind. Mind owes to your attachment and salvation with this mundane world. So, condition its whims and emulate the undermentioned formulae in letter and spirit.

| | | |
|---|---|---|
| *Object to be conquered in life* | : | **Objective** |
| *Object to be swallowed in life* | : | **Anger** |
| *Edible object in life* | : | **Sorrow** |
| *Object to be gifted out in life* | : | **Wisdom** |
| *Object to be displayed in life* | : | **Mercy** |
| *Object to be accepted in life* | : | **Prestige** |
| *Object to be commented in life* | : | **Truth** |
| *Object to be preserved in life* | : | **Respect** |
| *Object to be discarded in life* | : | **Jealousy** |
| *Object to be forsaken in life* | : | **Attachment** |
| *Object to be read in life* | : | **Book** |

For, books usher the path to achieve success in life. French thinker Ismail Shaatir quotes, *'Books are the sources of wisdom. You need to accustom reading them.'*

A Sanskrit verse endorses this thinking, *Tamaso Maa Jyotirgamaya.*

*'Oh light, lead me from darkness to radiance. For, darkness is the symbol of ignorance, whereas the radiance relates to that of wisdom.'* Any ignorant fellow couldn't make way towards welfare out of ignorance, which calls for some basic knowledge, from which one could reach the portals of wisdom.

**The biggest objective in life is to live determination, for determination is such power influencing man to do some deed.**

A few attaches wisdom with destiny, for man carves out his fortune out of sheer efforts, as he had been bereft of that during present birth. Everybody is bereft of such education, success, affluence and happiness, except through systematic dreaming. One needs to convert such illusion into reality through hard work. The skyscrapers you visualize today owe to the hard work and creative thinking of architects galore. Infuse your mind with constructive ideas, for these alone would reorient your dreams.

Let me recollect some anecdote. A young girl stayed atop some valley. She was always watching a beautiful mansion in the overlooking valley through her windows. The windows looked extremely beautiful as though they're made of gold ingots. The girl dreamt of some wonder befalling on her to be its owner. For, her thoughts resembled golden hue in contrast with the windows made of golden ingots.

> **Success is got from courage and spirit, for spirit prod you move ahead and courage would influence you to work more.**

She became an adult along with such dreams when she went on playing in the precincts of its garden.

Some day, she inquired her mother, 'Could I peddle the bicycle on its pavement?' Her mother objected earlier, but permitted on finding her unstable mind. She warned her to stay within her home without peddling afar. The girl knew whither to proceed. The weather was fine, for the path through that pavement lead to her overlooking valley.

Lo, her bicycle stopped near the gates of golden ingot lattice window. She stood before the entrance after parking the bicycle aside. She became an adult with that dream of reaching that window.

Alas, she found the windows pretty soiled and dusty, which she believed earlier as made of golden ingots. They remained unclean, but appeared as golden with the sunlight falling on them.

The girl was extremely disappointed. She got down from the bicycle with broken heart and was about to return home. She noticed another home whose window lattice shimmered like gold atop another valley. The scene, no doubt, looked astonishing, for it was her home, where she was brought up.

The anecdote hints how the girl's dream has been fulfilled. The scene appeared verily in front of her eyes, which was invisible to anybody. So, you need to adapt some strategy and attach with some discipline. Success will knock at your doorstep when you work day through night.

It is true that success would be hardly got from enthusiasm and action. You could become so whatever you have desired. For, the book has some effective formulae and secrecy of achieving success. You could plant the seed of any dream. You could visualize the sprouting of such seed.

**Objective is acquired when you equate with others, for an adage claims one swallow does not make a summer.**

The sprouting of seed needs utmost discipline. The discipline is such capability, which orientates someone arrive at taking decision without any sentiments. Many problems could be sorted out through discipline systematically. Success would certainly kiss your feet provided you involve the craze and planned organization with your sentiments.

You won't visualize the some thousand-hour long hardship behind the movie you've been observing. For, the success of that movie owes to the box office revenue. Many veterans have admitted of becoming *successful overnight* through discipline as their success owed to many years of perseverance.

The discipline is that key, which could transform the impetus to reality. Observe the aura around athletes who participated in the recent Olympics at Beijing. The guys have acquired the utmost objective in short span through sustained practice day and night, sparing the least happiness.

You need to hone such skills in your mind for attaining success. Every opportunity knocks at your door accompanying many challenges. Disciplined guys always look through the stairs making you ascend without much ado.

Dependability owes to certain discipline. Discipline and dependability are interrelated. However, disciplined fellow acquires the fundamental behaviour of keeping track of the issues and attempts to finish the objective before schedule. For, discipline extends suitable strength and makes him avail the best possible option for becoming the successful giant.

A farmer prepares the fields with utmost efforts before planting seeds. The plant would remain so clean during the occasion. The analogy equally applies on you. For, *the ground is your brain and the seed happens to be your dream* in the aforesaid process. You need to cleanse out your brain cells before receiving the plant of success. You have to brush off your memory, which has sprouted like steppe around your dreams.

The dream tree would yield such fruits as they've benefited Dhirubhai Ambani. For, his dream was some issue, which he planted in his memory field with utmost hardship. It led to the growth of another formula anew,

Enthusiasm + action = Success

**Discipline would qualify you as befitting person so that you could achieve objective without ado. For, discipline is dexterity that could be easily acquired.**

Enthusiasm is that force capable of giving birth to creativity. It would turn you out as the successful entrepreneur. For, enthusiasm sprouts out when you have faith in your work.

Any work anew calls for hardship. It will create some craze within you. A few wonder what is there amongst successful giants, which they didn't have. How did they accomplish such achievements? Why do they get utmost bonus? Why was their pay cheque appreciable? No doubt, everything looks pretty astonishing. Successful giants too have experimented in their lives. The secret remains of their achievement in short span of time following the implementation of such procedure with utmost confidence.

Any Deos, the management guru advises, 'the seeker should have such learning traits of children. Children coming to this world remain prepared to acquaint with everything they come across. The guys observe everything seriously and learn without ado. Similarly, you need to learn everything you're unaware for becoming successful.'

You have to admit yourself of remaining unaware of everything since birth. You need to make attempts to learn everything provided you spare extra time. For, successful giants always adopt new formulae amidst their routine. It doesn't mean that they've mastered the art. However, they wish to assimilate them in life through trial and errors, without being frightened over any failure.

Observe any child for an hour, especially when he learns to walk. He falls quite frequently, wakes up, and continues his attempt wondering why he fell. He learns by reasoning to attempt anew without fall. He couldn't assimilate himself to walk unless he does so. Similarly, successful giants have the capacity to wake during sudden fall, thereby learning the process through trial and error, adapting sustained reforms. The guys would go on working through fine-tuning so long as they emerge as successful in their debut.

The guys do realize about sudden reforms. They acknowledge such conditions and transform flopped business somewhat that unbelievable. The folks seldom learn anything through old experiences other than making things at ease through new options.

**Life functions like some program machine. You ought to de-program in exploring something anew.**

You come across one common feature among successful actors and leaders reaching at the zenith, which others don't have.

You need to deliberate like those giants unless you wish to become successful. Imagine how to do this? I shall let you know another anecdote. Perhaps, you might recall the incident of sprinter running one mile within four minutes. People often believed it as next to impossible in fathoming one mile within four minutes. The opinion hung on till 1954 A.D. when the sprinter Roger Bannister disbelieved them. Some 37 sprinters broke that record after his debut, which made over 300 to outperform that distance in less than four minutes.

The anecdote makes us believe that most of our facts were shibboleth. You could visualize things in different hues provided you change the colour of such pair of spectacles.

However, reality is somewhat different. For, you could visualize things without the pair of spectacles, when nature appears spell bound. Probably, this is the cause for many of the geographical and scientific explorations were the outcome of changed conceptions.

Some generations before, people believed that sun revolved around planet earth. Innovations have transformed that concept. It is true that our brain gets controlled through concentration. How could such concentration be defined?

Our physique resembles a mansion. It has many storeyes and cells. It gets divided into physical and mental spheres. Mind gets differentiated to ethereal plane known as consciousness. The physical body is the cemented structure of flesh and bones. Mind reigns over that mansion making it sturdy and beautiful through aesthetic props.

**Anybody's fortune can't be changed without struggle like diamond seldom shimmers without polishing.**

How to beautify our physical body? You know our physical body could be decked up in its outward appearance. The most appealing factor in such decoration subsists at the interior level. How to cleanse and decorate our mind? What debris needs to be evacuated?

Mind becomes the debris on being corrupted with negative thoughts. The situation warrants for evacuation of such debris. Evacuation of worthless and detrimental thoughts from our mind is the sine qua non. For, the worthless thoughts have spoiled not only our outward and interior appearance but also become detrimental to the multiple growth of our personality. One needs to break the legal barriers to acquaint with issues anew, which proved pretty disastrous.

People advise not to be jealous of anybody. I advise you to be jealous of people. Be jealous appreciably, especially through the depth of your heart, but not with your neighbour. Be jealous of giants like, **Tata, Birla and Ambani.** You ought to become so on certainly. Feeling jealous of your neighbour could make you as your neighbour. You will be a giant beyond your neighbour when you feel jealous of **Tata, Birla and Ambani.**

Hold yourself if you're taking off through an aircraft. You need to adopt the strategy of Carl Yangzenski when you're exploring the option of acquiring strategies anew. A news agency reporter queried the guy on his completion of 3,000 hits during 1979 Red Sacs Baseball event at Boston, *'Are you not being frightened of the spectators observation?'* Yangzenski rebutted, *'I have batted beyond ten thousand times in my life. It substantiates the failure of my earlier seven thousand hits, which could keep my mind poised.'*

Yangzenski knew that success and failure are the facets of the same coin. Errors sprouting through positive thoughts work like staircase.

You could find what the IBM's founder Thomas J. Watson has spelled, 'Doubling up of your failures could lead to your emerging successful. Anybody finds impossible to achieve success without fathoming his mind. He alone will emerge successful who's able to conquer his mind.'

❑

"Failures galore in life will get you assimilate with real aptitude and capability. The same failures will usher you towards success."

—Tarun Engineer

# THINK WELL ABOUT OTHERS

A journalist often sought the automobile giant Henry Ford, *'What is the secret of your success?'*

The gentleman Ford replied over smile, *'I owe my success to courage and confidence. I believe that confidence and courage could make anything impossible on earth possible.'*

The poor journalist insisted, *'I disbelieve what you claim. Could you explain anybody relocate water through sieve from one place to another?'*

*'Why not?'* the comments of Henry Ford kept the hapless journalist surprised in anticipation of his answer, justifying something possible through impossible.

Gentleman Henry Ford continued, *'We need to keep waiting upon courage and confidence till such time, when water won't freeze.'*

Indeed, the automobile giant Ford's answer was absolutely true. For, the characteristics such as humility, courage, self-confidence and tolerance contribute to the overall development and growth of our personality, qualifying us to become successful in every sector. This is possible when those characteristics are in order without any ostentation.

The characteristics exceeding the horizon of self-confidence become the root cause of man's misery. Man bereft of humility, courage, self-confidence, and tolerance becomes unstable, indecisive and intolerant.

One couldn't interpret something as long as one disbelieves in its accomplishment. Imagine how could one emerge stronger as long as he conceives, *'I could accomplish this job.'*

You shall get perished the moment of prioritizing weakness in mind disqualifying yourself as incompetent. You shouldn't hope for his success when he has forsaken to struggle ahead. For, success pivots forever on confidence. Confidence is the heavenly gift within us. It is also glorified as courage or poised mind etc.

Always keep your mind steady like a rock, irrespective of favourable or unfavourable circumstances, interpreting such circumstances as transient. The situation resembles harmonic ripples sprucing on throwing some pebble into still water. A rock remains inaccessible to the impact of ripples. Similarly, bravery and adventure of anyone keeps him unmoved. Saint Tulsidas has said–

*Dheeraj dharma mitra aroonari,*
*aapatkaal parakhiye chari.*

**A stone on being hid for many years underneath earth qualified to become diamond. Similarly, the rock of success becomes diamond after extreme hardships, but one needs to scratch either for empowering them with beauty.**

Anybody could emerge as triumphant irrespective of encountering sorrows, or pains, or fear through courage, abiding by principle, Stop and observe.

Tulsidas has advised beings to encounter life through courage. For, any courageous guy could accomplish unfinished task without much ado. And so, beings could end up in failure on undertaking task upon harsh attitude or unstable mind.

Fortitude is also the root of comfortable life. For, change is the basic law of nature. So, you're bound to adapt some change, making something possible from impossible, at the cost of conditioned stable mind, concentrating on your objective.

Let me recollect some traditional anecdote. The charioteer of Hastinapur king Suta, Adhiratha sought guru Drona accompanying sons Basu and Shona,' *Oh gurudev, I desire my sons should get trained in warfare under your guidance.'*

Drona refused to entertain his request on the ground that princes alone are eligible for training on warfare.

Adhiratha returned home. His sons began targeting the onlookers after acquiring warfare skills, when everybody fell asleep.

Drona undertook the final test after the princes got one-year training on skills of warfare. King Dhritarashtra and eldest sage Bhisma were present on the occasion. Basu and Shona came to witness the event. Arjuna was told to experiment with ultrasonic arrow.

emoved that stone pebble again. The verdict was in
farmer and his daughter when the stone pebble turned
e. For, the farmer's daughter has inserted another white
after discarding two black stone pebbles, out of sheer
However, the financier couldn't visualize her tricks.
dote substantiated how the farmer got waived off the
ed his daughter from getting married to the financier.
u paradise seekers need to favour destiny on you, by
avocation according to your taste.
olutely true that hobbies have some deep relationship
dge. For, scientific innovations galore are beyond such
e recent outcome of Linux software package owes to
some amateur student.

**haracter is
undation
of your life.
evate your
ter for your
ive rests on
h stone.**

You could imagine the fate of sustainable development movement sprucing up as hobby during 1970s across the continents got transformed to become the giant movement of world politics.

The danseuse Mallika Sarabhai shaped her destiny out of amateurish interests while pursuing studies for her doctorate through
dabad unit of Indian Institute of Management. Indian
singer Shankar Mahadevan becomes so out of amateurish
fter qualifying through chemical engineering faculty of the
nit of Indian Institute of Technology. The hobbies sprouting
n Ali eking out livelihood for family on mining and timber
become world's sole ornithologist, or Palash Sen becoming
singer from the avocation of physician, or Rhodes scholar
d Farooqui turning to become the documentary film
r, or interior decorator Twinkle Khanna becoming the film
r mechanical engineer Raghu Rai becoming a photographer
e, are noteworthy. Hobby alone has lynched Mitali Raj, to
the cricketer from an ordinary dancer.
shall come across examples galore, wherein the hobby has
y shaped personalities but have also played unique role in



Masked Arjuna silenced some barking dogs aside by experimenting with the arrow. Basu shouted on finding his arrogance, *'I could also display this forte.'*

King Dhritarashtra refused the objection raised by guru Drona. Basu was about to shoot his arrows when someone harked before the dog was about to bark. It continued barking when he shot the arrow to silence the opponent.

Drona cried out, *'Arjuna is the day's archer.'*

Sage Bhisma intervened, *'Basu is the day's archer but not the grandmaster Arjuna.'*

*'How come'* asked Drona?

*'For, we have focused on barking dog. But, Basu and I heard some unimpressive voice before the barking dog. That chirping belongs to some bird after feeding its sibling with hay. Basu shot the arrow focusing on that scene, which silenced the bird on the pierced arrow.'*

*'His aim was pretty good to Arjuna. For, Basu concentrated only on the target. Anybody focusing on the target would emerge as successful.'*

**Review yourself for qualifying to be some giant. Nobody could identify about you better than yourself.**

Sage Bhisma inferred about the result. Basu became triumphant on the occasion.

My advice is that you should emerge triumphant like Basu. You need to emerge as Basu rather on Arjuna.

A devout sought lord Brahma 'Let me know master the way I could achieve peace, happiness and progress at one go.'

Lord Brahma said, squeezing two haversacks on him, *'One of the haversacks is replete with vices of thy neighbours. Do not open even after forgetting, nor show that to anybody, tying on your back. Another haversack is replete with your vices. Go on observing this frequently after attaching it to your bosom.'*

Unfortunately, the bum went on observing and allowing others see the open-ended haversack replete with neighbours' vice on his bosom, which put him on the path of annihilation.

So, proceed ahead by learning something or other from others, for life is the cue for success. Emulate that practically for sustained improvement in your life.

> **Quite often, you shall find all vistas for success being shut. But, sustained deliberation could ascertain you about one path.**

The Scriptures eulogize *man as the best specimen of creation. It doesn't mean that his skeleton is aesthetically more appealing than species galore, for he has been capable of reasoning skills. He could multiply happiness through amplification of radical thoughts as token of respect to the humankind.* However, he could emerge as the complete authority on earth through intellectual and spiritual skills of the available resources.

The Scriptures have also interpreted, 'Oh man! Excel thy life through splendid deeds. Get glorified through thy sustainable immense powers.'

Unfortunately, man for the era has moulded into stressful life while initiating into new deeds. Introspect thyself, 'What is the correct interpretation of my life?'

So, hold yourself with rapt attention, as long as you find some positive response. Perhaps, you might avail such positive response some day. You shall hear the legible voice from the spirit within.

My experience dictates about your life not only as responsible for your life, but also your splendid performance.

A rider needs to be inserted on such statement of turning you down. For, your destination could describe about your excellent performance.

Let me describe another anecdote to justify this fact. A bird attempted to fly towards the poles during winter. A horse treading on its path made its feed fall in space. The bird went on chirping from being enlivened out of the warmth of that feed. A cat gobbled that bird at one gulp swerving off the feed, on hearing the chirping noise.

Could you infer the secret of this anecdote? Let me share the secret on your failure.

- Make your destination according to your capability.
- It doesn't warrant the supporting friend suppress you in no time.
- The supporter doesn't favour you in the guise of unburdening.
- Protect yourself from stupid friends resembling the feed.

For, this book has been interpreting your proceeding on the



support of confidence. Ho
you achieve your target? You
go through another anecdote t
about this fact. A financier used
money for poor in his village.
farmer couldn't repay the mor
time. The crops in his field wit
on seasonal failure and destiny ba
him out.

The financier stuck to his gu
get the money back from the far
what to do.

The farmer had a daughter. Sh
has influenced the entire village. T
either to repay the overall debt or g

The rural folks have inferred th
put forward another condition be
warranted the farmer's daughter pic
black and white from the financier'

She shall get married to the fina
her picking up black stone pebble. Sh
shall repay the loan had she picked u
eventual refusal might get the farmer

The farmer and his daughter acce
thronged over the spot. The financier
in the bag through dishonesty. The gir
was left with three options. She was t
father out by marrying the financier a
pebble. The second option was to allo
without repaying the debt after refusing
third option was to expose the dishonest
her father to repay the debt.

However, the girl made up her min
out of the bag. She threw the stone afar
after its removal. The stone pebble mingl
street. The financier stuck to his guns on s
could be arrived even with the leftover st

individual lives. The probabilities of success could be more while frisking about your future in some hobby, for success owes to unique concentration or meditation. Hobby and meditation are facets of the same coin.

> **Nobody could emerge successful in life unless one risks oneself according to the adage –No risk, no reward.**

Prasoon Joshi, the creative art director and lyricist believes—'I am a downtown youth interested in writing. I was fond of rhyming verses. My couplets were published when I was seventeen years of age. I got qualified in MBA from IMT of Ghaziabad when my penchant for music theatre spruced up voluntarily. Often, I thought of making my career in the corporate world.'

However, I wished to fulfill my parents' dreams despite being rebel. Often I got through business management course for establishing my career.

It was optional to carry homework for vocation during my studies. I was to complete the assignment for summer vocation on *Gray Worldwide* in Delhi. I was virtually unaware of the requirements of the advertising media. I felt rather extremely involved in entering into the world of creativity through business management.

I knew every nuance of the advertising media business lobby. Moreover, I was also a writer.

Even then, the change over was pretty difficult for accomplishment. The assignment I had during summer vocation gave me the forte to sustain in my life. It made me to opt for that avocation for life, which kept me extremely euphoric now. I am outperforming in my avocation for the day out of that inherent hobby within me.

A 19-year old Rinku Singh has fulfilled his dreams to transform it into reality. It could be labelled as an *American Dream*. The youth hailing from small village Bhadohi of Varanasi district of the state of Uttar Pradesh fulfilled that dream which every citizen of the country was about to organize ahead.

Mr. Rinku Singh replied, when asked, 'I longed to become the cricketer like my fellow citizens. Me thinks, it was the game changing my fortune of becoming billionaire overnight. Messrs. Suresh Raina and R.P. Singh at Lucknow sports hostel advised me to evince interest in bowling during earlier interaction. Of course, I had another problem. I couldn't give up the habit of bending arms straight while throwing javelin. Often, I have disbelieved how a mere twist of arms could enhance my image.

My coach Mr. J. S. Bhatia informed my companion Dinesh Kumar and me about one million-dollar Arm Baseball tournament taking place in Mumbai, two months before. Mr. J. B. Bernstein, the South Asian agent and the managing director of Steve Figure Management Baseball Talent Hut was exploring some good baseball pitcher.

**India shall dominate as the numero uno economy in the world when her every second citizen plunges to become opulent.**

Mr. Bernstein insisted me often to get into practice when I haven't even heard of the game. My coach Mr. Bhatia prepared me face the event with pitching tips, a few days before.

I have learnt the game of baseball within those days. For, I was deeply dedicated to learn the skills anew, or else bending arms was next to impossible for some javelin player like me.

The event fetched not only one million U.S. dollar when I pitched at the speed of 87 mile per hour, but also availed the opportunity to present my debut through pitching at San Francisco Baseball training event.

I exhibited my skills successfully before some thirty athletes of major league baseball team. Now, I am getting some 160 million rupee in every match. I believe in a couple of years I could amass such money, which even the test cricketer Sachin Tendulkar has not earned during his cricket career.

A similar career recurs with Meerut based eleven-year old athlete Shilpa. She was subjected to some serious ailment, making her immobile upon the effect on her central nervous system. She began facing frequent troubles. Doctors attending on her had lost hope.

Shilpa thought she would stay on wheelchair for the entire life. For, the doctors often believed only a few people could survive after this ailment. The young girl seldom got disheartened out of this deformity. She used to converse with every patient admitted in the hospital of her optimism to walk some day.

**Look not behind. Whatever has bygone becomes gone forever. The path of success does manifest as endless on doing so.**

The girl was relocated to some specific hospital in nearby Partapur. Specialists have attempted making her recover from such ailment through many treatments. They're extremely influenced from her courage. They advised her to imagine herself of walking through comfortably. She began exercising herself on bed upon extra efforts as though she was trembling out through stretching.

Some day she has wondered of moving legs on fantasizing herself proportional to the retrieved complete strength. She screamed out, on reaching the other end of the room, when her cot was found shaking, *'See, I am shaking myself, I could move, I could do everything. Observe me that I am moving around.'*

Everybody in the hospital was found moving at sixes and sevens to spare selves from this ordeal. For, the teenaged girl shook the entire hospital out of her euphoria. People were shouting, when things went on falling with broken glass vases, as though some quake has shaken the entire hospital.

Learn to gift in life except acceptance.
Speak not about what you give.
Harass not forever to accept something.
Speak less and slowly
but do so appropriately.
Think quickly for something
good but something big.
Listen more about all
**but do according to your conscience.**

The girl began moving to her school on foot, after a couple of years. Neither had she supported her movements with the calipers nor any wheelchair. I wondered that Shilpa could shake the entire earth from her imaginary powers.

You should shake the entire earth like our teenager Shilpa. You need to have constant faith and claim proudly, *'I would stick to my objective so long as I won't shake the earth.'* The book will let you know about the subsequent details how and when should you undertake risks in life ahead. For, giants among human beings will do such feats for they're habitual to make determination. So, give a thought again how you wanted to become successful.

**"Men disheartened from failures equate themselves to cowards. Failures usher them to the path of success."**

**—Tarun Engineer**

# AWAKE YOUR POWER OF CONFIDENCE

I have wondered how an author used to write thousands of novels when I was pursuing my engineering studies. How do they think about new plots? How do they play with their own jargon? How do they end up the stories?

I was always attempting to decipher the data, which remained an outer world. The more I pondered over the subject, the more I was swerved from the track.

I was extremely curious to unveil the mystery upon the penchant to become a writer of eminence. However, I didn't have any other option other than penning my thoughts through smaller plots and getting them regularly published through newspapers and periodicals. I got relieved from the college after nearly a year.

I was enjoying my vacation at Nainital, the resort on Garhwal valleys. I used to observe the pond seriously sitting near the main bus bay during my evening stroll across Mall Road. I came across the gentleman who resembled some writer on a particular evening. I came to know him as some vernacular novelist Ranu during my conversation. He used to write pretty well during those days, for many of his stories were filmed. *Kati Patang* and *Jheel ke us Paar* were some of his filmed novels.

I have also read many of Ranu's novels during my childhood. The author was pretty influenced when I shared about my experience. He disclosed of his arrival to the valley resort was to write some novel *Puja* based on the real incident. Puja was a nurse at Pant Hospital situated near the main bazaar, who met with some tragedy a year before.

I coordinated with writing of his novel, after getting the writer introduced to nurse Puja in the hospital. Ranu appreciated over my script after ascertaining my acumen.

Some day, I shared my anxiety with Ranu, '*Sir, I wish to become a writer like you.*'

The writer responded earlier over smile, '*You could become so certainly. My blessings are always with you.*'

Subsequently, I followed him and scripted '*Ek Aur Laila,* which got published in 1980 from Roorkee's *Prem Pocket Books*, which qualified *me as novelist Tarun Engineer.*

Awake the spirit of confidence in you. Achieve complete success over your dreams. You won't become victorious so long as you have the self-confidence in any work to be initiated. For, confidence meant your attachment to something, without abandoning that work or accepting defeat.

**Every achievement in life resembles line drawn on that disappears before dragging. For, mind shall realize about the scarcity of some object when one of your desires get materialized.**

Let us revert to Kargil War. India and Pakistan were on full-scale war across the line of control with appreciable casualties on either side with manpower and ammunitions. The atmosphere becomes awesome, when the Indian border guards have bayed for enemy's blood. A lieutenant and his pal Vinod Bhati, who happened to be their colleague, estimated over the loss. One of the soldiers was wounded, who happened to be the friend of Mr. Bhati.

Vinod Bhati sought his protection from the lieutenant. The latter replied that doesn't mean he was alive. It could be unbecoming of putting the soldiers at risk for some dead soldier.

The lieutenant permitted Vinod Bhati when he said, '*Sir, I wish to save him.*' Vinod Bhati was successful in reaching his wounded friend despite facing slew of odds. He was also wounded during his return with his wounded friend.

The lieutenant found him dead on justification. He told his colleague, observing Vinod Bhati, '*I have already told you that it won't be worth saving him. Your friend is no more. You were also severely wounded in your attempts to protect your wounded friend.*'

Vinod Bhati replied, *"Sir, it was essential to protect him, as a friend. For, he was alive when I reached there. His final words were pretty precious. For, he explained before breathing his last, 'I was confident of your arrival at this moment."*

The confidence subjects us to some impetus. It would usher the way, get us introduced to people of virtues. It eliminates challenges coming on our way towards success, even such difficulty relates to financial hardship. Confidence triumphs over scores of odds.

Delhi, the Indian capital city has scores of industrialists, who have raised the business empire worth some billion rupee upon absolute confidence by injecting little money. Dr. Surinder Kapur, one of such industrialists is related to Sona Group of Industries. He has lynched his industry to reach the market value worth some thirty billion rupee, through concentration, consumer satisfaction and confidence.

**Man born on earth has to die someday. Do such deeds like the industrial giant Dheerubhai Ambani in getting glorified.**

The automobile ancillary unit, Sona Group of industries, has over 4,000 people in its workforce. Sona Group became the market leader in producing fifty per cent of the steering products required for assembling Maruti car in India. Earlier, Surinder Kapur was dealing with ornaments. You could find his jewellry showroom even today in Connaught Place.

However, he did the homework well abroad. He disallowed losing confidence in any of the jobs he undertook, running the cab or working in some restaurant. He went on hunting pastures anew on his return after getting doctorate from Michigan University. He began working with Bharat Gears Limited in 1972.

He laid the foundation stone for Sona Steering Company, producing automobile components in 1987. His family was virtually related to making gold ornaments. His business was joint venture with Maruti Suzuki of Japan, where his family invested half million rupee. The initial turnover of the company during its first year of operation was one billion rupee.

Today, Sona Group of Industries has a turnover of some thirty billion rupees, of which the overseas share amounts to some eighteen billion rupees. The company has over 2,500 people in its workforce at home and some 1,800 people working abroad. It has sixteen and four plants respectively at home and abroad.

Sanjay Kapur, the son of Surinder Kapur is associated with the business, who happens to be the spouse of film actress Karishma Kapur. He has also initiated Polo Cup, in the name of his daughter Samaiyra.

You could also become successful on the impetus of Surinder Kapur. I have absolute confidence, for you have been reading this book with rapt attention. Such self-confidence will glorify your personality with certainty. You need to focus on the following parameters.

01. **Have positive approach in life:** It is necessary for anybody to have positive approach in life. You need not go away from the country. You could derive the result from nearby. Be in touch with people, from whom you could learn something for future.

02. **Do not step into others' shoes:** The virtual drawback in one's personality is to step into some others' shoes. It inhibits us from conversing or dealing straightforward without any embarrassment. We lose self-confidence from such experiment. You should have the relevant data on which you wish to converse with anybody. Enhance your personal knowledge. Keep serious track of the lingo, grammar and style of conversation and let that known to others. Be a good listener. You could subsequently be an influential speaker.

03. **Keep track of the fashion and trends:** Your facial features, height, physique would seldom back you. You could condition your etiquette, attire and body language without much ado. Could you ever appear abhorrently with poor body language? Bear in mind to always wear branded garments irrespective of the place of visit. You will realize about this through enhanced level of self-confidence.

04. **Utilize your imaginary powers:** The simplest method to keep remembering about things is to drop the image of the object in your subconscious mind. For example, you had to recollect the spot where you have left the key, memorize that spot in your subconscious sheath. You shall realize later whether you have not left the key at that spot. You will certainly get the key on your revisit.

05. **Adapt yourself to constant practice:** Constant practice alone improves your retention power. Take a small incident. You

need to remember the birthday of your family folks. Commence with your birthday. Imagine which day fell on your last birthday. Accordingly, try to recollect about the birthdays of your folks. Try to remember such dates of famous athletes. You could bring your memory power more after recording such information.

06. **Always take nutritious food:** Good memory could be retained through nutritious food, which is anti-oxidant. A study appearing in the *American Journal of Chronicle Nutrition* reported the investigators to have found the people under the group 60-90 consuming appreciable quantity of fruits and vegetables, which kept their retention power maximum.

> **Your issue shall ascertain about your frequency of sentiments. Your sentiments shall swiftly share with you whether you're resonating at such frequency.**

07. **Keep track of your physical body:** Physical fitness would sharpen your memory. It would also enhance reasoning power. For, the retention power goes on decreasing with increase in your age. Most of the people couldn't remember the telephone number, name of the person or the country code. Your brain would work at lightning speed if you were pretty healthy. Your retention skills won't be affected with increase in your age.

George Bernard Shaw believes, *'People often dream of becoming giants but couldn't create such thoughts in them. I always work through such giant thoughts and transform that into practical reality.'*

The Sermon of the Lord interprets this as, 'Transform your deed into reality.' It is practically true that even the giants of such management establishments have taken recourse to the formulae appearing through the Sermon of the Lord.

*'Hey Man, do the deeds without anticipating its fruits.'* We find ourselves pretty embarrassing on frequently hearing the formula of completing any act without anticipating any resultant fruit. Neither are we hermit nor any sage. The formula suggests you to go ahead with your work, ignoring about its resultant. The formula prescribes you to survive amidst present state of developments. The formula advises to survive for the moment. One's survival of course, relies on momentary pulses.

For, momentary survival has some structure, irrespective of stay or condition around; one shall live to the fullest possible level.

Enjoy the moment fully by imbibing in it. It describes us to get fully lost in whatever work we've been on. Your immersion in such thoughts could enliven you forever. You're projecting that as the forte for your survival. You're doing everything as though you've encountered just now.

**Go ahead. Munnabhai signifies not to accept defeat in one's life. It was not M K Gandhi but film producer has discussed it by cherishing his career at stake.**

Imagine whether you could accomplish any thing without mobilization or expending yourself in that work? So, focus on the work without diverging away in any other object, nor swerve your mind away.

The saga of lord Krishna is the living embodiment. His life was away from any swerves. He was ever attached to his work irrespective of any odds at such moments. Neither had he the past nor future in mind. Such was the splendid effect of lord Krishna, as human being on earth.

The lord was concentrating on such pranks when he got involved during childhood. He knew that the moment of involvement means absolute attachment with the work. Have you ever imagined of diverging from anything in life? There won't be any other splendid work other than what you've been doing in your career.

**Education is not necessary.**
You ought to become the master of your trade.
**It is not necessary to study more.**
You ought to assimilate what you have learnt.
**Formality is not necessary.**
You ought to know to keep your words.
**Money is not necessary.**
You ought to know how to recycle money.

You have got the assignment on that ground. Try to be honest in your work. You need to do everything in it. Cherish yourselves into that act when you've lost virtually about your identity. How could you think of the future or the events gone by? Always focus on the bird's eye during concentration like archer Arjuna. The bird's eye happens to be the fundamental formula of management world of the day. The formula would come only into force when you get lost in your work. You won't remember even about its outcome.

Such is the interpretation of '*Ma Phaleshu,*' or '*think not about the result.*' So, get into act with full concentration and virtual involvement, when somebody else would look after that. For, the spiritual foray has this as the fundamental truth.

The gurus of management of the day have been realizing about the significance of this formula—think about the present work, when worries unseen would get resolved automatically.

Imagine for a moment of your excellent performance ignoring other thing. You wouldn't be successful in life when you worry about the outcome.

*The Sermon of the Lord* interprets about another formula, 'Keep quiet while working on something. Act under absolute submission. Seldom unrest would scuttle your performance during such moment.

A leader gets disturbed when his team fails to satisfy. The team gets waylaid when the leader disorients the objective. He might not be properly influencing the team to act.

*The Sermon of the Lord* substantiates for the followers to get involved in performance. Is there any other formula for one becoming successful?

❑

**"Any task won't be big or small.**
**Only your thinking makes it so."**
**—Tarun Engineer**

# ATTEMPT TO POPULARISE YOURSELF

I returned to Delhi, exploring pastures anew, after completing my engineering studies. I had dreamt of becoming purchase officer in some good establishment.

The company where I had been for interview had selected somebody else for the job. The director of the establishment asked me, keeping in view of my ambition, 'Now, we have been left with the position of draftsman. Could you work with us?'

I have replied often, 'Why not? I need a job badly. I shall certainly work with you.'

The director said, 'OK, you could join our establishment after three days.'

I reached the establishment as per the promise I had made.

The gentleman was taken aback when he observed the modus operandi of my work. He queried, 'How come you're drawing so nicely with finesse when you have completed electrical engineering?'

I replied, 'I brought the necessary equipments from the market, when you hired me for the job of draughtsman. I went on acquiring specific skills when I assimilated with the techniques of drawing at home.'

The director said, patting my back with warm affection, 'You are overconfident of what you do. Certainly, some day you would reach at the pinnacle of success.'

A year rolled by. I was appointed as the purchase officer in some other establishment. The director of the company reacted, on my leaving the job of draftsman, *'Man always becomes some giant banking on his ideas. He would become so proportional to the thoughts he had earlier.'*

You could shake even the solid earth on such confidence. You could be successful on such confidence provided you have belief in that. You could rewrite history when you win over the universe.

For, faith or belief on something doesn't have any secret. Faith works in this manner, *'I believe that I could work upon that.'* You shall be empowered with energy and aptitude through which you could work. You will gain self-confidence that you could accomplish the job without ado at the cost of exploring all options.

An old anecdote recollects some expertise inquiring a rustic; *'Any giant took birth in your village?'*

The rustic replied coolly, *'No, only kids are born here.'*

You could laugh on hearing such response over the belief it was a joke. However, that rustic couldn't assimilate with the query of the expertise. The response of the rustic justifies none of the giants to have taken birth from any village or metro city, irrespective of the status of such elite. She had been born as ordinary infant from some mother. You will know that the birth of any species will always happen in the form of infant or sibling.

**Objective could be secured keeping life subservient. For, the laws will put you in such mould after grinding all vices where you could visualize all objects positive-oriented.**

Imagine the means of some seed amplifying to become the giant tree? Imagine also how much fertilizer, rain, sunlight besides wind, is required for its growth? Similarly, any child needs the requisite environment, adequate protection and good formal education and etiquette.

We often listen to some adage, 'morning shows the day.' It means the childhood of many giants sport such importance during their childhood.

There won't be any specific rule describing the important features of anybody at his childhood. A few personalities will emerge so, whose childhood crawls through ordinary boundaries, facilitating them in ascending at the zenith of success, which they've not imagined at any stage.

The will power of some personalities remain pretty rigid. The folks will become giants some time later despite living under ordinary environment, on reinforcing their will power quite frequently.

We have appreciable number of Indian giants in their own spheres, such as Mahatma Gandhi, Abraham Lincoln, Raja Ramamohun Roy, Swami Vivekananda, Saint Gyaneshwar, Rabindranath Tagore, Chhatrapati Shivaji etc, who have established through such deeper allegiance, masochism and sacrificing nature. Their mothers have played the remarkable role in their upbringing.

It is absolutely true that virtuous mothers become successful in transforming their ordinary wards into important personalities. Let me recollect an anecdote related to gentleman Ravi, hailing from Jaipur, the western Indian state capital Rajasthan. He was sent to study in local school while he was a child. The teachers expelled him on proclaiming as disabled and incompetent. Ravi wrote to his mother, what his teachers have spelt out ***'Your child is incompetent for studies.'***

Ravi's mother was empathetic for a while. She interpreted in the next month, upon her self-confidence, ***'Who adjudged my son Ravi as disabled? I shall get him tutored.'*** His mother made up her mind with specific objective, when Ravi began leading his class with appreciable marks.

Perhaps, our Sage Tulsidas has interpreted, with this development in mind,

*Guru Sangati guru hoi so laghu Sangati laghu naam*
*Char padarath mein ganein narak dwarahu kaam.*

The verse interprets—any bigger thought could transform man to become the giant in his field, and a smaller thought could demote him, on the contrary. Our reverend playback singer Lata Mangeshkar says, *'The fundamental formula in my life was to remain afraid of myself. Introspect within you whether the path you tread was OK. Proceed ahead without any second thought, when your answer is in the positive.'*

Her father Deenanath Mangeshkar has initiated this formula for her welfare. She had been emulating the formula in letter and spirit even today.

Introspect thyself on your ordeal whether you wish to hog into limelight of success.

For, your inner spirit alone could judge about your potential of becoming successful. We label this spirit as the *conscience.*

Today, appreciable number of people disown their identities on being baffled over certain potential. However, self-castration and ego prove to be detrimental in our path of success. Self-confidence arises in us when we accomplish the job with absolute faith and diligence, when our conscience comes into the picture. For, you're squarely responsible for training yourself. Anybody else won't appraise what, why and how to proceed.

The book helps you in proceeding ahead, but you alone know about the way out. For, you alone could direct yourself that how the book proceeds ahead.

You could evaluate about your progress. You could achieve the splendid part of success in your mission within a couple of days, the moment you gain from such characteristics.

**Fathoming the destiny astride the chariot of hopes with ambition anew shall give different form altogether, for nothing could be gained on being lost in darkness of pessimism.**

I recollect something about three friends desiring to become spies. The folks sent their resume to New Delhi based firm **Red Alert Detective Company**, and got the response for an interview.

The interviewer sought from one of them, on showing some photograph for about five seconds, 'He is a criminal. How could you identify him on your sudden encounter?'

The fellow replied without batting eyelid, 'It is extremely easier. He is one-eyed fellow.' The interviewer fumed, 'He is not the one-eyed criminal. He has two eyes. It is his side profile, from which you're estimating him to be one-eyed fellow.

The second fellow was repeated the same question, after showing the same photograph, when he swiftly replied, 'I shall trace out this criminal quickly. For, he has only one ear.' The interviewer roared, on being furious, 'Both of you're stupid. You folks don't understand that I have been showing you the side profile of the criminal.'

Now, the turn came for the third friend. He was also shown the same photograph. He replied, after giving serious thought, 'I could identify him, for he has used contact lens in his eyes.' The interviewer was taken aback, for he was unaware of this information. He went through the record and found the data exactly true. The interviewer congratulated the third guy for his acumen and asked on being inquisitive, 'How do you know that the criminal has been using contact lenses?' The folk answered, 'What is anew in this? The man neither having one eye or ear, how could he wear the goggles?'

The anecdote has hidden many details. The third folk's answer was exactly correct, for he replied in haste, for his two friends have already answered. Had he replied this much, 'I am telling this from my experience.'

Certainly, he could have got the job, but his destiny has backed him out. Do you mean everything could be had from such destiny? It is a matter of serious thinking. Does anybody get everything from his destiny? A psychiatrist has experimented about this to substantiate the scientific validity. He thought an improved version to ascertain was to explore possible options whether people are more fortunate or unfortunate.

The gentleman inserted advertisements in newspapers and periodicals inquiring who else will adjudge himself as the fortunate and who else not? The people from many fields and ages accessed him.

He got realized from whatever data and experience the people had on their fortune subsisted on the following four parameters.

- They are good in preparing and identifying opportunities.
- They take fortunate decision on the basis of their experience.
- They get voluntarily influenced by positive hopes.
- They embrace virtuous principles in their career, which transforms them as the fortunate from misery.

Let me recollect another anecdote. A poor farmer was traveling somewhere astride his mule. He came across some giant mysterious stone. He tied that stone around the neck of the mule. Another trader astride some camel was taken aback on noticing him. For, what the farmer thought as stone was nothing but some precious stone.

Do's for becoming a rich person....
**Keep up your mind cool, Warm up your pocket,**
**Be ashamed through your eyes,**
**Have control over your tongue, Have compassion through your heart.**
The opulence of entire world shall be at your feet.

The trader realized that the farmer was pretty ignorant. He told the farmer, 'Will you sell this stone?'

The farmer replied, 'OK, give me a rupee.'

The trader said, showing his sagacity, 'One rupee is damn expensive. I shall pay you eight annas.'

The farmer proceeded ahead without compromising. The trader thought him of selling the stone on his return. How come he shall find any buyer in this vast stretch of desert? The destiny has something else writ. Another trader held the farmer ahead. He took the diamond by paying him one thousand rupee.

The earlier trader asked the farmer, on his return, *'Come on, what will you recollect. Give that stone and have this one rupee.'*

The trader snubbed, beating his forehead, when his farmer has narrated the entire development, 'You fool, you have sold one million rupee worth diamond at one thousand rupee!'

The farmer replied, *'OK, I am the fool, you're paying me eight-anna, despite your intelligence. What should I believe you?'*

The anecdote emphasizes us that the trader couldn't arrive at any decision despite having no confidence. *For, confidence is that forte capable of shaking even earth and making heaven stoop before you.* One doesn't know how many impossible tasks have been accomplished, as the believers were having had deep self-confidence.

Nobody knew how many innovations have taken place in the world on such confidence. So, we shall reiterate that one gets accessible to that on having more self-confidence. A few people find incentives very quickly, for they have been charged with self-confidence in every infinitesimal part of their conscience.

The Third War of Panipat was a matter of self-confidence. None could have survived from the flare up of violence across the battlefront in which s/he couldn't have cherished. The folk numbers recollect even today that woman folk in every household broke their bangles. So, you need to harness self-confidence forever.

❑

**"Politeness makes a man great. Hard work leads him to opulence because hard work and fortune are in the ratio of 70:30."**

**—Tarun Engineer**

# WAKE UP FROM SILLY ISSUES

During the creation of universe, Lord, the Supreme Absolute had raised higher altitude valleys, materialized the existence of oceans with tides, gave birth to invisible species, and roaring animals threatening the space, when he established planet earth during his creation of cosmos.

One day, he thought of creating some species enjoying nature's flora and fauna. Then 'Man' was created.

The maiden man was extremely happy. He realized himself alone on observing some tender shrub attached to the giant tree branch.

The maiden man told lord, the Almighty, on approaching him, *'Your Excellency, I feel something short in your creation of planet earth. But I don't have happiness in my life. I don't have any desire to live anymore.'*

Lord, the Almighty understood his woes. He created 'woman' to enliven man's life in solitude.

Woman, as such, was heavenly gift for man. Man was extremely baffled at woman's beauty, hue and smile. So, he was found entrapped in her body language.

He approached lord, the Almighty again, accompanying her, *'Excellency, my lord! Woman is an icon of infinite desires. I feel myself incompetent to fulfil her desires galore. She desires often to have special floral fragrance to dress her up or some waist band anew. She gets estranged on my failure to bring them. She makes fun of me. I was extremely happy and unconcerned earlier. So, take her back.'*

Lord, the Almighty made the woman return to him upon smile. Maiden man cried again before lord, the Almighty, *'Sorry for the error, my lord. A woman remains obstinate and impatient. I have found my life to have been worthy. Now, my life's sentimental values and happiness have been caved in her conscience. So, return that woman for my company.'*

Lord, the Almighty found his request as anticipatory, but replied coolly, *'Now you couldn't return her. You folks need to stay cohabiting despite many anomalies.'*

The division of opinion proliferates about woman since time immemorial. Man and woman live together in the universe of lord, the Almighty. The duo has been bestowed with intelligence, and aptitude alike. Nobody knew how many women have entered the zenith of success, where it has kissed their feet.

Reena Shaw is a living example to have brought something anew in the world of accessories. The designer shoe, money purse, vanity bag etc have fetched the market across the continents.

Her accessories were found as the branded ones not only at home but also abroad. However, she couldn't have had the success overnight despite deciding upon her own future. Something else has hidden behind her success, i.e., hard work and struggle.

**It is not important how much is the level of your intelligence. What you have shall be more important on how you utilize them under circumstances.**

One could imagine in the competitive world about the marketing of some product but maintaining its utility and excellence is not so easy.

The thirty-year old Reena Shaw based in Mumbai, of course, entered into her business, by injecting some thirty thousand rupee, but she got the flag of success flying aloft after nearly eight years.

She has glorified the world of woman's accessories such as wallet and designer shoes, by launching the franchises at New York, Paris, London, Milan, and Dubai, through *Renaldi label* logo. She replied, when sought about the secret of success, 'Everybody buys fashion products from anywhere. It is not limited to fashion world, but other accessories such as footwear, wallet will also enhance the woman's personality. That is why; I have opted for this avocation.'

Reena became mature with the opulent family, but she had taken utmost pains to carve out her niche in the world of accessories.

She should have opted for some other extraordinary avocation, which has not gained any importance so far. It was not so easy for her accepting defeat, other than making business of several millions.

You could also bring some revolutionary changes in the world of business and trade. So, you need to think and deliberate like Reena

Shaw. You should rect·'y the errors options to rectify errors crept in earlier attempts with sui·ıble amendments.

You need to deliberate over such experiments afresh. Note down the anomalies you have come across, mentioning those anomalies one after another, responsible for your inherent failure in life.

01________________________________________

02________________________________________

03________________________________________

04________________________________________

The book shall share with you in rectifying such anomalies. For, you need to evaluate the difficult propositions, think afresh constructively, which calls for some splendid connections in the society.

Think about reaching the zenith of success of any field. Your thoughts would be aloof from what you shall ponder constructively. For, the solution to difficult propositions calls for constructive plans and splendid connections in turn.

Imagine you had to reach at the zenith of success for any problem. You should deliberate over the constructive phase of that proposition. Obviously, solution finds pretty interrelated in between various ideas, which derives its forte from the central nervous system through trial and error of developments. Exercise alone could make you reach the path without much ado in the blueprint of success.

Ascertaining ideas in between the lines simulates finding some destination on an unknown two-dimensional map. You could initiate such path through the map appearing in this book. You couldn't experiment over such instantaneous solution in practical life, for you would be involved in tracing such path in the complex map.

A similar incident occurs while exploring such option. You could disbelieve over such option apart from learning techniques galore, which could make you trod vicious path. Most of such paths appearing rosy away from such links or episodes seldom prove to be so, other than making your life pretty complicated and the procedures goof up.

Your thoughts could refine your identity provided you explore interlinks in between such thoughts.

Imagine how far you were resourceful? How much command you have had on language? How much sonorous is your utterance? The evaluation relates to that era capable of ascertaining your progress, influence and success. So, make up your mind to embrace them with utmost self-confidence.

It is true that your deft handling, sweetness and smile could make every proposition favourable. So, you should have some self-confidence to venture ahead. You would find yourself capable of achieving something, by means, 'Yes, I could achieve something in life.'

Look around on finding yourself pretty disturbed. Please deliberate seriously on developments such as what you have come across and realized about the outcome. You shall find that people around you were successful and have been at the climax in their respective fields despite belonging to ordinary background.

**A rifle doesn't fight in war but the soldier handling that. He fights through strong self-confidence rather from his heart.**

However, such people alone could emerge as successful, who have been accustomed to hard work and firm will power.

You could become unsuccessful for your lack from such self-confidence and your attempts were seldom foolproof. It might happen that you won't be successful in the preset gestation period. You won't be successful despite making efforts in this direction.

Self-confidence is such forte in life, which makes any laity accomplish something unbelievable in life. For, the power of his spirit would symbolize his will power. It doesn't mean that you could achieve in no time. So, you need to follow the tips mentioned underneath.

- Aesthetic mind is always precious. Enhance its beauty. Interact coolly with whosoever coming across through sweet dialogue.

Shahrukh Khan told in the super hit movie,
**'Om Shanti Om,'**
**'The possessions galore shall attempt to mingle with you the moment you make up your mind to accomplish something through heart.'**
The lines shall get implanted in your heart
**like this book attempting to present facts.**

- Everybody should live without any stress. You would find yourself pretty helpless and exhausted under stress. Seldom could you arrive at any significant decisions.
- Acquaint with the techniques of forgiving and tendering due apologies. Generally, your self-confidence gets intensified when you forgive and ignore others' weakness. You will be empowered to get unbelievable respect in the society.
- Condition your own fear. Nobody had been some complete persona on earth. Face that haunting object troubling everybody. Attempt to dispel such fear haunting you boldly addressing the audience. Jot down the points you wish to share with them. Address yourself before some mirror upon absolute self-confidence.
- Explore and stabilize your source of positive thoughts. Everybody is bestowed with some negative thoughts of virtue. Circumstances warrant you to expel them on ascertaining their weakness.
- Avoid breaking anybody's faith. Share not his (her) opinion expressed in confidence, for s/he might be your coeval or member of your household.
- Avoid insulting whosoever concerned about the behavior or deal. Try to appraise him (her) through poised and legible comments.
- Avoid making any silly issues as the matter of your repute. For, you will be facilitated from those folks cashing in on silly ideas.

Introspect yourself after emulating these tips practically. Love your life, for this life seldom comes again.

Always bear in mind, *Lord, the Almighty will keep infinite access open for you, if He shuts anyone inimical to you.* But, don't bask your eyesight under sorrow on being disheartened over His wonders. Hazy eyesight couldn't find out His ways and means, which He has kept already earmarked for you.

Rio Moiré said, during some workshop on self-confidence, held recently at Japanese capital Tokyo, 'There is no job across the universe, which man couldn't accomplish unless there is practical truth. Yes, it calls for some self-confidence in us.'

❑

**"Your laughter could make the entire world laugh. Nobody shall cry, if you cry."**

**—Tarun Engineer**

# CHALK OUT YOUR DEFINITE OBJECTIVE

My mother used to inquire me during childhood, 'What could I be on becoming an adult?' Often, I used to coolly reply on becoming an engineer like my maternal uncle.

For, my maternal uncle Kailashchand was an engineer in Kalgarh dam. I was pretty influenced by his splendor, pomp and grandeur in the society. It moulded me to become an engineer, but I couldn't well concentrate on my studies. It made my household folks to make fun of me.

It doesn't mean that I was least intelligent, but my mind meandered through insignificant things, which made me failure at my eleventh standard. My uncle Shanti Prakash told me, *'You couldn't get through your studies. Proceed ahead in involvement through your father's business. Dispel the dream of becoming an engineer.'*

My uncle's pricking comments hurt me badly. I made up my mind to get through the examination, score good marks for entering into engineering degree. Subsequently, I got involved in studies, worked hard and made day and night equal during such experiment.

Consequently, I got through the twelfth standard with highest marks, and was admitted into an engineering college for electrical engineering faculty. My uncle blessed me when I met him, *'Son, I had admonished you harshly because you're farther away from your goal.'*

So, this came to be my practical life of swerving away from the objective. For, I went on dreaming to become a film hero, though my personality seldom matched iteratively for the role. You know, I was expending my valuable time and energy over such fragile objective.

Why shall man swerve off his objective? Have you deliberated seriously upon this? For, he could utilize some two or three per cent of his mind, putting appreciable part invalid for life. Scientists around the world testified Albert Einstein's brain after his death how come he became scientist par excellence.

The practical results have visualized some eight per cent of Einstein's brain cells to be active, while he couldn't experiment the rest of his brain for the purpose. However, lord, the Almighty has bestowed us such brain to innovate such results throughout our life utilizing twelve times the potential of Albert Einstein.

The experiment calls for your absolute concentration. Concentration owes to your values (hobbies). For, your hobbies alone could hone your skills while watching some movie, test match or serial episodes on television. The creativity in such observation could affix your brain in such manner that makes you have least interest in developments devoid of creativity. Studies form part of such concentration. My swerving off from the objective owed to this syndrome. So, you should improve your concentration power and deliberate only on such objective.

**A man lacking potential to live shall find himself slave to circumstances. The circumstances alone shall circulate in him daringly.**

However, one finds obstacles galore during stabilization of such concentration. It doesn't mean one flirting away from such objective. One could be successful on positive thinking provided one's faculties back on penchant for something.

Pulela Gopichand has accomplished such mission. I am deliberating on him, who has made significant debut as an ace badminton player. He happens to be the second Indian champion in All England Badminton Championship after Prakash Padukone.

A tragic event shattered Gopichand's dreams during 1994 Pune's national championship event. He felt as though his dream was shattered when he fell on the court during a row with his double seed. He groaned under severe pain, for it was beyond his control, keeping him off playing for sometime.

Gopichand was admitted to a local hospital. The swelling of the joint was so severe, which called for some serious surgical operation. His knee was severely affected from the fall in the court. Doctors disbelieved of Gopichand play badminton ahead with similar swiftness and punch, as he did earlier.

He was bedridden for four months. Whosoever athlete have heard or came to know about Gopichand felt that he was finished as an athelete forever. That personality scoring points by rushing like some leopard began facing hardships even to take mere turns on bed. For, any athlete could find pretty difficult on being bedridden, staying away from grounds. However, the doctors operating him have subsequently confided him to be back very soon with reset knee.

**Success will move farther on your swerving from objective. It shall kiss your feet provided you align with the objective.**

But, Gopichand would return to badminton court hale and hearty, irrespective of delay. He was enlivened of doctor's confidence, when rays of hope made home in him afresh.

Gopichand began practising simple physical exercises, following doctors' advice after some ten months. He returned to badminton court after a couple of days but without zest and enthusiasm. He didn't accept defeat at any cost. His sole ambition was to fulfill the dreams of becoming an established champion. He began working hard anew with renewed vigour and vitality.

Gopichand got into the pitch after nearly two years to play in some tournament. The spectators were bewildered of wounded badminton ace preparing him on the court facing opponents.

His performance was far from good. For, his failure to win made him learn lessons afresh, and reaped the benefits in subsequent event. He began retrieving the old zest and enthusiasm, as the time rolled by.

Gopichand became the numero uno again in the badminton arena. Every athlete across the continents has lauded the courage and determination of Gopichand, made through winning of the 2001 All England Badminton Championship upon renewed vigour.

You could also establish record like Gopichand. You could establish business record with appreciable dividends. You could be promoted to higher levels on acquiring additional values during avocation. You need to fix up the goal like our Gopichand. You need to find out appropriate sector. You have to qualify through our questionnaire of attitudes. It could fix up the sector in which you ascend at the zenith of success.

Get into the business. Read through the questions carried underneath. Please tick before each question with appropriate answer befitting your personality.

1. **What will you do before any work?**
   - (a) I won't deliberate seriously ☐
   - (b) I shall do so before handling the risk. ☐
2. **What is your approach towards such work?**
   - (a) Work simultaneously in all projects. ☐
   - (b) Work seriously in a few projects. ☐
3. **Your behaviour often could be**
   - (a) Speak more, but listen less ☐
   - (b) Listen more, but speak less ☐
4. **Your self-apperceation could be**
   - (a) An ordinary man like others ☐
   - (b) Serious-minded with novelistic approach ☐
5. **The objective of your mission**
   - (a) Roll on according to life ☐
   - (b) Work on specific mission ☐
6. **How far are you practical?**
   - (a) Get lost in dreaming ☐
   - (b) Believe in practical proposition instead of hallucination ☐
7. **What do you think of future?**
   - (a) Worried quite frequently ☐
   - (b) Live according to the present phase ☐
8. **Working on project anew?**
   - (a) You remain slipshod during the process. ☐
   - (b) You will sketch out the blueprint coolly. ☐
9. **How do you think on ideas anew?**
   - (a) Shall accept when things are practical ☐
   - (b) Shall remain inquisitive on things anew ☐

10. **What is significant in your life?**
   (a) Relation, happiness, opulence and familiarity ☐
   (b) Respect, creativity and peace ☐
11. **If entrusted with some job?**
   (a) I love taking very important job. ☐
   (b) I wish to work peacefully behind the curtain. ☐
12. **On what basis do you arrive at the decision?**
   (a) Do that which is appropriate. ☐
   (b) Do after serious deliberation with utmost vigil. ☐
13. **Encountering time constraints**
   (a) Usually get delayed ☐
   (b) Limitation is there, but will reach on time. ☐
14. **Your point of view about others**
   (a) I do appreciate good jobs. ☐
   (b) I couldn't appreciate swiftly. ☐
15. **The effect of your sentiments**
   (a) Shall dominate on work ☐
   (b) Hide such sentiments without ado. ☐
16. **What's your priority?**
   (a) Honesty and professional approach ☐
   (b) Professional approach prior to honesty. ☐
17. **How are you rated in the office?**
   (a) Keep myself well informed ☐
   (b) Limited up to my colleagues ☐
18. **Someone inquiring about something**
   (a) Shall respond swiftly and comprehensively ☐
   (b) Answer after serious deliberation ☐
19. **The plus point of your interaction**
   (a) Shall befriend everybody ☐
   (b) Couldn't interact with everybody ☐
20. **What should be the benchmark of decision?**
   (a) Argument and justice ☐
   (b) Empathy and condition ☐
21. **Life's philosophy?**
   (a) Why should I work every day-Let there be rest in between. ☐
   (b) Leisure is unlawful. ☐

22. **Your interest in work**
   (a) Relaxed environment expediting job swiftly ☐
   (b) Organized work under phases ☐
23. **Your response under adverse circumstances**
   (a) Adapting according to the situation ☐
   (b) Always try to change the environment ☐
24. **Any new idea sprouting in?**
   (a) Share with dependable kith and kin ☐
   (b) Could share with anybody ☐
25. **Your thought towards life**
   (a) Exploring of probabilities ☐
   (b) Accounting for the reality ☐

**What is this Attitude Test?** It is a questionnaire, incorporating certain hobbies, working tack, ability of interaction, aptitude and associated questions on your behavioural pattern. You shall also find similar tests asunder:

**A. Mental Aptitude Test:** The test analyzes about your discriminatory aptitude incorporating either on numerological argumentative capability or arithmetic angle or squarely evaluating your retention potential.

**B. Work-compatibility Test:** This test would be conducted to ascertain the problems encountered during your performance.

**C. Special Aptitude Test:** The questionnaire remains assorted. The test is conducted to ascertain the technical know how about your objective.

**D. Personality Test:** It is conducted to find out whether the subject would work according to requirements of his objective. The questions such as, *'Are you interested in reading poems or flying kites? Are you interested in reading books or flying an airplane?'*

**E. Fidelity Test:** These tests are conducted in sensitive and professional areas. The questions such as, *'Do you wish to play chess instead of reading poems? Do you read poems instead of playing chess?'* Often questions such as *'Have you ever uttered lies?'* were asked.

We shall let you know about the points you have scored.

You would certainly work in such manner, when you answer **(a)**s which involves your appreciable interaction with sundry folks. You need some freedom for excellent performance. You prefer leading the life with some freedom and excellence.

**You could steer the life in proper direction on stabilizing your objective. For, strong thinking power is the mother of complete actions.**

Cultivating relationship and befriending would be significant in your career. You dislike staying alone, often impatient and speak with some care. You hasten yourself while answering, but seldom hides your sentiments. You always like affection, love and appreciation from others. You will be seriously influenced by other's opinion.

**The befitting career waiting for you:** Stock broker, secretary, receptionist, director, advisor, marketing executive, advocate, advertising executive, medical representative, public relations executive, travel agent, hotel management, income tax organizer could fit the bill.

If you score **(a)** and **(b)** equally, you could be constructive, imaginative and professional in life. You prefer working alone behind the curtain without anybody noticing your performance. You have lesser number of friends. You're a good listener. You dislike blowing your own trumpet. You are really a professional, for you take decisions with seriousness.

One could seldom get answers from you. For, you analyze about the pros and cons of the developments. You prefer to work in seriously involving with some project. You are extremely tolerant and honest towards others. You hardly appreciate anybody in the arena. You keep vigil to the utmost level while conversing,

**Do you want to know how opulence could be earned within a short span of time?**
Mr. Haldi Ram Aggarwal is the suitable example, as he had opened a small sweetmeat shop in Bikaner some 70 years ago, which got transformed to 7 billion rupees worth massive industry.

concentrating on adapted words and the lingo, convincing about the content impeccably. You dislike working in make-shift environment.

**The befitting career waiting for you:** Artist, historian, novelist, academician, photographer, graphic designer, banker, webmaster, producer, managing director, nursing, advertising executive, and cartoonist could fit the bill.

Perhaps, your mind might have been overpowered with some hazy picture after attitude test. You might have made up your mind on which profession you should get in. Which could be your career? What should you be? Please write down about such objectives in the row under mentioned.

*I ______________________________________ wish to become ______________________________ on the acquisition of my added values in ______________ which was ascertained after the Attitude Test.*

Give some frequent thought over what you have decided, uttering, *'Yes, I am capable of doing this job,'* and *'I should achieve the objective at all costs.'* Certainly, you could hone your self-confidence when you could visualize hazy picture of such objective, when you're alone. The image would carve a niche out in your heart, reminding you while you're busy on routine activities.

The behavioural science explains that our inner conscience certainly backs us whenever we arrive at accomplishing some significant mission, by transforming the catharsis (thought process) of such objective into reality. For, your life reflects your ambition and ideals forever. You could become so as you wish. This is the fundamental formula of inevitable success.

❑

"Leader seldom surfaces from anywhere any moment or any incident But, such people rehearse in solitude for they dream to become better than others."

—Tarun Engineer

# THINK LIKE GIANT PERSONALITIES

Indian movie producer Tarachand Barjatya told celluloid hero Amitabh Bachchan, on finding his lanky body with elongated legs, when he sought to enact as hero in his movies, '*You are pretty taller and lanky. How could I make you as the hero in my movies? The heroine working with you needs to enact by standing on some stool. So, it could be fair, have you had abandoned dreaming of becoming hero. For, you're misfit. Get back to your home.*'

Amitabh Bachchan ignored his advice and struggled to eke out livelihood by his stay in Mumbai. For, his conscience was replete with self-confidence endorsing him to be the hero on the celluloid screen.

Amitabh, thereafter, displayed his essential quality as an actor, enacting in *Saat Hindustani*. After his debut in *Zanjeer*, he was recognized as the super star. Tarachand Barjatya, who disowned him in admitting for his production, accommodated him in his latest venture, *Hero,* where he got qualified of becoming the super star. It is justified from such incidents, how far one should be attached with his objective in anticipation of success.

Benjamin Disraeli on accomplishing extraordinary success on being the British premier was an outsider, as far as his birth and lineage. He used to say, '*Man is not the slave of circumstances, but he enslaves them. For, the world is an arena of ideas. The environment around us gets transformed proportional to our issues, desires and confidence, as and when we go on thinking.*'

There won't be any such desire, which couldn't be accomplished. The sermon of Lord Jesus Christ insists beings to listen to the voice of one's conscience. It might be possible; one had to renounce anything to get his dream fulfilled. Proceed ahead confidently with your objective by sticking to slew of desires.

People would go on criticizing, and put innumerable obstacles in your way. It is possible of people labeling as some stupid or crazy guy.

However, stick to your objective, for followers of Jesus Christ troubled him in similar manner. Worry not and fear not, on finding your life being enveloped by hardships hovering with pessimistic clouds. Your confidence and firm will power would make you reach at the zenith of success at the cost of dispelling tentative obstacles.

Yes, the instantaneous requirement is to create such self-confidence within you. Keep your objective at every moment without losing any moment. This fact had been interpreted in the verse below, as

*Vacham Niyacchatmani tam niyachcha*
*Buddhou dhiyam yachcha cha buddhisaakshini*
*Tam capi poornatmani nirvikalpye*
*Vilapya shantim paramaam bhajaswa.*

The verse is being interpreted as—'Adsorb your voice in your mind, mind in your intellect and intellect with thy spirit. Enjoy the eternal bliss by submerging thy spirit in Supreme Absolute Consciousness. Life calls for some etiquette rhythm for survival. Concentration is necessary for achieving every objective.

Concentration is nothing but merger of both entities. Your intellect needs to be merged in thy spirit. It could be so, for your mind needs whatever act you accomplish should find endorsed by the intelligence. Let the act of intelligence be earmarked for thy spirit. To say, thy voice, mind and intelligence be aligned to fulfill thy objective. However, you could encounter with scores of competitions.

Success won't knock you off unless there is some competition. You need to encounter such obstacles with full zest and renewed vigour. Nobody could safeguard you unless you arrive at the set target.

Professor Himanshu Roy of Indian Institute of Management believes, '*A proper selection of competitors could endorse your major role, howsoever insignificant be that business. It is essential to ascertain for yourself, which field you desire to enter under the logo of such USP.*'

Certainly, the selection of competitors' thinking and action could bring absolute transformation in the arena. The tacks of accomplishing tasks go on changing. The circumference of deliberation might contract or stretch. Competition alone could be some turning point irrespective of your reaching at the zenith of success or the nadir of failure. You could reach the goal off mark provided you're the trailer in such race. Your fight could be on the footboard in reaching objective as the runner-up, unless your competitor gets stabilized and farther than you.

You need to face acute competition in the race towards success. Of course, the issue could be significant had you get into competition.

How could you arrive at the procedure when your clientele is busy in deliberating on some other group other than you? What formula should you embrace luring the clientele endorsing your reaching at the zenith of success? Adopt the formulae explained underneath.

- *Accomplish some giant objective through small components.*
- *Bear in mind about the creative aspect of your brand image.*
- *Observe the opponents with positive point of view.*
- *Fix up your objective with some flexibility before entering the market.*
- *Competition is the yardstick of your progress. Stay fit to wallow in the race.*
- *Your image improves howsoever the competition be splendid. Have good terms with your competitors.*

Many of the fellow seafarers have disbelieved during 1485 A.D that Columbus could return alive, when he reached the Atlantic Ocean. His compatriots advanced ahead though they were frightened earlier to do so. They returned to Spain after exploring Americas without caring for scores of obstacles on their journey. They were given red carpet welcome by Spanish countrymen and were felicitated for accomplishing successful expedition. Some of his own supporters were jealous of his service to humankind, when they derided, 'It was not somewhat Herculean task of exploring Americas. Anyone could have invented. You completed the expedition on reaching west off Atlantic Ocean.'

Columbus went on quietly listening to their comments. He addressed his supporters on the following day, despite their sarcastic remarks, 'Friends, get me the boiled egg stand on the table, if there is no complicated task on earth.'

Columbus' followers attempted to accomplish the feat, but in vain. Eventually, he told them, after making the squeezed horizontal portion of such egg stand, 'See, doing so would be easier.' His followers felt embarrassed on realizing about his tack.

So, it is true that success could be achieved by those, whose thought remains positive towards life. The folks could accommodate

**It doesn't take much time to inaugurate any task anew. Everyday rolls in anew for such inaugurals. Achieving objective without forgetting the past is something extremely difficult.**

selves to the changed circumstances. Such folks seldom condition selves without being frightened of the swings coming across in life.

It could be substantiated that positive thoughts and success are the two facets of same coin. So, your point of view would infer about the overall life lying ahead.

Your thoughts alone could condition about the future position. Obviously, you could be successful and the success would kiss your feet when your thoughts swing positively.

An example could be seven feet and three inches tall weighing 191 kilograms, Khali, as record ace in the smack down contest of WWE.

India took some six decades to hoist her national flag, open the wrestling record putting Europe and America as the runners up. Khali, whom we are proud of, could have stayed underground had not the senior Punjab police officer S.S. Bhullar recognised of his good physique and capabilities. He took the charcoal hero with him and made him a diamond. His triumph was extolled not only at home but abroad.

Khali, born on August 27, 1972, to some poor family of Himachal Pradesh had his christened name as Dilip Singh Rana. His friends at home began cutting jokes about his height and horizontal building up of the physique. It is somewhat unusual, when people began staring at his well-built body, forgetting everything on hand.

He reached Shimla, the capital of Himachal Pradesh, to eke out his livelihood. His fortune took turns, when police office S S Bhullar met him on the streets. He took Khali along and got him enrolled in the state police as constable. He prepared him for the Beijing Olympics wrestling contest.

The *Great Khali* participated in the U.S All Pro-wrestling contests for the first time during 1966. He trailed behind but eventually emerged as the budding debutant. The trainer Brian Ong died from his punch during 2001 contests. WWF got him signed over some contract in 2006 A.D. He knocked off the wrestler undertaker during 2006 April. At the end of July, he trounced the wrestlers like the Great American Bash and Barista to qualify as the world's wrestler in the free-style wrestling.

You also possess such inherent capabilities like the Great Khali, which remain unnoticed. The capabilities could be aroused even at the slightest pretext. Our Upanishads claim, '*Aham Brahmasmi,* interpreting 'I am the Brahman, the Creator.' The interpretation has been carried out within different faiths in different manners. For, the seed won't sprout from tree other than having the probability to become giant tree. One could not imagine over such tree without any seed.

**Your perspective determines your life, but what you wish to become owes to your thought for the day of objective.**

Anyhow, it requires the warm climate for seed transforming into some giant tree, viz., soil, sunlight, wind and water. You could also reach at the zenith of success on availing such support in any field. You have such parameters, for lord, the Almighty has begotten you, so achieving such success could be much easier task. You could enhance your capabilities through systematic approach, when you couldn't reveal such mission before anybody. You could blossom out voluntarily, for you know your plus points very well.

You could access the path of such objective disregarding your minus points. It is only possible when you differentiate and compromise between the plus and minus points in you. For, confidence alone could play such dynamic role, which could be harmonized through personality oriented development.

**Evaluate Thy Self-confidence:** Psychiatrist Michael Lee justifies, 'You could set off this parameter through self-evaluation. Identify about your psychic capabilities. Everybody is born with such instincts. He does identify such powers at certain stage.'

The most effective technique of identifying our capabilities shall remain with our hobbies. However, many people seldom could ascertain about such capabilities under social pressure, on being over

**You could visualize the contours of objective legibly once you fix up and could fructify that through the medium of dissection.**

ambitious, which could have been atrocious. We could see this syndrome in the fall of our Y-generation to swerve off their objectives.

You could be successful in the world of music provided you have such capabilities. For, your capabilities get amplified in that field. The necessity however, remains that you should excel in the field you enroll. So, it calls for selecting your objective on identifying such capabilities.

**Explore Thyself:** The next phase of development could be your self-evaluation. It could explore your inherent capabilities, which you entertain wholeheartedly. These could help in seeking out your livelihood provided they are developed in appropriate manner. Keep the correct targets through suitable plans for development by entertaining criticizing points of view.

**Imagine thy predicaments**: Often it happens that you couldn't identify about your capabilities. You could realize of your fleet during such hours of crisis. You find that you couldn't accomplish the task despite being trapped in such uncertainties.

For example, you disbelieve that you could sing well. You're frightened whether anyone would deride you on singing. Prepare for such ordeal alone well before such real encounter in anticipation of satisfactory performance.

Try to attempt in singing folk numbers or rhymes all alone. Do the rehearsals for a couple of days to enhance your level of self-confidence. Make your friends listen to your recorded version. Accept my advice of not getting disheartened on people deriding about your singing traits.

> Anyone depending on his intelligence
> shall certainly reverse his path of progress.
> His immaturity of wallowing in his sentiments would make
> **him suffer for the entire life.**

**Initiate the task in solitude:** Any creative personality sport his activities alone before entering the arena. The society enjoys the bliss from music, but its rehearsal always takes place in solitude. The singer could certainly develop some rapport with his mentor. The formula applies not only for playback singers, but also for other fields. You could be a successful painter or write good verses or invent some process, accordingly. Even the wrestlers assess about their capabilities alone before going public. Such rehearsal could serve as the benchmark of their mission.

❑

You know about your interests. Your becoming over-ambitious and getting crushed under social pressure could certainly neutralize them.

—Tarun Engineer

# ASSIMILATE ABOUT THE OUTSTANDING PERSONALITIES

Perhaps, you might have been unaware of Dr. APJ Abdul Kalam to have sold newspapers during his childhood in Rameshwaram (Tamil Nadu). For, he had his formal education from a poor family. He completed his education after availing the scholarship. He was admitted into the faculty of aeronautical engineering at Chennai-based *Madras Institute of Technology*. Later, he qualified in the field of space science.

He gave new direction to India's space mission as a scientist. He developed *Agni* and *Prithvi* missiles thereby innovating modern technology for the country in missile technology for the century. He was recognized around the world as the *Missile Man*. Dr. Kalam proceeds with certain objective in life, visualizing the country as the superpower by 2020.

A few personalities in the world visualize accomplishing success through their destiny. A lyricist has commented about them,

*Ram Bharose baithkar, raha khaat per soch*
*Anhonee honee nahin, honee ho so hoye...*

We attribute this as the point of view of the fortunate, which could drop the people away. Such folks while away with the thought whatever is inevitable shall happen, while things staying cool shall remain so. However, such paradise seekers cashing in on destiny remain cowards.

*Ajgar Karen Na chaakari, panchi kare Na kaam*
*Daas maluka kah Gaye, sabke data raam.*

Lord Ram happens to be the saviour of everybody on earth. For, Ajgar (Python) seldom works. Birds never work. The species get their feed despite flying and chirping idle. So, what is the necessity of us working? We shall get something in life what has been destined for us. This is the negative thought we have had.

The interpretation warrants that one should not get disheartened of one's ambition. One should dare proceed. The fortune shall obviously transform him. For, your destiny and hard work will function at their own levels. Scriptures uphold the view, 'Destiny is the mightiest on earth.' However, man on earth could be graced well shedding his destiny. For, the world is a battle field, which has been cited by poet Rahim in his duet.

*Rahimana chup ho baithiye, dekh dinana ke pher*
*jab nike din aayenge, banat na lage der.*

It means, *don't get discouraged, but venture ahead, the destiny shall certainly change you.* For,destiny does its work and hard work shall do its work. Scriptures have said, *Destiny is mightiest.* but man becomes fortunate by breaking the shackles of destiny.

**A hard working person gets what all he desires but he shall get everything on working towards the objectives.**

Accordingly, you could notice how the founder and managing director of Hero Honda Group, Brijmohan Lal Munjal has transformed his hard work into success. Munjal was the disciple of an ashram. He worked in ordnance depot of the Indian Army for two years, after completing his formal education. He was subsequently shifted over to CEOG office.

However, Munjal longed to do some business leaving the defense job. So, he began deliberating over self-employment after quitting the plum job. He disbelieved on what to do, when he found one of his cousins manufacturing bicycle pump. He advised Munjal to manufacture ancillary parts of bicycle, for India was not allowed to import spare parts of bicycles.

He established the firm *'Munjal Brothers'*, associating with his brother, after borrowing money from the bank. He began regularly supplying products for bicycle manufacturers at home. He began producing bicycles under the trade name, *'Hero.'*

However, why did he christen the bicycle as *Hero?* It has some anecdote behind. The celluloid hero appeared to be the mightiest during 1955. So, Munjal christened his bicycle as Hero, outperforming other market models. The then Punjab government granted licence for his company, which made the company join the corporate world.

Munjal began manufacturing mopeds after nearly five years. Honda Company of Japan during 1986 got with the Indian counterpart Hero jointly to produce two-wheelers for Indian market. The joint venture Hero Honda produced 100 c.c. motor bicycles *CD 100,* which outperformed *Yamaha* and *Rajdoot* models familiar on Indian roads. Lo! Today, *Hero Honda* is the outstanding motorcycle available in the world.

**One who dares to dream finds the entire world as the pitch. For, every elite dreams something, which materializes through hard work.**

Dispel disheartening trends in your mind. For, it is justified in the world that there is no successful personality, who has not encountered minor obstacles on his mode of success. The path could get blocked for successful personalities. However, such guys remain deprived of the final portals, who avoid in becoming crazy, which don't have the bent for success.

Could you recapitulate how the father of Sikander the Great was an insignificant soldier, who didn't have any province, or any prince, other than Sikander dreaming to be an emperor subsequently? His father's background seldom posed any obstacle in his son achieving success.

US president Roosevelt lost his legs. However, his lameness seldom put obstacles in his path of becoming the president of the three-century old democracy. Another president Harry S Truman had not even joined the college for studies. He happened to be the true man of reaching the apex house of power after the cold war skirmishes.

Success seldom objects anyone from reaching its portals despite having ill health, poor education, lesser age, old age, misfortune or bad luck. For, success knew well that whosoever insignificant shouldered shall remain stuck to its wings.

The proponent wonders why not he proceeds ahead under pretension. We need to recapitulate the comments of evergreen celluloid Indian hero Dev Anand. He has completed some 80 summers and winters, but he continues to think, *'I am still 24-year old youth.'* He continues to deliberate himself as some 24-year old youth, qualifying him to stay on in the business of film production.

*'For, the world doesn't have any such royal path, treading on which you could have had success. This is my utmost opinion, which I have inalienably adopted throughout my life.'*

Former president of India, Dr. APJ Abdul Kalam is a unique personality, as the world is replete with such personalities. The giants were mobilized to work hard, irrespective of their objectives in becoming triumphant.

❑

"You could reach the short cut path provided you divide the objective into infinitesimal objectives."

—Tarun Engineer

Health, money,
intelligence, love,
supporting society and
purity of spirit in
minute level are suffice for
**short-term success,**
whereas
biggest success
calls for
**strong will-power**
**and**
**insanity!**

It is true that whatever we think would influence our age. However, our positive thoughts would certainly extend our longevity. For, positive thoughts shall tone up our metabolism and various cells and veins through different chemical compounds.

The scientists of Texas University have propounded through some studies that man would have longer life without getting disheartened even during his euphoric moments or adverse circumstances.

**The opulence of universe owes to lone fact. Hard work was just to transform that fact into reality.**

The development could be a matter of self-confidence. Swami Vivekananda hoisted the flag of excellence about Indian culture in religious congregation at Chicago, when he was barely 29-years old. His eloquence made philosopher John Lubbock comment, *'The world could become some paradise and aesthetically appealing had man awaken upon his individual self-confidence.'*

Our women folks are not behind in accomplishing something impossible to some specific mission, by virtue. We could find South Asian maiden woman Bachendri Pal to have scaled Mount Everest as bona fide Indian. She found poor supply of oxygen the moment she reached the summit ignoring the plea of Bulgarian mountaineers. She fulfilled her mission on reaching the summit with her own cylinder. So, you have to admit the capital of self-confidence is more precious than nature's gift—oxygen.

Joan of Arc, a herdswoman dreamt of becoming the commander of French army during her childhood. She was absolutely confident of being born to liberate her country from the colonial

Tell you conscience to do something
at the cost of excessive
**Hard work.**
Come out of your dreams to achieve superiority and
show some wonder.

yoke. It substantiates anybody born with self-confidence hardly gets disturbed from any adverse phenomena. He (She) goes on breathing comfortably on accomplishing mission one after another under the influence of such self-confidence.

Let us think what our industrial giant Dhirubhai Ambani claims, *'The term failure is unavailable in the lexicon of self-confident person.'*

Let us think of ants, how do they carry even the heaviest objects with self-confidence from one place to another. They fell down frequently, despite ascending the walls, and become successful in reaching the destination.

Success and failure frequent like harmonic tides of some big ocean. Some get neutralized on hitting the rocks, while others were found successful in hopping beyond. Cool yourself even for slightest failure. Keep attempting on becoming triumphant. It doesn't mean the magnitude of brain power but the way you are putting that to use. The significant part however remains about the deliberation, which could steer you ahead.

My query to the renowned physician Raj Kumar Gupta as, *'Does any child become scientist?'*

Dr Gupta replied, *'He could become so, for it doesn't call for stormy brain, or any abnormal retention power. It is also unnecessary that he should have scored good marks. However, it is necessary that he should have good aptitude. He could become the scientist par excellence proportional to the quantum of his interest.'*

Make up your mind about your objective. Get into action for becoming successful. For, the outlets of success had been kept open. Yes, you ought to enter through them.

❑

"The time to attend for wear and tear of debris of terrace could be sharing sunlight. Arriving at the correct objective is possible at that time when self-confidence has bloomed from within."

—Tarun Engineer

# CONDITION YOUR ANGER

I fetched some proposal to look after in a firm as the sales engineer on my return to Delhi after completing engineering studies. I reached the firm on the following day. The boss of the firm kept me on the job and sent me on some task to Jaipur for two days. I was to discuss with the client for getting the final order.

I left for Jaipur on the same evening and reached the client's factory on the following morning. The client was expecting my visit. He began discussing with me about the supply order. I was extremely hungry overnight for I hadn't taken food on my way. I told him to discuss the deal after he fetches me some breakfast.

The proprietor of the factory said, on becoming furious, 'Have you come to have your food or get the supply order?'

I had convinced him, 'Sir, I left Delhi last evening. I haven't taken food on my way. I have reached straightaway to your factory so that your waiting shall come to an end, the moment I alighted from the bus. Consequently, I have been pretty hungry.

The fury of the proprietor lynched heaven, for he wished to discuss the supply order hastily on being involved in some other task. He shouted out on finding me unprepared, 'You can go now. I won't order your company for any supply. For, I don't have time to wait till you finish your breakfast.'

I got extremely angry on finding his behaviour. I told him, when I was on my feet, 'What sort of human being you are? I have shared about my helplessness. What for you found yourselves peeved? Is it for my breakfast? I don't want your order. I am returning to Delhi. Get your supply from some other company.

'Go on man! Who has objected you? You should have reached the factory after completing breakfast. Your company might expel you from the job very soon, if you stay in this manner.'

So, his statement came true. For, the boss of my firm removed me from the job, on realizing about my return without getting order.

I thought of the consequences sitting alone whether my beahaviour was wrong. I should have met the proprietor of that factory after finishing my breakfast. I should have discussed the supply order. He couldn't have been fumed had I spoken about the breakfast after the deal.

I was pretty sorry for the firm lost its supply order out of my maiden error in life. So, things got frozen of me becoming the sales engineer elsewhere.

So, you shouldn't get fumed. For, the anger would destroy your personality. It would trail your future behind. It has been summarized in the

*Dhyayato vishayanpumsaha sangasteshooshajayate*
*Sangastmanjayate kaamoo kaamakrodhadhobhijayate*

It interprets that the root of anger has destruction. The nature of minds remain becoming over-ambitious or stay on desires. Anger fluxes in when the desired objective is unfulfilled. Anger would disturb the retention capabilities.

For, anger and discretion are counterproductive. Anger would eclipse beings with darkness. However, darkness gets dispelled on receipt of some rays of light. Anger disappears on being enlightened from discretion. However, any human being fails to arrive at any decision of fair or unfair.

Let us recollect an anecdote. A Brahmin lived happily in a village with wife and son. He domesticated a mongoose at home. His wife loved the mongoose as her own son.

One day, she reached bathing aside riverbank, leaving her husband to look after the child. Meanwhile, an aide of the prince told the Brahmin, 'Angel, His Excellency has summoned you for offering charity.'

Well, how could the Brahmin ignore of His Excellency's orders? Moreover, the prince has summoned him for accepting the charity. He thought some other Brahmin might accept the offer in his absence.

Aside, his child was asleep alone. Suddenly, he recollected about the mongoose. He thought of addressing the animal to look after the child and return home on accepting the offer.

He left home by leaving the mongoose over the thought it could take care of his son. A black cobra observed mongoose guarding the child, when it slithered while Brahmin left home. The mongoose threw the butchered snake aside after extracting blood on swift attack. Its skirmish with the snake has made mongoose mouth bloody. The mongoose kept on waiting the Brahmin near the entrance of the home.

However, the Brahmin thought that the bloody mongoose has slain his son, the moment he returned from accepting the charity offer from His Excellence. The mongoose died of continuous beating on him being angry.

The Brahmin found his son sleeping comfortably, the moment he entered the room. He noticed the splintered cobra aside. He realized that the mongoose to have slain the cobra for saving his son.

The Brahmin atoned for his sin. For, he slew the mongoose out of his raging anger, which saved his child.

So, we had to recapitulate Osho, or Acharya Rajneesh's precept, *'Anger is extremely insignificant object. You could visualize its favour provided you cool down for sometime. For, anger would access from one end and drift apart from another. You need to condition yourself without allowing that override upon you.'*

**Seven out of 20 richest persons in the world including Bill Gates haven't completed even the formal education.**

The characteristics such as anger, jealousy, malice, greed, and competition are pretty insignificant, but your ego could flare any of them. Anger accesses without hurting you. You have successfully encountered during its earlier approach.

Allow the shower of delight envelop you. You will realize the disappearing passion without approaching you. Your fortune will smile when the reality glorifies you.

Everybody dreams of becoming a glorified personality but fails to fulfill. You're the most fortunate amongst them, for you have got the book with such formulae, which shall go on ushering you of the ways and means, keeping your mind away from swerving apart.

*Uttisthata jagrata, prapya varaan nibodhat*
*Khsurasya dhara nishita duracaya,*
*duranga pathasa tat kavayo vadanti.*

It does interpret you to become enlightened in regulating your anger, on waking up from the mire. You ought to walk on the edge of the sword to meet with the objective. You ought to prepare your mind. For, people interpret about the mind as some accessory of the physical body, from which the being arrives at any decision of accomplishing good or bad.

Any automobile without steering wheel couldn't be propelled. Similarly, life is directionless without mind. It could also be futile in some aspect. However, man is oriented through mind. He had been quite capable of traversing through earth, ocean, valley and planets, by remaining stationery at some point. Mind, as such had been the cause of his salvation or emancipation.

*Bandhasya vishaya saange mukto nirvishayam taya.*

Mind is of that characteristic that transforms the man slowly, following his objective. He will have similar features, nature, appearance and hue.

*Mano karoti Karmani mano lipyate paatakaih*
*Manascha tanmana buddhaya na punyamanascha paatakaih*

Every object in the universe is on the move. Mind is also on the move. It always remains unstable. It is ought to move, ought to think and work upon. The brain becomes so on the manner in which mind thinks. Anyone becoming the scientist, or becoming a billionaire or a writer of eminence, he could become so, for mind's function is to assimilate and deliberate over the idea.

*Manevam Manushyaanaam Kaaranam bandhamokhsyo*

However, mind owes to attachment and emancipation. It has equal control over dominance and strength of the inherent man, which we interpret as sentiment, when he resorts into taking decision without sifting through the fair or unfair aspects of the issue. Any decision arrived at, whether fair or unfair, had been the outcome of his discretion.

Let me recollect another anecdote. A child was extremely furious. He was found not uttering any unpleasant invectives on anybody. His father told, on handing him with a bag filled with nails, 'Nail one of them on the wall, when you find yourself irritated to utter nonsense.'

At the outset, the child nailed some fourteen nails up on the wall. The wall was pretty hard that made him sweat out after nailing them.

He often thought of controlling his anger rather than striking those nails on the wall. He already nailed appreciable nails on the wall.

A week rolled out in this manner. The child replied, when his father sought on finding no nail on the wall, 'I am not getting angry now.'

The father replied, 'OK, now you remove those nails.'

The child found removing the nails was pretty difficult in contrast with fixing them up. Somehow the child removed them without ado.

**An open cash box could even shake the mind of honest person. Do not reveal your thoughts forever.**

The father told, on finding the wall without nails, 'My son, you have removed the nails, now observe the punctured wall. So, any invective uttered will puncture your mind likewise.'

The child realized his father's comments and vouched not to utter any invective again.

Anger is somewhat dreadful. Man dislikes in recollecting the developments. Anger could convert him extremely sensible, making him volatile, nervous and extremely irritating. However, anger hangs on with the person for some time on reaching the apex, affecting the person seriously.

For, anger metamorphoses with humans like other sentiments. It sports such feelings, visualized by anybody since childhood. However, man sports his anger in two modes. Either he would lose senses, or express anger in some mode. Often, it is noticed him of expressing himself in varieties of modes, on conditioning such anger. He would stop mingling with the person on whom he finds angry.

**You shall think about your objective when reading some wisdom vigorous-oriented manual. Your objective shall get slackened once you finish reading such book.**

Not only this, he would drag himself under ordinary circumstances. Such practices could be known as repressive in nature. For, our brain has cerebrum as the major column, amidst other columns, capable of accomplishing the complex and hard work. The smallest column is known as the cerebellum regulating sentiments and their intensity. It is also known as the emotional brain.

Cerebral cortex could sift through the objects under various circumstances. It seldom endorses incomprehensible things, or apperceives to sort out. Anger will be the outcome of its intensification.

You will become outrageous when your friend fails to keep words or backs out of his assurance. Anger will also affect your health. It is extremely necessary to condition upon one's anger. Anger could be conditioned through following tips.

- Keep in mind not to become volatile irrespective of circumstances. The extent of anger could be gauged from your behavioural pattern.
- Appreciate others' point of view. You shall be enlightened on appreciating others' perception about the development. You could regulate health without blowing such development away. So, try to gauge from others' perception.
- The probability of frequent skirmishes could get pruned accordingly on your relaxing through tense development. Stay cool and relaxed forever.
- One stops interacting with others on finding volatile through self assessed pronouncements. Others pronouncement might be appropriate on the occasion. Try to understand about others' perception.
- All of us have some weakness. Anger is inevitable when some comments upon the development. Try to sort out the uneasiness after proper assimilation.
- Do not make a mountain of a mole hills. Try to gauge over the developments. Have a guffaw on such occasions without inhibition. Certainly, it would expel your anger amassed from frustration.
- Anger overpowers for anybody sitting constantly at one place. Have a break amidst routine and take a stroll in cool breeze. It would automatically result in optimistic outcome on your mood getting refreshed.
- We complain against others on the changed circumstances. It would prevent us from plunging into our thoughts. One could handle the scenario by injecting some change.

For, everybody is being worried and getting insecure under the present state of developments. He is either busy in grabbing or losing something. People are storming out in some mad race affecting our physical health. The psychiatrists believe the issues could be incorporated in one's mind without much ado, provided mind is unattached from any development.

Moreover, it is essential to anybody staying healthy on accordingly assimilating through life. A few folks believe our health remains secured through physicians. It is untrue. For, most of the ailments owe to wrong lifestyle affecting our physical body. So, one ought to undergo the tips given below, for enhancing one's health.

- Healthy life calls for clean environment with regular bath. Our dwelling should have sufficient air and sunlight. Our body should take good food, beverage, besides regular physical exercise.
- The next formula is to have balanced food replete with fat. Green vegetables are must in our diet. Meat diet could be stable with appreciable protein, with appreciable amount of cholesterol. Subsistence on meat would enhance the quantum of uric acid.
- Good cooking of the food is essential. A menu cooked by some helpless, agitated and enraged cook could affect his guests badly. Any cook with stoic mind cooking menu could remain pretty tastier.
- A healthy life needs contented, deep and balanced sleep. Sleeping for appreciable time won't be necessary. A completely relaxed sleep is a must. The folks would get sound sleep after working hard for the day. The disheartened and helpless folks sleep lesser. A sound sleep calls for peace of mind, security and euphoric thoughts.
- Undertake regular physical exercise. It could bring euphoric mind with improved blood circulation. Jogging in open air could improve your health. A sound mind dwells in sound body. It would make obesity, the root cause of ailments, virtually disappear.
- Any enhanced look of your body could be stressful. It could subject the person to drink liquor. Let the person decide whether such condition could subject him to drink liquor.
- Stressful mind is always detrimental. Some peace of mind with external relaxation doesn't enhance splendid health. Spiritual bliss could be derived from conditioning one's senses. Mind's state

could influence our physical body in good or bad manner. So, it calls for steady stream of positive thoughts.

- The state of jealousy, helplessness and fear would usher negative thoughts. The state of peace, optimism, truth, friendship and good manners enhance our health through positive stream of thoughts. So, adopt the correct mode of thoughts with poise.
- The state of mind and relation with the environment could influence our performance. So, plunging according to introvert and extrovert personalities could be more beneficial so as to live life without any stress.
- You need to depend on the guidelines of your lineage deity. A regular prayer could work wonders. Shield yourself from blind faith and obsolete manners forever. Living your life at ease is possible through coherent thought system. A verse appearing in the epic Mahabharata, interprets,

*Yen yen sharirena yad yatkarma karoti yeh*
*Ten ten sharirena tat tat phalamupashnute*

**Share not personal views with competitors for they could blackmail you.**

The verse endorses us stay hale and hearty. For he alone could gain everything, he who sports less anger and remain overambitious in life. I recollect an incident when I studied in the fourth standard during my ninth-year. I stood amongst my friends on the school ground. The prizes were distributed for the meritorious boys after they played for the day.

The announcer beckoned the players. The players entered the ground amidst the clapping spectators one after another. Often I thought of becoming some cricketer on becoming an adult. I told my conscience that a day I would also emerge amongst clapping spectator, after the prize distribution event. I told my friend, "Suneel, I shall play cricket on studying in higher classes. The spectators would receive me amidst clappings". My friend smiled on hearing my response.

My father bought the cricket playing kit on the following day, when I informed of my desire, 'I wish to play cricket.' I went on playing cricket after summoning my friend on transforming our house terrace into cricket pitch.

Such objective was unmatchable for my personality. However, my friend bowled the ball after enhancing my morale. My friend clapped his hands on finding my good batting. The clapping kept me hearing repetitively when I told him to bowl the ball again. He bowled when the ball swooped off after hitting my bat.

**Anger could swerve men from their objectives. The determination to accomplish objectives could destabilize your anger.**

My friend went on watching me surprisingly. I accessed him one step ahead when I was dreaming to become a cricketer of eminence. I didn't have any guru who could have taught the formula of me playing the game without ado. So, one ought to have a guru in one's life. The guru could be someone alive or in disguise as some book. Our life would become an ingot of raw clay like a potter churning earthenware afresh. A guru alone could give the form of some ware. We ought to work seriously for getting such form.

Perhaps, *the Mahabharata* has valued karma some highest position followed by fortune. *It is being said that goddess of wealth Lakshmi ahead of some loathsome guy but trials behind some dynamic folk.* Neither could it be hardship other than an enterprise as per description in the *Mahabharata.* Anger would drag us behind and entrepreneurship could propel us ahead.

The erudite believe him in conquering the world at the cost of self-conditioning. He alone emerges to be the trained guy, who could regulate himself without ado. For, he gets glorified on regulating his instincts and traits.

However, self-control shall remain the sine qua non in one's life. For, those guys lacking self-control get irritated even under slightest pretexts and hang on without accomplishing any of their ambitions. The situation has made many meritorious guys trailing behind in their career. They remain unsuccessful despite the desire to proceed ahead.

The radical thinker Crowe believes, '*Man remains an innocent child to some extent. However, the core issue in his life remains the acquired values under circumstances. The power of becoming triumphant is the most significant. It couldn't be ignored at any cost for its utmost reality.*'

**You will not feel about heaven unless you die. You cannot experience success unless you pass through the phases of failure.**

The developments under changed circumstances influence human life. For, opportunistic moments glorify man in becoming triumphant. However, giants need the support of others in reaching at the zenith of success. He needs maximum support from followers unless wishing to break the pot hung from the highest altitude, replete with curds. The more will the pot of curds hang above, the more shall he need the support to break.

At the outset, there might be many people standing below with absolute might, while their followers waiting for the ordeal above. Still there might be more people above their plane, leaving the man with the objective of breaking such pot. He will extol his followers as the partners of success on being triumphant. He would proclaim of his triumph as the sum total efforts of his complete set of followers.

Fight till the end.
Allow not your urges blown off.
Do not leave the hope of
becoming successful.
Some lyricist has believed.
A weeping man shall weep.
A man laughing shall always laugh.
A man sustaining shall do so.
A drunker will always drink
**but he ought to have been thirsty.**

It is true that man has achieved whatever success for the humankind; he has achieved them with certain set of objectives from time to time. The success might relate to surgery, engineering, or any other sector of importance. They were achieved in certain time frame, on being framed of their respective objectives.

However, one gets success in business for one's objective to accomplish the target. The satellites have been orbiting around earth in such manner as though some scientists have determined to emerge triumphant about space mission. The objective is beyond one's target. It signifies one to work in fulfilling one's dream.

Nothing could be achieved in the universe unless one has arrived at some objective. Man strays across without such objectives in life. Seldom could he find out whether had he been roving around, making him getting into some abyss. So, make up your mind whether you wish to proceed ahead.

For, our industrial giant Ratan Tata believes, *'Work could regulate one's anger. Act well across your path. Renunciation is the cure for selfish thoughts. So, renounce well. Firm faith is the cure for weaker thoughts. Have firm faith in whatever you do. Mobilize yourself in accomplishing the mission through your mind, body and opulence.'*

So, I believe, this is the fundamental formula to annihilate vicious sentiments. The emergence of dynamic thoughts could annihilate those thoughts of no-confidence, mobilizing the lost self-confidence in you forever.

❑

**"Courage but not anger shall be the forte for becoming successful in life. He becomes glorified who smiles forever in life."**

**—Tarun Engineer**

# ALWAYS BRING POSITIVE APPROACH INTO MIND

A couple of years ago, I was addressing a business congregation at Mumbai. The topic of discussion was '*How to improve sales?*' Sales crew from many of industrial giants was present on the occasion, who were hearing with rapt attention.

Perhaps, I deliberated for nearly an hour. One of the sales crew asked, on approaching me, when I completed my address, 'Mr. Engineer, I wish to know much about your personal life. Could you spare a few minutes with me?'

I replied, 'Why not? At the outset, I wish to know why you are interested in ascertaining about my life.'

'For, I came to book the supply order for some limited establishment, when I met you fifteen years before. Often, I have discussed with your subordinate when you're the purchase officer.'

'But, today, I am taken aback on your role as management guru. So, I wish to know comprehensively on how you reached this position, whereas I continue work in the same position for the past fifteen years.'

I knew the storm arising within his heart. So, I asked him to meet me in a restaurant nearby. He accompanied me instantly. I told him, 'Now tell me, what you wish to know about me?'

'That is all, what I have spoken to you,' saying so, the gentleman sat by dragging some chair lying aside.

I replied him, 'Listen, I was damn influenced during my career over the personality of industrial giant Dhirubhai Ambani. I was always thinking why not I become when he becomes the world's fortune industrialist by getting into the business by mere injection of some Rs. 15,000. Later, I bought a small office in Delhi during 1994, with appreciable efforts when I was on job. I went on deliberating over the thought of proceeding ahead in the business through positive thinking. Often, I was to differentiate with many thoughts arising in me.'

'Eventually, I selected trading with engineering products. For, I was always purchasing these products, when I got qualified as an electrical engineer. Moreover, I had good rapport with the suppliers galore.'

'Subsequently, I began concentrating on the business; working simultaneously with earlier firm, on availing the opportunity. My acquainted lot and old colleagues extended their cooperation on bulk supply orders.'

'I used to buy the goods from suppliers having good rapport and re-sell for the needy, which benefited my business. Often, I emulated the working formula, '*Think Big, Think Quick,*' of Dhirubhai Ambani, in letter and spirits. I was appointed the official supplier for Germany's semiconductor giant Jean Mueller. Since then, I haven't looked back in my profession.'

**A successful man won't be so from birth but will be triumphant on treading ahead making others' imagination as his base.**

'The list of buyers went on amplifying, with the names of exporting agencies. One of my friends Mr. Brijesh Sharma suggested why not I impart the skills of management on my pulling through the business without expending anything. He believed me of having appreciable instincts endorsing a management guru.'

I was rather influenced by his advice. At the outset, I have imparted such management tacts to the crew of his firm, *Das-Paus Sales Corporation.* It has worked wonders, when the company has had ample gain within the span of two months.'

'I was pretty confident of achieving success in the sector. I have signed similar contracts with many firms, one of which was yours, for which I have been imparting the *skills of improving sales.*'

The gentleman intervened, on being taken aback in listening over to my saga, 'Mr. Engineer, I have been the most stupid guy in the world, on observing your astounding performance. For, I hung on to the profession, since fifteen years, without any change.'

I have emphasized, 'You're not stupid. You're the most dexterous guy. That is why, you have been working coolly. You lack yourself from self-confidence. For, you dislike bringing positive thoughts in you. Our mind factory is replete with thoughts. For, it churns out thoughts galore within some day.'

You have two production supervisors for the factory churning out such thoughts. We could label them as Mr. Success and Mr. Failure, respectively. Mr. Success is in-charge of churning positive thoughts. He lets how you could become successful. What plus point have you had in the task? Why are you becoming successful?

Another production supervisor with you is Mr. Failure. He produces pessimistic and negative thoughts. He is pretty sagacious in exploring the cause of failure. He queries why don't you switch over? Why are you weak to proceed ahead?

**The fragrance of flowers will always advance in that direction where the wind will alter the position. A man's successful fact gets highlighted across every nook and corner in the universe.**

Mr. Success and Mr. Failure have been damn obedient. They would interact the moment you think over. You ought to point either of them with mental gesture. Mr. Success would come forward, if your thought has been positive-oriented. Mr. Failure would drop in to mobilize your thoughts the moment you seek support. I vouch you with certainty of becoming successful in venture, proportional to the thought you've expanded.

You ought to ponder over the spectrum of your criticism. You have been left with five alternatives in response to such criticism.

- **Acceptance:** You ought to introspect whether such criticism is appropriate before accepting facts. You should endorse that fact, through 'Yes.' For, acceptance of fact could highlight others of your correct perspective in the light of errors.
- **Refusal:** It shows your point of view on the fact was different. You could say, *'My work was pretty slow for the day, but I won't work so,'* when someone interprets, *'You work pretty slow.'* The phase of criticism to some extent justifies your responsibility. It would also enumerate how far your point of view is different.

- **Confine to your limits:** This alternative conveys of how others interact with you. Confining limits could make you extremely self-confident. You could say when someone disqualifies about your competence, *'Certainly, I have had the experience but without any capability and intelligence.'*
- **Defend yourself:** This option would uphold your opinion, in letter and spirit, like *'yes'* in yes, and *'no'*, in no. It could be followed when there won't be any argument of the sort.
- **Evade yourself:** The solution to any inference could be through mere evasion. You could spare some time to relax. For, such criticism ends up as though it has not sprouted under any circumstance, through such evasion.

However, majority of people are not intelligent and temperamental by nature, and would react on hearing somebody's criticism, *'Let us react through Tit for Tat.'*

It is not somewhat improper. For, you could have evaluated after such deliberation of your being pretty stupid and misfit. However, you continue becoming temperamental without attempting to reform yourself at least for once.

Criticism, in fact, belongs to two categories—positive and negative. Positive thoughts could mobilize the concerned person towards positive thinking, as your boss tells you, *'Congratulations for your assessment report. I have been observing the efforts you undertook to complete the task. The report could have looked extremely better have you added some line graph?'*

> **Anybody couldn't be evaluated properly so long as he lives with comfort and peace of mind. He shall get qualified in the examination when he analyzes about his position amidst challenges and adverse circumstances.**

Such criticism, of course, would come under positive stream of thoughts. As, the deliberation has taken place on the real core issue, when you were asked how to make the report more effective?

However, negative-oriented thoughts could hurt the objective of anybody's nature. The issue of importance veils away, when the argument sustains through abuses and invectives galore.

As your boss would flare up, 'How have you erred with stupidity? I don't know what sort of people get the job from alien background.'

Just as your boss insists, 'How come you sported stupidity? I don't know what sort of people have got into the profession?' Here your boss would pinpoint about your weakness in place of reforming thought.

Such criticism has only answer of leaving the job instead of reforming yourselves. However, a few people would criticize anybody just to influence others. It doesn't become any criticism other than wire pulling. So, seasoned folks should discourage such mediocre personalities.

**Nobody remains glorified from birth but becomes so from deeds.**

A positive approach could be the appropriate solution tiding over slew of criticisms. Any instant response remains proportional to the personality concerned. The folks would endorse others criticize when they couldn't evaluate about their personalities. It is absolutely true of such folks seldom sparing lesser time in ascertaining about them.

The folks would hang on with slew of negative thoughts. So, try to spare sometime to focus on some issues for your stabilization. Evaluate subsequently over positive potential within you.

Estimate yourself about your behaviour towards nieghbours for your criticism turning positive upon second important issue.

Feel the pulse, whether your argument justifies your behaviour as positive, or acknowledgeable, or negative? You have been left with three options.

*I am not wrong, but you're wrong.*

*You're not wrong, but I am wrong.*

*You're OK, I am also OK.*

However, the criticiser turning positive would endorse such style, 'I am also OK, and you're also OK.' It does signify that I have justified myself through honesty. I would disallow you in overpowering me.'

It is evident of positive thoughts disallowing others in politicising. How could you proceed about your honesty sans anybody's interference on firm will? This could keep inter-dependence alive and lighten the intensity of such criticism. However, it is essential to keep the tips mentioned below on reacting positively.

1. Listen carefully to such criticism. Keep quiet without any response. Hold yourself in expressing defensive and instantaneous responses.
2. Control your anger on hearing such criticism. Exhale yourself slowly. Hide not yourself from such criticiser except keeping yourself under poise.
3. Evaluate on the outcome whether it was positive or negative through natural instincts. Concentrate seriously on the response had the criticiser been dependable and worth adoring. Else, there is no necessity of getting disturbed from such criticism. Leave the spot coolly.
4. Ask him politely where have you erred? Keep yourself whispering without admitting his comments without letting anyone label you as '*misfit,*' or '*poor guy.*'
5. Ponder coolly about such criticism. Admit the comments by heart had it been positive. Uphold his comments with assurance of reforming about your performance.
6. Attempt to reform according to his criticism. Ask him whether every reform brought was satisfactory.
7. Justify satisfactorily in your subsequent performance whatever you've acquired so far. Do not be afraid on being criticised. For, there could be likelihood of your improvement.

It is quite natural of us being afraid of such criticism. It doesn't mean of your self-realization as poor guy. Bear in mind of such criticism always pointing towards one common issue. Quite often, such criticisms could transform you to become serious, industrious and refined in outlook.

I shall reproduce an anecdote for small justification. A young lady told her mother, on being sapped out of her energy following her obsessed with spate of issues in her mechanical life. Her mother experimented on her after ushering into the kitchen. She squeezed carrot in three different containers. She added egg and crushed tea leaves in second and third containers respectively.

She made the three containers boil on the hot plate without speaking to her. She inquired her daughter, after extinguishing gas cylinder, ***'What do you see now?'***

The lady responded, ***'Carrot, egg and tea.'***

The mother queried again, ***'Observe them seriously.'***

The young lady observed the carrot turned soft on being boiled. She found the egg to have turned soft from within, but could have been peeled off without ado. She found the container having crushed tea leaves in emitting the fragrance of tea decoction.

She couldn't stay back. She asked her mother, 'What do you wish to say?'

The mother intervened, *'The three objects have encountered similar situation under different circumstances. That means, they're made to boil under constant temperature. The contents have responded indifferently. Now, tell me, which position you occupy amidst them.'*

**A negative thought oriented folk always searches difficulties and hardships galore despite awaiting opportunity while positive thought oriented folk avails such opportunities amidst umpteen difficulties.**

The experiment has justified human life experiencing similarly. For, everyone undergoes similar situation, but reacts according to individual potential and understanding. The manner, in which you respond upon encountering issues however, remains significant.

*'Do you resemble the cooked carrot, looking pretty solid from outward appearance, but getting soft on little boiling? Or do you reflect an egg, whose viscous heart is pretty soft, but precipitate under extreme condition, when the hard rind breaks upon light stroke? Or do you sport the decoction of crushed tea, transforming acidity of water replete with some fragrance?'*

Probably, you might resemble one of the above conditions. For, treatment is necessary before neutralizing the effect of any wound.

Most of the problems arise from human interaction with appropriate means of solution. So, it calls for identifying of the cause on finding such issue.

What has brewed from within? Why does it happen? What could be its outcome? You could evaluate the problem through series of such questions.

Classification of issues after evaluation is a must. Find out whether the objective is against your decision. You could explore the long and short impact of such issue. Also find out whether the problem calls for instant or delayed solution? The problems need to be deliberated systematically on various facets and shortlist facts and effects accordingly.

**Books are fruitful to idiots like the mirror for the blind.**

For, the industrial giant Kumar Mangalam Birla advises, *'Don't find fault, but find a remedy.'* To say, you need to focus on the outcome. Move ahead, as early as possible, about the alternatives to the redressing of grievances. Else, you might trail behind over the unpredictable outcome. You ought to think of the alternative.

However, the better consolation could have been the individual satisfaction. Dhirubhai Ambani has advised, *'Prevention is better than cure,'* to say, before the sprucing up of any crisis, one had to find out suitable measure. Take the help of someone if the situation warrants such timely support.

Do you wish to make your children giants?
Read this book at least once.
For, your children haven't read
this sort of book.
Certainly, they become giants on reading this.
This is not my oath but confidence,
**which you could emulate.**

For, problems are inevitable in any life. That is why, Dell Carnegie has said–

*To every problem under the sun*
*There is a remedy or there is none.*
*If there be one, try to find it*
*If there be none, never mind it.*

This analogy applies equally upon you. You ought to speak positively. For, practicality, uttered syntax, and accent owe to mind, which reinforces positive energy at the cost of dissipating negative energy, on barging through your mind.

❑

"Nobody should show innocence in practical world.
For, the tree appearing upright in the forest gets fell.
Similarly, innocent folks become target
in the world at the outset."

—Tarun Engineer

# TRAIN YOURSELF TO CONFIDE ABOUT OTHERS

**Boli to unmole hai, har koyee bole bol,**
**Liye taraju tol ke, tab mukh bahar khol.**

Saint Kabir prescribes beings to ascertain about their voice. The human beings should not speak about insignificant things. They should weigh what they wish to put forth before others. For, giants seldom speak indifferently, but adopt positive-oriented words while interacting with others.

Abhishek Bachchan queries his firm's shareholders eventually, in the movie, *'Guru,' Shall we stay back or proceed ahead?*

He finds enthusiasm in return from his audience. He could have had the vapid response on his shoddy questioning. Such is the art of questioning and one ought to learn the varieties of posing questions at the outset.

You shall find in what manner could you use such syntax. The book would explain about such questions, whose answers remain hidden within them. Such questions could be posed to make the respondents confide over the issue.

The questions seldom had any answer. Generally speaking, such questions won't be questions, from which we could expect answers. They remain mere statements, which were plunged in the form of questions, as '*Does Mahesh Bhatt make good film or not?*' The answer could either be *yes*, or *no*. You have ushered an alternative for others, while the earlier question hardly had such alternative.

The drafting of such questions could stabilize you, like *'Does the book not appear pretty good?' 'Do you know how the slew of issues was explained in phased manner?' 'How the book has created big thinking with brevity?'*

You could improve your condition very well on adapting the syntax through serious deliberation.

For, questioning has been an effective medium to stabilize relations. The public would attach with you on your questioning positively. As you query someone, *'What splendid point has been highlighted in this book?'* You have availed opportunity for the respondent to answer from which he could cool his passion.

You ought to pose like this for influencing somebody, *'Do you mean I should read the book again?'* Such questions confide the audience to the best possible level.

How far were you successful in life? It depends upon your point of view. It also depends on your point of view whether the glass remains half-filled or remains empty. Similarly, if you ascertain like— *'Alas! How merry it is with rose saplings sprouting without thorns? It couldn't have been less charming without such thorns.'*

**When you get disheartened in life from every angle, you ought to shelter self under somebody's love. For, such love remains infallible medicine to forget sorrows galore.**

Accordingly, your thinking treads through such path of success. It gets developed through positive oriented thoughts. You could shape those thoughts keeping such shades of opinion. The inference could certainly influence your life ahead.

For, poised and good shades of opinion could bring utter happiness. Others would evaluate you on such shades of opinion. You could express your opinion before others in three possible ways.

*1. Through words, 2. Through accent (tone), and 3. Through indifferent gestures.*

However, positive shades of opinion ought to be shaped out of correct efforts. It won't sneak voluntarily. You ought to learn something anew every day. It could relieve you from the habit of objecting someone.

You ought to remember none of the tasks remain insignificant in one's life. It shall apply well through your shades of opinion whether the task is appreciable or insignificant. So, observe such opinion through your apperception. Always realize that your mind remains sanctified like some shrine. None of the shitty ideas could trespass in that shrine without your endorsement.

**Absolute relief from negative thinking:** A pessimistic thinking remains an enemy of your persona. Avoid such sort of thinking. Always befriend with optimistic personalities with their serious views.

For, psychiatrists believe that mind gets subjected to such negative thoughts under depression. Such ideas would exhaust your psyche rather than mobilizing. Nobody could accomplish anything without making desperate attempts. He couldn't even venture ahead under the state of pessimism. For, your shades of opinion alone could end you up in success or failure.

**The impact of positive thought:** History has been silent witness over the failure of scores of disheartened and insipid people in their career. It doesn't mean that positive thoughts bring panacea over sprouting of issues galore. However, you could enjoy peace under extreme conditions.

**Overconfident guys won't find as successful entrepreneurs. For, positive thought oriented folks shall achieve success through swift attitude.**

For, positive thoughts alone could console host of challenges sprouting in life. A lyricist has commented upon,

*Zindagi Zindadili ka naam hain*
*Murda dil kya khaak ziya karte hain*

Non-coordination, consequently, is against your shades of opinion. For, the condition of non-coordination could transform the environment around. It signifies that you shall seldom recognize such transformation. You insist to bring such transformation from which you would reach the opponents, or to justify that opposition is beyond non-coordination. It highlights some specific shades of your opinion, which might entertain some friction.

The circumstances alone shall determine how far one remains honest upon his views. Such non-coordination shall affiliate with some peers, mobilizing non-coordination to transform into some movement.

Similarly, Bal Gangadhar Tilak, one of the freedom fighters, gave the slogan for the country during colonial rule, *'Swaraj is our birthright. Gandhi,* the father of the nation, embraced non-cooperation movement. So, we have to realize that opposition to such movement could make us hang on to frozen level, from where our voice would hardly reach them.

I believe that you are pretty afraid of such non-coordination. You are trying to proceed shielding from such path, for such path could be damn easier.

**How do you think? How do you realize? Every activity depends on your behaviour. For, everybody's mental configuration remains pretty different.**

You should bring some transformation within you. You ought to make any struggle steer unto such movement. At the outset, you need to evaluate about your capability and persuade others what they want from you.

You ought to apperceive with the antecedents of Mohandas Karamchand Gandhi, on how to persuade with the state of development, without being worried or raising any storm.

M. K. Gandhi adopted non-co-operation movement at South Africa and India, struggled a lot, brought the country into the ambit of fight against imperialism, but British lawmakers disallowed in making the country independent. The civil disobedience movement assumed the form of virtual opposition. For, Gandhi knew about his capabilities besides the role of opposing the British rule. He disallowed the continuation of dialogue of compromise. However, he kept a platform anew afloat, where he seldom compromised on the state without opposing the alien rule.

The manner in which Gandhi transformed the movement, assumed virtual constructive opposition, which involved the form of compromise. He showed his debut to the second party, simultaneously apperceiving them of his limits.

So, you need to imbibe with the opinions of Gandhi for becoming successful. However, you couldn't become successful so long as the bitterness freeze within you. So, the best option available would be to forgive yourself and others about the creeping errors.

Keep the sentiments of gratitude. It gets flooded with happiness. Gratitude towards the public remained the hallmark of M K Gandhi's public relation. He got into the annals of Indian history as remarkable persona out of his comprehensible power of forgiveness. He hardly lost his courage despite being humiliated from the British.

Identification alone could glorify your personality. The elite remain happy and contented out of their glorified personality. Cambridge lexicon endorses *your personality as the way you interact proportional to your dealings, sensitivity and ideals you adopt.*

Longman's lexicon has also defined *the personality of anybody as the complete nature and conduct.*

The practical aspect of personality however, calls for, the development of your physical and mental attitudes. For, coherence in one's life owes to your internal and external development. The development of persona remains aligned with your sentiments. Your persona would remain brightened the more your sentiments remain conditioned. Our psychiatrists believe the rearing tack of the family and the environment around alone could mould the child's personality and its interaction with the society. So, the child's personality could replicate sabotaging nature had the child been brought up amidst arsenal, where he enjoys things on violence.

You will find some formulae enabling the development of your personality, from which your personality could be more effective.

- Avoid insulting or complaining about others' behaviour.
- Extol the virtues of others with diligence.
- Attempt to present yourself honestly so that others always get impressed.
- Get yourself interested with others' dealings. They will reciprocate on being impressed by your changed role.
- Attempt not to harm or malign others unnecessarily.
- Be a good listener. Allow others extol about you.
- Give up beating about your own trumpet through prioritizing others' values.

> Your ambition owes to desire.
> Your desire makes you to perform karma.
> The way you perform action,
> **you shall fetch fruits.**

- Always give regards to others about their importance in the society.
- Endorse other's opinion without berating (You are wrong) him at any cost.
- Always present yourself in befriending manner.
- Avail others the opportunity to present their views.
- Attempt not to challenge others. Hear, understand and respond naturally about them without hesitation.
- Explain the weakness of others indirectly.
- Evaluate and extol the insignificant deeds of others.
- Congratulate those working according to your tack.
- Explain about your errors before your critics.
- Always try to remain happy with beaming face.
- Always entertain positive-oriented thoughts at the expense of negative thoughts.

For, self-regulation remains your motto to uphold positive-oriented thoughts. It is an art, which calls for your adequate training according to the crisis. However, the art within such training could make man's persona glorified, to become the most triumphant personality.

❑

**"Your important problems couldn't find solution through thought phase on which level you have developed but you ought to think at higher level for resolution."**

**—Tarun Engineer**

# CHANGE THE ENVIRONMENT AROUND YOUR SURROUNDING

*Paranchi khani vyatrinaat swayambhuh*
*Tasmaatparanga pashyati naantaraatman*
*Kaschit dheeraha pratyagaatmaanamaikshat*
*Aavrittahachakshu amrtitatvamichchinnaha*
*Paranchaha kaaman anuyanti balah*
*Te mutyoraha yanti vitatasya pasham*
*Ath dheeraha amritatvam vidhitwa*
*Dhruvamdhruveveswah Na prarthayante*

It signifies that lord, the Almighty has multiplied our sense organs. So, people observe things from the extrovert angle rather from introspection.

For, ignorant persons eulogize tangible objects in the world. However, venturesome folks keep track of the nectar in each object without being entrapped in such maze. For, the reality remains that splendor of such tree could end up at any moment when one depends on hollow roots.

The same analogy applies equally on you. For, anybody appearing from outward appearance seldom looks so from within his personality.

You might have observed when you drop a slab of ice in water, ninety percent of the slab remains within water, leaving ten per cent above the surface. So, anybody should keep his personality like the slab of ice, keeping appreciable part of his grandeur within himself, which is necessary for the mundane affairs.

The secret of giants proliferating in the world follows similar analogy. For, the people who acquaint themselves with the art of life through excellent tacks equate their outward appearance with the inner persona. The folks expose ten percent of their persona hiding the ninety percent within selves. However, many people survive through unnatural motives like plastic and paper roses, which appear aesthetically appealing but farther away from the inherent fragrance.

Ninety percent of such personalities appear socialised from outward interaction with the society. The folks look hardly ebullient from their inner persona. The folks sport false smile resembling unnatural laughter. So, live afar from such double-sided personalities by removing the mask of pseudo personalities. End up such persona replete with machinations, else you could outshine like some brass ornament plated pure gold. Such people are labeled as wolves in black sheep, interacting with the society dreadfully.

Once, I visited the museum of snakes in Calcutta housing varieties of reptile species. Its curator accompanied me during my visit. Often, I inquired, 'Do you have double-headed snake, as enshrined with the Scriptures in your museum?'

The curator replied smilingly, 'The birth of double-headed snakes have ceased on earth since the time double-headed men were born. However, the double-headed men are more dreadful in contrast with such snakes.'

**Our character blares aloud beyond words and acts for our character reflects success and reflection never utters lies.**

So, you won't find them performing any good deed in life. For, they always remain aggrieved about their lives. The folks were well aware of life turning some battlefront. The folks, as such, lose interest in arguments on being disheartened, as enumerated in the *Mahabharata*. The principal character Arjuna disliked fighting on being disappointed. His fingers shivered when the bow fell off. He began shooting arrows when lord Krishna mobilized him to pick up the bow.

The analogy reflects one dispelling such disappointment through firm will. So, proceed ahead on firm will by remaining diligent on your conscience.

Let me recollect an anecdote. Hamid was a familiar merchant in Saudi Arabia. His business spread to far off countries. His ship was submerged out of powerful tornado during his journey to some far off countries across Mediterranean Sea. He lost his slaves on entourage except Adil who reached ashore safely.

Adil found a town little away from the shore. The citizens besieged him on his reaching the town. He went panicky disbelieving about their behaviour. However, the people made him sit on a platform bedecked with precious jewellery.

'What does it mean?' questioned the people surrounding him.

'We follow this tradition here,' replied a gray-bearded gentleman. 'We select him as our emperor for a year, noticed near the outskirts of our town. We would throw him off atop the valley after such gestation period, when the wild animals would feast on his body. We shall crown whosoever arrives near the outskirts subsequently as our emperor and discard him after one year. The tradition has been on since eons.'

'So, you mean I could be your emperor for one year, and do whatever I wish,' explained Adil to the old man.

'Absolutely without any doubt,' replied the old man, 'Everything about us rests on you for one year.'

Adil levelled up atop the valley in a couple of days through his orders, where he was about to be thrown off one year later. He got transformed that spot into a beautiful garden. He got the garden planted with shadowy and flowery trees with fountains and ponds, and raised hundreds of apartments for residential purpose. He did many philanthropic works for hundreds of families, which kept them euphoric forever. Adil got everything he had longed for, and got saved from the throes of death.

**The biggest lie in the world is that the cue of your life is not in the grip of destiny. You ought to get benefit when destiny plays along with you.**

The Sermon of the Lord interprets, '*Man should do such thing for his emancipation. For, he alone happened to be his friend and his foe. He doesn't have any foe in the tangible universe. Enmity arises only through his befriending or vengeance. However, he befriends voluntarily through conditioning of his self and won the battle through objective.*'

A recent traffic snarl across New Delhi's Karolbagh area entrapped me. The vehicle owners were moving in slipshod with repetitive head-on collisions. I imagined the importance of traffic lights during such impasse. Imagine how the three coloured lights assume importance.

A change in environment was evident with sudden change in colored light. A few vehicles drove past made me to proceed ahead.

The development makes us realize some incident on apperception about the pros and cons of the situation. For, that is vehicle, which remains mobile, that is beard, which grows, and that flying aloft is life. It means sky, nether world and earth, respectively, across which, we desire to create havoc in life. We could neither fly, but wish to take off. We couldn't live under water, but wish to swim across.

The speed of such horizontal movement, drifts apart and flying from life. The issue arises about harmonizing of events. For, our splendid movement is dependent on its harmony. Generally, the red light indicates the condition, green shows movement, but yellow harmonizes the position in between. This colored light determines your haul from proceeding and virtual movement. However, you ought to focus on green light, which is positive-oriented. The green light alone could mobilize your self-confidence.

**The mission of success depends on confidence. Anyone thinking through negative oriented mode couldn't become the significant personality in life.**

So, the green and yellow lights sport the first and second stops in reaching any of the portals of self-confidence. How could you believe about others, when you disbelieve on yourself? How could any physician treat his patient on losing his self-confidence? He, who lacks self-confidence, finds his journey quite cumbersome. Do you mean nervous person untrue and frightened ever initiate any business?

However, find out how far you're self-confident on recharging, on finding yourself disappointed from such condition. For, everything is being observed from afar. What do you speak? What are you doing? How do they proceed or what is your body language? All such things reflect your extent of self-confidence. However, answer the following questions just to assess the situation.

1. Do you wish to undertake risk or find yourself frightened in attaining good target? ☐ Yes ☐ No
2. Do you hesitate in admitting your mistakes and attempt to learn something from such mistakes? ☐ Yes ☐ No

Find out through introspection how far you're self-confident. If one of your answers is 'yes,' then you need to proceed ahead with seriousness. You need to study the story, if both of your answers have 'yes.'

It is an old anecdote. A moneylender decides to undertake pilgrimage. He told his three sons, before departure, handing three bags of marigold flower seeds, 'I shall return and see them later. Keep them as they are.'

The moneylender visited all the pilgrim centres. He returned after a year, after offering special puja and archana (offerings through flowers over chanted hymns) to various shrines. He inquired about the marigold flower seeds from his sons, when the eldest replied, 'I have kept the seeds within the cupboard for they required absolute protection.'

The moneylender found the stinking seed-bag on opening the cupboard. The seeds have turned black on decomposition. The moneylender was pretty aggrieved over his act. He asked the second son about the condition of the seed bag, when he replied, 'I have followed the routine every morning, for the seeds called for fragrance of incense and spray from the conservative aspect.'

The bag of seeds looked pretty decomposed on opening. The seeds looked damp with stink. The bag sported the fragrance of incense from regular exposure. The moneylender was pretty aggrieved. Now, the term came for the third son.

The third son took him to the outhouse, where he inhaled the fragrance of flowers with breeze. The moneylender was taken aback. He found blooming marigold flowers in the outhouse garden. The third son garlanded his father with marigold flowers. For, he has

Initiate the day through morning walk.
It shall make you brisk for the day.
Have confidence on yourself.
You could become positive in thinking.
Analyze about failures earlier during spare moments.
You could seldom err in future.
Ensure your potential every day.
It shall sustain your confidence forever.
Attempt to transform your dreams into reality.
**It could enliven your spirits.**

cultivated the garden through regular spray of pesticides and use of fertilizers. The bag of marigold seeds could have yielded hundreds of such bags. The moneylender said smilingly, 'I have tested your intelligence. Only you understood my objective.'

The anecdotes give an impetus that the wisdom resembles seeds, which gets lost on assimilation. It proliferates daily on regular assortment, making us evident that self-confidence arises from firm will. Your mind will be subjected to stream of positive thoughts on accomplishing of any job. Your objective reflects from closer angle. So, be positive in your approach derived from positive thoughts. A gentleman, accordingly, inquired from bank manager, 'I want some loan worth twenty thousand rupee for six months.'

The manager asked, on being stunned, 'You could get the loan. Have you got anything to be mortgaged?'

'Yes, I have a Mercedes car, which I wanted to mortgage. These are the related documents.'

The manager seriously scrutinized the papers and lent him the money after completing the basic formalities. He kept the car in the garage under surveillance. The gentleman redeemed the pledge with the accumulated interest undertaken after six months. However, the manager said, without keeping his words, 'I couldn't understand the circumstances that led you take loan, after mortgaging the huge Mercedes car, on being its owner.'

The gentleman said smilingly, 'I shall clarify about the cause that I hardly needed any loan. However, I came to know of one leaving abroad by mortgaging one's car in a bank against nominal interest. How could one leave one's car safely in a bank at such lesser interest?'

The manager was taken aback on hearing his response. He couldn't find anything wrong with the gentleman. It was the specimen of his positive thinking, which he has accomplished without much ado.

You should also arrive at similar decision. For, every impossible task gets solved automatically, when people have utmost faith on you. ❑

**"Success is a journey but not the destination. For, thinking about destination could end you up through stairs of success."**

**—Tarun Engineer**

# LEAVE THE PATH OF PRETENSION FAR BEHIND

A gentleman queried Albert Einstein about how many feet make one mile. He replied, *'I don't know why I should charge my memory with such data? I could tell you within two minutes through any of the books.'*

Einstein has imparted something in this answer, where we should shield ourselves from making our memory with data about facts. We should allow our mind to think properly at the cost making pretension. For, he believes, *'There are two ways to live your life—one is as though nothing is a miracle, while the other is as though everything is a miracle.'*

For, you won't find anybody in the universe becoming unsuccessful in life despite possessing some self-confidence. He alone could become triumphant, claiming with firm will power. Certainly, I shall be successful as I had the stamina to achieve victory.

Columbus was an ordinary sailor, but he had tremendous self-confidence. He arrived at the inference that earth is spherical in shape. People were deriding at him as his statement was against the then religious tenets.

The sailor explored Americas after being successful in finding Indian peninsula. None of his sailors longed to accompany him during the expedition to Indian plains. He couldn't have any signs of land during his voyage sustained for several months. His fellow oarsmen stopped rowing the ship and decided to slay him despite being irked of his crazy mission. They stormed out, 'We shall confine you in some cell on being handcuffed for misleading us.'

The oarsmen began roving the ship despite acute persuasion. The sea has turned violent with dreadful tides but had disturbed them. However, Columbus relied on firm self-confidence, which has surcharged his memory with some visualized goal anew. Meanwhile, the storm went ferocious when one of the staff disappeared.

The oarsmen found the polar meter defective when the ship sailed some 200 nautical miles, west of Conrad Islands. He seldom backed out of his enthusiasm despite facing many objects. For, he overlooked some dream. He has found some spot anew where he hoisted the flag on October 12, 1492. Similarly, Napoleon Bonaparte's life was replete with self-confidence. His observation was quite famous, *'My lexicon doesn't have the term impossible.'*

For, he had firm confidence in his will-power. His convoy of mounted cavalry in the army on observing Alps Valley wondered, *'What will happen? That valley has extreme altitude.'* He replied over smile, *'Nothing matters. Work hard. That will vanish from our way.'*

**Success is significant in every sector of life. For, those successful entrepreneurs alone shall get into the annals of history.**

His army abided by his firm will and made way to move out of Alps Valley. It has been justified that people would emerge prominent on finding challenges wholeheartedly. Subsequently, Stephen Hawkins did invented many theories on the footsteps of Columbus and Napoleon Bonaparte. He believed, *'Success is life's shadow. So, life is full of struggle. Life could have turned vapid had there not been any struggle other than monotonous developments.'*

It is true that the negative ideas won't exist like the way darkness seldom exists. It is so due to the shortage of light rays leading to darkness. Scarcity of positive thoughts sprouts negative thoughts. Ignite the light of positive thoughts in mind when negative thoughts shall perish forever.

For, failure is neither defeat nor misfortune. But, ending up of life with failure is the most unfortunate phenomenon. For, success is not difficult to acquire as one needs to tread few paces ahead despite ending up in failure. Imagine of you having not doomed despite moving like aunts.

Why are you disappointed despite ending up in failure? For, your life is four paces ahead on pavement. So, jog ahead steadily.

The pavement trailing behind vanishes the moment you tread ahead on pavement. The next step would turn the future into the present. Do not embrace the past attitude. Avoid roving across tying the dead child on to your bosom like some monkey. Have the impetus from the past and proceed ahead with your objective for life rolls on wheels.

**One should work more to become successful. There is none in the world who became rich and glorified through pretension.**

Saif Ali Khan queried Harry Baweja, the movie producer very recently when Baweja put him on insignificant role in the movie *Qayamat* along with Ajay Devgun, 'Why don't you provide analogous role to Ajay Devgun? Harry replied curtly, 'You couldn't sell yourself as the star. You ought to struggle in the career. So, you won't get the role as long as your movie emerges as box office hit.'

Today, Saif Ali Khan's struggle not only has transformed into success but also has put him at the top echelon. Everything becomes inexplicable for Saif Ali after the movie *Hum Tum*. The film for Saif Ali becomes the maiden hit. The image has felicitated him with best actor award for that year.

Saif Ali acknowledges himself, 'Solo movies became the difficult task for me when I was struggling for some role. The celluloid world has three-Khans—Shahrukh, Aamer and Salman. The films involving the trio indefensibly were well produced. I was always thinking, 'I was yearning forever whether I shall become the fourth khan. I became so following the hit venture of *Hum Tum*. However, I am farther away from such thinking. I became the selling artist as per Harry Baweja. I had the desire of becoming so.'

The most successful objective with Saif Ali Khan after the success of *Hum Tum* was that he has changed the opinion of many movie producers. They have been offering him such roles which he has never dreamt earlier.

Saif Ali says over smilingly, 'I have enacted different roles in movies such as *Kal Ho Na Ho, Ek Thi Haseena, Parineeta, Dil Chahta Hai* and *Omkara*, which made producer-director acknowledge that I have been the fourth Khan, capable of setting box office record. However, it took nearly twelve years during which I have had long struggle by working extremely hard. I have reaped the benefit. The producers are not only now offering me the roles of my choice but also lucrative price.'

Kargil war hero, Major Pratap Singh has recounted keeping perhaps Saif Ali Khan's role, 'We have thought about our warriors as ordinary folks. We have been astonished on hearing the sagas of unusual chivalry.'

**Sowing seeds of opulence shall yield the crop of opulence. Similarly, that of poverty could yield the crop of poverty for soil disregards which variety of seed you have been sowing.**

My sane advice to the paradise seekers, *'Do not berate your intelligence at the cost of others'*. Sell not your services cheaper. Focus on your plus points. Explore your good traits. It doesn't mean how much intellect you have had, but how much intelligence quotient you have secured.'

Remind yourself frequently. *My opinion is most important than my intellect.* Adapt positive oriented thoughts at home and on job. Explore the tack of doing job rather than avoiding yourself. Amplify such opinion within you. *I become successful.* Experiment positively and constructively of your intelligence. Hone your intelligence in that manner where you could emerge triumphant. Bear in mind the aptitude of thinking has been more precious and significant than chanting. Convert your mind for constructive purposes at the cost of thoughts anew. Explore working tacks anew and introspect

Your capability to hear
or
see gets seldom stretched out, for you
could perceive what you ought
to visualize and listen
what you ought
**to do so through ears.**

yourself. *Am I using my mental aptitude for creating some history or mere ranting the history?*

Perhaps, you might have heard about the failure of people of all ages in this manner. *I am beyond this age limit for becoming successful. I can't execute that role that I wish to accomplish for my age.'*

It is a matter of astonishment that very few people in the world realize that *their age is appropriate* for any slew of challenges ahead.

So, Vimlesh Mishra, the script writer of president of India, believes—*Always bear in mind that there are two types of personalities in the world—the realists and visionaries. The realists knew whether they're proceeding while the visionaries have already reached the destination.*

You ought to introspect to fulfill and enhance the value of your dreams. You ought to prepare yourself for hard work while dreaming for your future.

Do not permit yourself under pressure under the belief that your dreams are vapid.

❑

"Successful giants disregard how many days they'd have to struggle, but focus on the number of days through which success could be derived."

—Tarun Engineer

# RECAST YOUR THOUGHTS OF BECOMING SUCCESSFUL

Mr. Ajay Sharma wrote me a letter from Lucknow, when I was busy in writing this book. He spelt, *'My three attempts of meeting the optimum results have ended up in vain. I have got myself into some doubt. I wish to fulfill the dreams of my parents. However, I have lost such confidence, which kept me agitated, when I relapsed and proceeded with extreme enthusiasm. My fourth attempt of thinking brought me success beyond my comprehension.'*

The anecdote relates to a youth who have secured second position in Indian Administrative Services. Mr. Ajay Sharma writes, *'My ambition was not shaky, but I got disturbed. However, I have never accepted defeat, but sustained failure transformed my mind to become obstinate. I have worked extremely hard, mobilized myself with diligence and ended up in success.'*

The contents of his expression justifies that man could achieve any objective provided he attempts such task with hard work.

Akshay Kumar, the celebrated actor, who got into the Black Belt status, was giving the screen test for the maiden opportunity. A producer asked him, 'You should return home for you won't be successful in acting forever.'

However, Akshay Kumar absolutely disregarded his comment at the cost of honing his self-confidence. He went on practicing acting, staying in Mumbai. Today, he has been accorded as the most saleable hero, emulating some infallible formulae, as

- *Ignore about someone unpredictable to comprehend.*
- *Destroy the signs of your maiden failure completely.*
- *Lend some money to someone frequently chasing you to avoid him.*
- *Do not work before breakfast. Have that breakfast at least unless the situation warrants.*
- *Two tragedies manifest on the universe—not getting the desired object, and getting that object.*

- *Evade not any work of the day for morrow as you couldn't complete the day-after.*
- *Expend beyond your resource without uttering lies. Follow your duty.*

The same formulae have been encapsulated in our Scriptures, as *Satyam vada, Dharmam Chara. It means, "Speak truth and follow dharma."*

A proverb interprets, *Lies seldom have foot*—which is absolutely true. For, lies couldn't be kept hidden for many days. It would be exposed some day. Liar won't remain trustworthy for appreciable time in the eyes of public. Confidence remains the greatest capital to be acquired in life. Celluloid hero Akshay Kumar has justified this fact in two of his recent movies.

**It is the tongue of enthusiasm and inspiration, hard work and action that could be perceived by every individual being across the universe.**

I believe many of you folks get lost for the day, but waste your appreciable part of the day in worthless jobs. It is very essential for them to think about time management. It is such capability which badly needs some discipline and diligence. You will get appreciable time to get the task executed have you managed the time properly.

How could we manage time in our diurnal practice? Follow the under mentioned tips with utmost care.

- *Appreciate about the value of time.*
- *Assort the day systematically into appropriate tasks.*
- *Do those jobs in hand with utmost care.*

Perhaps, you know well that time is absolutely precious. However, only the few personalities know about its importance. Time often rolls out, and gets away from us forever. So, respect the value of time better than money.

For, you have been left with twenty four hours. The personalities like Helen Keller, Mother Teresa, Louis Pasteur, Michael Angelo, Leonardo da Vinci or Albert Einstein have deftly handled that with whatever they have had. Everything depends on how you make use of the available time.

Industrialists make use of their time effectively. A few industrialists have kept their identification of working beyond the tacks of others. They alone could spell out by addition of dimensions anew with the means of economy.

India had a host of industrialists during 1868, when Jamshed Tata initiated production of steel. He glorified the plant in his desperate attempt to bring some unique approach. For, he had spent every minute of his work hour in splendid manner.

Similarly, Orchid Ply Group commenced working with small Ara group. However, Deen Dayal Daga, the company's proprietor has ascertained the future requirement of plywood in the country fifty years ahead of the preset target. Today, his products—variegated sheets of plywood has made unique image abroad.

The giants are such personalities who had been purely dependent on their own efficacy. The folks opted for other paths, which made them 'Little beyond' variety of giants across the country.

Mukesh Ambani said, when he was a student, *'I ought to work extremely hard in comparison with others to fetch the opportunity of becoming victorious. I used to expend my time in studying when my colleagues were watching movies.'*

*'I went on studying even after them going asleep. I used to work hard staying at home, when my colleagues go for holiday making.'*

**The direction of your life gets evaluated proportional to your desires and requirements. For, efficiency depends upon available resources.**

Nusli Wadia, of Bombay Dyeing believes, *'He alone shall emerge as triumphant who wakes up before his friends and works within the comfortable limits of health.'*

Super star Amitabh Bachchan commented during his 65th birthday, *'Man ought to work upon very hard tasks, to become splendidly successful in life. He had to work day-and-night, keeping attuned to the environment.'*

# RAISE OPPORTUNITIES AGAINST SUPPRESSING ISSUES

Man certainly believes to keep him at stake as the epiphany of his life. For, you couldn't achieve any objective without risking yourself. Keeping oneself at stake remains some unconditional danger. You ought to condition yourself while taking the onus of accomplishing a task.

Throw not your leadership on somebody at the cost of accepting onus of life. For, leadership is quite capable of assorting one's dreams flummoxing the objective, propelling efforts towards success.

The book will usher through such formulae, conditioning of which could lynch towards scores of opportunities through containing issues.

- **Vouch with thyself:** Dhirubhai Ambani has advised, *'Do such job that brings you utmost happiness.'* Assort over some hobby that could transform your personality. An example of vetoing prospects. Vouch with yourself that you could accomplish some job with positive approach without deliberately hurting anybody.
- **Age won't deter you:** You ought to loose umpteen opportunities when age conditions you. It would influence you on such disinterested jobs. Perhaps, you might plunge into jobs through ready-made approach, when you believe yourself to be damn aged.
- **Break the laws:** This is the best possible mode, though it looks pretty awkward. Sneak through issues anew and deliberate what have you went through earlier. Get into another issue on being separated quickly. Breaking of preset laws could be the most challenging aspect when they're framed to regulate some order. It could sprout issues of deliberation anew.

- **Keep communicating with your memory:** Your memory shall guide you what is good or what is bad for you. You could function like some pendulum in quiet atmosphere, when the memory would respond to each of your queries, *'yes,'* or *'no'*.
- **Mobilize your sentiments:** Allow the sentiments swam across your sub-conscious sheath without making them pile up. This is essential for relieving through negative thoughts. You could have rich experience on exhibiting such skills. Visualize them like some raised structure. The issues remain agog on being buttressed in phases through the portals of negative thoughts, destabilizing the base and thereby the raised building. Methinks, you could save yourself from such loss arising out of apportioning of sentiments.
- **Lighter touch like some leader:** It doesn't mean of your leadership traits could equate you to Supreme Absolute Consciousness. Allow yourself to become an independent idealist for utilization of memory and discretion.
- **Communicate with laity:** The procedure could justify through *'giving'* but not *'receiving,'* preferably through the approach of politeness, derision and fun. You could become familiar amidst spectators provided your reliance gets enhanced on reforming of errors, amidst spectators. For, derision and fun could end up the division between the people and you.
- **Do regular rehearsals:** Frame some project for achieving the objective, chiming with some mannequin for initiating some event. You could materialize with your objectives through positive-oriented thoughts.

Substantial facts are significant like solid objects for life. So, think something solid, something big.
**For, the author Napoleon Heel**
emphasised his wish
through *Think and Grow Rich* about
something solid, some big idea
and
**become richer in life.**

- **Introspect yourself:** You ought to relax when the will power pressurizes your objective. You could avail an opportunity through introspection. You shall get some strength anew for your career, success and life.
- **Cool your mind:** Do not focus or persuade voluntarily on any issue of importance for few moments. It could empower you to deliberate with utmost confidence.
- **Stick to your lane:** The beauty of your objective remains proportional to the pace at which you have initiated. You will celebrate the occasion when the pace gets ratified till you reach the destination.
- **Moments of relaxation:** Spare some moments during work so that muscles and limbs of your body get stressed out. Light exercise amidst work could reinforce you into work afresh.
- **Always remain receptive:** You will find yourself elated when someone comments about you as the most dexterous personality, whether you're in business or avocation. You could work splendidly with utmost experience, when you could comment proudly,
- I am heroic. • I am intelligent. • I am dependable.

Believe on elders' advice and reset your thermostat afresh. Expedite the drive of triumph with confidence so that you could emerge triumphant. Certainly, you could become successful provided you have confidence in your approach.

❑

"Acquisition of objective correlates with triumph in some war. For, a war is won forever through self-confidence rather from arms."

—Tarun Engineer

# ALLOW FERMENTING OF BIGGER IDEAS

*Natam Kammam Katam Sadhu yam katva Anutappati*
*Yasya Assumukho rodam vipaakam patisevati.*

This hymn of Gautam Buddha interprets such deed as unfair; performing which could put you rather disappointed, or makes you weep or cry. However, any small idea could transform your world provided you anticipate in drafting some giant plan.

The fact is absolutely true. For, assembly line production is such an idea on which the United States of America cashed in on successfully. Automobile giant Henry Ford has developed such model, which has led to the establishment of giant plants galore, elsewhere across the world. He verily believed, 'You are right, whether you think you could or you couldn't.'

India doesn't have any scarcity about such activities, where people have raised giant establishments through least possible ideas.

The idea of pesticides came to the mind of Mr. Shripada Rao, when he was posted in the Gulf of Aqaba. He established a pesticide company at home on his return with manpower exceeding some three thousand.

The beautician Shahnaz Hussain raised an empire of manufacturing herbal cosmetics Shahnaz Cosmetics on being extremely aggrieved of the suicide of her colleague.

Vishnu Talwalkar has opened array of giant franchises of Talwalkars Gym across the country by converting his passion into reality.

Many of the people have raised the *empire* of billions of rupees transforming the ideas sprouting in them.

The 26-year old Indian Army soldier Nalkur Shripada Rao has pondered seriously in opening some pesticides company. He has lead the relief and rehabilitation drive across the erstwhile Soviet Union after World War II during 1946, where he acquired the effective skills of using pesticides in cultivable land. Mr. Rao made up his mind on his return to establish supplying of pesticides at home with whatever money he had saved. However, Indian farmers and gardeners were unaware of pesticide use. The people of first generation often believed killing of cockroaches or rodents could amount to sinning.

Mr. Rao commenced his business ignoring adverse comments. He got some contract in eliminating termites during construction of Raghuvanshi Textile Mills after a year. He opened a small office in Lora Fountain at Mumbai on being elated of availing of his services. He floated a limited firm in July 1956, with an investment of some Rs.3,000. The tiniest outlet has been transformed for the day into some Rs. 750 billion worth public sector enterprise Pest Control of India (PCI).

The anecdote of Rs. 50 billion-Indian beautician Shahnaz Hussain's cosmetic industry was entirely different. The 19-year old Shahnaz Hussain got influenced after the suicide of her colleague to initiate cosmetics business from producing herbal ingredients. She believes, *'My colleague, who was one of successful models, got badly bruised on using Suntan Lotion derived from some rare chemical elements, when I was studying at London. The girl suicided on finding her complexion badly bruised. Often, I have made up my mind to manufacture herbal cosmetics for our aspiring models.'*

**Motivation is the key to success. For, it works like an elevator to keep pace with state of development.**

The developments sport the saga of becoming giants through least idea. Now, I am sharing with you about young lady Ms. Parul Tewari, who has justified through her successful activity. She was an oarswoman to eke out the livelihood for her family. She also studies and gets obsequies rites for manes.

The mother of Parul Ms. Rekha says proudly, *'My daughter Parul has taken care of the entire household, and she has accomplished such role, which my sons couldn't do.'*

The 19-year old Parul has been studying for second-year B.A. from Lucknow University. Her family has been put up at Thakurgunj. Her father Lallu Tewari was an oarsman earlier, but his daughter came to care for the family, when he was bedridden.

Parul has learnt seven years before how to row the boat near Kuriyaghat on the banks of river Ganges. Now, she takes people for boat ride across the river, and runs the family through raised income.

The former premier Atal Behari Vajpayee reacted, perhaps, on observing Ms. Parul, *'Hard working people seldom estimate the days required for becoming successful in their lives. For, they knew well the deeds should be performed for the welfare of someone, irrespective of its slow pace. So, always think about raising flowers, but not about thorns. The labour shall always remain sacred and paramount, irrespective of its performance.'*

Now, I shall let you know about a meritorious child, who had been serving as the CEO for a firm at the age of 14. He established his business through some game, a few days before. The business became effective for the student community, who remain frightened on hearing the name of Chemistry.

> **Leadership capacity means ushering path for oneself. For, directing somebody is so easy as giving your visiting card to somebody.**

The boy has explored such idea through games, which would solve all the problems coming under chemistry. The boy is none other than *Anshul Samar*, whose first produce in the alchemist empire would be *elementio.*

However, the product derived from Anshul Company is simple. Here, two players play some exquisite game through elementary cards, sitting face-to-face.

The game has some 121 cards, each representing some usable chemical element and compound. The game rules specify in elimination of electrons orbiting around valence shells. You ought to use the cards to the best possible level.

Remain unafraid of the devils coming across chemistry. For, Anshul's product could solve problems through correct procedure, justifying over the fact that people with preset values and constructive ideas reign over the continents thereby ending acute competition.

It is absolutely uncertain whether hectic competition and transformation annihilate or excel professional beings galore in respective fields. The present dynamic world has two phases— where you could either bring change through competition or partake in such competition through change. Certainly, you would be successful in either of the ventures. You will work on some idea anew, leading to the invention of some process or product.

The conservation, pasteurization and distribution of milk on massive scale from Dr. Verghese Kurian, some three decades ago, has proved to be some floating idea. The supply of lunch boxes to employees across Mumbai's industries and office establishments was also certain idea like some *Nano* car.

**Rebel doesn't relate to brain, but a knot of heart. It doesn't warrant anyone to plunge into battle front to disentangle other than diving into the ocean of others' heart.**

The invention of modern two-dimensional web pages through Larry Page and Sergai Bridge was similar to the design of online shopping through Piere Omdiyar. It is true that the organization exploring value system has established leading market today.

Harold and Mac Lyndon explain– 'The people leading our value system and constructive ideas were now found in leading other sectors.'

For, value system comes into picture any type of enterprise. Take the incidence of American car manufacturing company. The three U.S. car manufacturers were ahead in the market, but began trailing, when Japanese aces took over.

They began the ebullient competitors in the manufacture of small cars on emulating the inventions of value system, and have ushered the way in the competitive markets through second variety of cars. Majority of Japanese automobile giants came into existence either as small or medium scale enterprises, or the small scale ancillaries.

**The power of imagination ought to be used to make way for some objective. For, some people generally depend extremely well on such power.**

The managing director of Electromac, Mr. Tushar Mahardale says, 'Now, the budding companies sustaining on developing customized production calls for innovative technologies.'

However, you could achieve two objectives simultaneously blending the engineering and design skills, which are juxtaposed to each other—to say, availing cheaper products for customers, or keeping higher profit margin for the goods produced.

The CEO of Autodesk India and SAARC, Mr. Ajay Adwani says, 'The design technique for digital prototyping could be more effective in the days ahead. It would facilitate not only the economic use of resources but also easier access to the market.'

Frost and Sullivan's programme manager Mr. Vaishnavi Anantanarayan believes, 'The important aspect of innovation strategy commences from conception to production and design, which fetches an appreciable value for the company.

But innovation has certain risks but you ought to realize that such benefit aspect is directly proportional to the slew of risks. Not only this, the most appealing topic in the present world is danger doesn't involve through exploration of originality but dissimilating it in routine. It resembles the way physicians treat sagacious patients through psychoanalysis.

The living example belongs to Delhi's Mandavali based doctor, who has been treating joint patients through some splendid mode, working wonders. It leads to continuous swarming of crowds near his house.

One day, an old woman, pretty lean with hunch on back reached there, stamping her supporting stick in hand. She entered his clinic slowly, when her turn came.

Her exit was noticed not with hunch but she came out straightforward. A woman waiting her turn outside couldn't hold her patience. She inquired what wonder the physician has made upon you, by which you came out with straightened back.

The old woman replied, 'So, my daughter, he handed me a long stick replacing my old short stick, which has made me to walk straight.

It was merely an idea, adopted by that physician. You could find many such people, who have become industrial giants through their intelligence. Mr. D K Jain, who ran small shop in Sadar Bazaar of old city, Delhi became the owner of Bluemax Industries. His prioritising of the formula of diligence and consumer satisfaction has facilitated him to emerge with turnover exceeding some nine billion rupees. Mr. Jain couldn't study through missionary school due to circumstances beyond control during childhood, subjecting him to heavy losses at the earlier phase, due to his inability in communicating impeccably in English language. He shared with me, on learning lessons anew from such losses, 'I had been to hand over the specimen of wind sheets of my car to Stanley Company when I was barely twenty-years old. The glass broke when I fastened it to my vehicle window.

The proprietor of the company Mr. Tailor Apia yelled, when he lost senses. I couldn't understand what he often spelled out, when I began to cuckoo as 'Sorry Sir, and 'Yes Sir.' However, Mr. Tailor realized subsequently that the man to whom he addressed couldn't understand what he spoke. He wrote a letter, after a few days mentioning that I had the perseverance to learn about things.

**Man becoming rich doesn't depend on his destiny but on his actions and common sense.**

Mr. Jain has not forgotten those days when he used to pedal all the way from home to Kashmiri Gate. He recollects the number of his first Ambassador car. He constructed first plant of his company at Mayapuri, in south-west Delhi, during 1968, for which he took loan worth Rs. 300,000 from Delhi Financial Corporation.

Meanwhile, Hero Honda became his prominent client when Maruti Suzuki had not even set off operations from Gurgaon. Maruti initiated some twelve joint ventures, out of which Bluemax happened to be one such establishment.

The matter doesn't end up here. One doesn't know how many people got glorified through such establishments. Bhai Kulbeer and Bhai Harjeet, pursuing studies at Oxford, London became billionaire-duo in record period.

The destiny of the duo outshone during the establishment of *Boso Dot Com* during their HNC examinations. Oxford Standard Business School has extended cooperation for his website. The website achieved prominence, from which the Silicon Valley of Bangalore began getting finance. Later, he established *'Octomatic'* website after gaining the experience.

Rice derives its fragrance on being
**separated from paddy.**
Creativity gets anew treading through courage.
A refined gold becomes intrinsic ingot
traversing through firepot.
Men become immortal
**traversing through failures.**

A buyer approached the duo when they're about to raise money. Later, a host of companies swarmed to buy his website, when three establishments were in the fray to bid through auction, when Live Current Media bought it for 2.5 million pound sterling.

However, there are some people who long to become giants, but remain unsuccessful. Accordingly, someone reached a shop to buy books. He queried the vendor, 'Do you have the title, *How to become billionaire?*'

The vendor curtly replied, 'Yes, you'll get it.'

The gentleman said, 'Get me one copy.'

The vendor handed him a copy, but the gentleman intervened, after browsing through a few pages, 'Half of the book is found missing.'

The vendor replied smilingly, 'What difference does it make if half the book has been found missing, Sir? What hard work you need to do for earning money? Won't you be contented with five million rupees, Sir?'

One finds the swarming of such people. Such people would dream of becoming billionaires by mere ideas. However, the reality rests on such point that man is being enslaved of his desires. However, very few people know about this fact that desires alone contribute to one's development. You could have hung on Mesolithic age had you not been flooded with desires. You could have put up within trenches or tree bushes after hunting through stoning.

Desires need to be conditioned. For, the fundamental formula of becoming billionaire would be from apportioning your objective on conditioned desires.

For, the folks who have become billionaires were not only replete with desires but also have dreams galore, perseverance and self-confidence. The condition has transformed them to reach at the zenith of success. The secret of success will be hard work, big thinking and courage. The venturesome would hang on to his work as long as he is capable of reaching the final stage of success.

❑

**"An intelligent leader doesn't have patience to identify the path of success but imparts his supporters relevant qualities through better means."**

**—Tarun Engineer**

# CHALK OUT PLANS OF BECOMING A BIG SHOT

People often believe that some personalities are genius by birth. But this is not the truth. For, introspect yourself, whether Dhirubhai Ambani took birth as a genius. Was Nusli Wadia born as genius? Was Henry Ford born as genius? Was Bill Gates born genius?

No. Not at all. The folks were being born, brought up as ordinary folks. The personalities remained pretty independent in outlook except one characteristic of perseverance common to them. So, the folks became genius.

However, the antecedent of proprietor of Archies Departmental Stores, Mr. Anil Moolchandani becoming some genius has different background. He ran a sari shop in old Delhi's Kamala Nagar. He used to sit with his brothers in the shop, when the customers used to listen to English songs.

Nobody was able to understand those songs. Anil felicitated the customers through writing texts of those songs, when they realized from such lyric contents. Anil got another idea in enhancing business, especially, selling the songs after writing the contents. His father told him, on his permission, 'Do you mean could we eke out our livelihood through this idea?'

Anil didn't lose his senses despite his father thrashing his idea. He borrowed some 5,000 rupee from friends and commenced his business. He brought the maiden title of English songs sung during 1960s. The first title, *Best of ABBA Group* was brought out with some 3,000 copies. Anil's better half Neeru said, 'When the book is out, who shall buy that?' Later, Anil began getting orders to fetch the book through value payable post from Dibrugarh, Cochin and Kanpur.

Soon, the orders stretched beyond five hundred thousand copies from various centres, which made him to reprint the copy.

Subsequently, he printed some 15 to 20 editions of Bonny M, Beatles; Top of Pop, Old is Gold, Top 50, etc.

Anil got into the business of selling greeting cards, opening the maiden shop Archies in Daryaganj, Delhi. He installed the offset machine to print such cards and opened another shop in Kamala Nagar, very nearer to Delhi University campus. The students of the university were more accessible to style and contents of such cards. He tied up with *Gipson* of the U.S., which helped Anil to amplify his business through such tie up.

Archies began establishing franchises not only across the country, but elsewhere in Sri Lanka, Bangladesh, U.A.E and Dubai. The public issue of the company came in 1996, which got subscribed in quadruples. He installed a plant in Naraina industrial area, New Delhi. The offset unit began producing cards, books of English songs, stationary articles. Archies turnover at the initial stage was some five hundred million rupee. The century observed phenomenal change in sending greetings through SMS, and e-mails, which mobilized Archies to proceed according to fashion trends.

**He becomes the winner who encounters challenges tooth and nail but not as winner depending on sustained winning of events.**

Archies went online through the website ID –*Stupid Cupid*, when it entered the trendy bazar anew to sell jewelry, perfumes and other fashion accessories. Now, Archies runs some 106 franchises across the world and expects to multiply to some 200 by 2010. Archies has proved to be Asia's numero uno brand, and the company has present turnover exceeding 1.2 billion rupee.

The facts justify that every giant task calls for some hard work and hard work has been the universal law of nature. Hard work is necessary even to secure your meal. Hard work is absolutely necessary even for getting gratification.

Kumar Mangalam Birla believes, *'Knowledge could be acquired only through hard work. For, in the present era, everyone has been successful through hard work.'*

Salman Rushdie, the second Booker Prize awardee believes, *'Momentary success could compensate years of failure in jiffy. We shall find on analyzing of the personalities ending up in success and failure for some contrast, destiny in one's life remains responsible up to some extent. His capability, efforts, hard work and shade of opinion could be responsible for his overall success.'*

Mr. Aravind Singhania believes, *'Courage alone could be your fast friend if you wish to become successful in life. Adopt courage to be your fast friend, experience as your prime consultant, and care as your elder brother and hope as your protector.'*

**Apportioning restricted approach as your style of work enables one to reach portals of success. For, you ought to accomplish the assigned task within the definite gestation period to reach preset objectives.**

However, you need to bring some utmost changes in your life to get recognition amidst limited giants. You could become successful on adopting such changes in your life. Do you know what the industrial giant, Mr. G. S. Poddar has believed? He claims, *'Seldom should we work hard for splendid achievements, but we should also dream them. We need not plan for such ambition but should have self-confidence over slew of plans. You ought to select your objectives before becoming such giant. For, some specific and certain objective alone could influence you to think ahead.'*

Three youths of around 25-year sipping beer in some pub regaled over such idea, which they initially disbelieved of transforming into some model of billion dollar venture. The idea has the provision of making the beer or wine guzzlers reach home comfortably through inn or pub's vehicles, when they're incapable of driving their vehicles back home.

The trio—Ankur, Saurabh and Mishal established *Party hard driving,* in Mumbai on last year end, December 15, 2007. Mr. Ankur says, 'We have finished bookings up to 1700 hrs of drinkers for December 31, 2007. We need to wait for chauffeurs for them at the last moment. We have been arranging the system in Delhi and Kolkata during 2008 year end.

The chauffeurs remain on their uniforms, carry mobile phones, could accept fee up to five hundred rupee per night, and might demand fifty rupee more overnight after three a.m. The company desires to establish its franchises in at least five cities, which is the specimen of some creative thinking.

Believe me about the twenty-seven year old Nayan Shah has already testified his idea. Shah & Co's Energy Drink **Current** became one of the international brands. Mr. Shah based in Ahmadabad city has already made his brand reach from Dubai to Delhi and London to Lucknow. Mr. Shah established the factory in Kuala Lumpur, when he launched this brand in March 2006. Now, his energy brand anticipates doubling the selling output, as it has been selling some 75,000 cans every month. Last year, Mr. Shah reaped some 35 million rupee sales turnover, expects that profit to stretch some 70 million and 500 million, respectively for 2009 and 2011.

Another company **Grid Boats**, based in Ahmadabad is little ahead with respect to sales turnover. The 25-year old CEO, Mr. Pulakit Gaur claims, *'The people disbelieved when I explained them of some robot scrubbing the place and keep not only surveillance of the area, but will also send SMS in the event of the entry of some trespasser. Today, we had orders to supply some educational institution for 30 such robots, and our expression of interest with some Mumbai based equity company is on way. We shall be successful at some stage through production en masse.'*

**Your life won't be rosy through success but such actions done for others' welfare could make you happier.**

The robot is capable of taking hologram of trespasser and could e-mail or SMS through fed numbers into the system. The basic model would cost some ten thousand rupees, whereas other models could be made available at around twenty thousand rupee. Mr. Pulakit Gaur says, *'Our target is to produce some 5,000 specimens by early 2009.'*

However, the condition was entirely different for Mr. Star Fernandes which took some thirteen years, for self-establishment in revolutionizing the advertisement world through some specimen anew. He made up his mind to name the production house as *Happy Dog* to unveil not as ordinary production house, but raise as the unique house to meet with trendy requirements. It could be especially so, when you need some crane to lynch luggage from tenth floor, or some pizza, *Happy Dog* could take the onus at your doorstep.

Established in September 2005, *Happy Dog* claims of corporate giants to have made use of their services. Fernandes says, 'I have realized on working for sometime with the production house that why not all services be availed, under one umbrella. I have commenced *Happy Dog*, after much deliberation. However, my ambition got fulfilled after some 13-years.

*Happy Dog* has its units established across the Americas and Australia but have the official rights being limited to homely shoots. The company is busy in producing vernacular film in Hindi, after securing some 90-million turnover.

**Self-confident people accomplish their work through delight and one who has the merit and skill shall complete any task courageously and outperform everybody in any contest without losing such opportunity.**

I am introducing you 24-year old Rahul Mahajan of how he has fulfilled the dream of becoming giant after giving up the job with WIPRO. He commenced *Joycom Solutions* through his website Alliance.com. He has only his personal computer with acquired values as the capital. Mr. Mahajan claims, 'My parents were pretty perplexed on my leaving the job in Wipro. For, I was ambitious of drawing more money despite getting some 50,000 rupee salary per month in my maiden job. So, I have established a company with the cooperation of my friends.'

Today, Mr. Mahajan has been earning over 100,000 dollars. He has earned some six hundred thousand dollars through the Alliance dot com business. He has now acquired many oversea clienteles and fetches some twenty dollar every hour from PHP, AJAX, ASP.net, and Flash, working through web 2.0 technology.

Alliance dot Com is a common platform for freelancers. It would affiliate the freelancers with some project or outsourcing companies. The freelancers, who are willing to get creative writing, editing, engineering design or the expansion of some portal or computer application could get such work through platforms Alliance.com, or Getacoder.com, or Guru.com, or Odesk.com.

***'Take any business or MNC corporate anew,'*** says Mr. Rahul Mahajan, *'More or less, the satisfying part of development therein remains equal as regards to enhancing the business aptitude. We ought to frame the strategy on* *three principles—(a) preparing the blueprint of success, (b) creating employment opportunity through certain specialist, and (c) reaching at the zenith of success through the emulation of such principles.'*

'You ought to know at the outset about the production of which object gains more mileage in any city. It means holding the pulse of consumer. You could end up in loss unless you focus on this aspect.'

'You ought to think of sales to supply under the existing economy when you should think of extending slew of incentives for the customer, which happens to be the fundamental formula of success.'

The executive director of Radisson MBD Group of Hotels, Ms.Sonica Malhotra is such unique personality to have carved a niche in the hospitality industry. She had the onus of making the blueprint of Radisson MBD Group of Hotels, where she oversees funding and marketing aspects of the group. Ms, Sonica studied through Mt. Carmel Covent and Jesus Mary College, after being born in Jalandhar and brought up in Delhi.

She got her postgraduate degree from Kathak Kendra, after completing MBA in Finance from International Management Institute of New Delhi. She was ambitious of doing something unique from her childhood and thereby got into hospitality unit.

She claims, 'I have never thought of me being a girl. She could become successful when the society thinks of her betterment.'

**A splendid thought could come from anywhere around with certainty but to make it practical needs effective leadership.**

Sonica believes Gen N to have realized of some women to have been versed with appreciable management capability. She could do well in hotel management. She longs to lead the industry for trailing behind could prune her creative skills forever.

It has been identified through this message that ideas are pretty significant in human life. Our epics claim, *As you sow so you reap.*

Certainly, you could perform well provided you bring some ideas in your mind. Any student ambitious of becoming topper in examination would emerge so after doing hard work through perseverance.

Meanwhile, lynch ahead with highest ideals to qualify in becoming the giant. However, man's mind is transient. It could have orbited around the earth in anticipating doing so ahead through planet mars. The pace of time retards in front of that of mind. The transient mind, consequently, has wonderful and immense power.

**Internal engineering is such procedure for personal development which could condescend some desire to visualize life anew.**

The sense organs are capable of deriving the knowledge about the present state of developments. For, Patel Roadways have justified the dictum, *'Pankhon se kuch nahin hota, housalon se udaan bharee jati hain.'* It was not an ordinary industrial group but the athlete trio—Reesa Patel, Rekha Patel and Komal Patel got the name through the world of sports. The daughters of farmers have plunged into the memoirs of the country after crossing its threshold.

The opponents also have biased them on being versed with their talents. Reesa Patel has secured medals in several competitions, while Rekha Patel has been the sprint queen and Komal Patel has been ambitious of getting record in javelin throw.

However, the credit of Suneedhi Chouhan entering celluloid world, after bagging maiden talent show—*Meri Awaaz Suno*, on the television at tender age of twelve, owes to Mr. Sonu Nigam. She says, 'Mr. Sonu Nigam has availed me an opportunity of singing through the vernacular movie *Mast,* after bagging talent contest on

Camel desists to move underneath the valley.
Lie desists to access any saint.
Truth desists from reaching any leader.
Snake desists from reaching some burglar.

**But goddess of wealth Lakshmi is unafraid of accessing anybody.**
**She accesses everybody but stays there where she gets felicitated.**

state-run television Doordarshan. The film songs became hit, which kept my singing career prosperous. People believe my inability to sing romantic songs. However, Sonu has often persuaded me hum and rehearse soft numbers at home. I had the opportunity to sing through the movie *Ajanabi*, which the audience appreciated much. I have been singing since then for various movies in Mumbai.

Mr. Lakshmi Mittal, the steel baron chairman of Arcelor-Mittal Steels, perhaps, believes in endorsing Suneedhi Chouhan's success, *'Young Indians have glorified the country. The new Generation has enthusiasm coupled with mission anew. India has been treading the economy at quick pace. However, it calls for creative thought, for that could be the first step towards the zenith of success.'*

You ought to hone the skills of constructive thinking, for the utmost success shall knock at their doorsteps. It shall keep not only their objective but of others through day-to-day reformed performance. They could deliver optimum production without much ado at least period of time.

Please deliberate over any task ten minutes before accomplishing, 'Today, I could improve the task in some format. I could do it better than my erstwhile performance. Do you know, how am I mobilizing the enthusiasm of my work force? How am I going to improve my performance? You could realize yourself of having reached at the zenith of success treading through constructive means.

❑

"Identify facts brewing in the minds of opponents to enhance leadership potential so that what splendid outcome could you deliver without ado in no time."

—Tarun Engineer

# COMPILE THOUGHTS LIKE SAVING MONEY

The incident goes back to some thirty five years, when I was on stroll near the pond of Nainital, the hill resort amidst cool breeze. I was studying at Nainital. It was the month of June, when the atmosphere reeled through scorching heat. I was jogging aside the shrine of Hanuman to secure blessings. Suddenly, I came across a hermit; when he said smilingly, *'Get basked well,'* in response to my offering salutations.

I was little concerned on receiving the hermit's message. For, I couldn't assimilate whether he has blessed or cursed me with bane or boon. The gesture in which he has often articulated made me realize that he has blessed.

Time has rolled out. I returned New Delhi, after completing my studies in engineering college. However, I haven't forgotten his blessings made on the other day. For, I have never received such blessings from any hermit or saint, which he showered me to hang on happy and cheerful forever. Live for hundred years, but remain well basked. His blessing has compelled me to frequently think over such blessings.

Slowly, I went on acquiring incentives in my career. I had got the position of purchase manager from mere purchase officer. However, when I roved from company to company for procuring purchase orders on opening my business of importing engineering goods, I came to realize the hermit's blessings. For, I have ascertained the extent of basking during my race to enhance business, which has made me achieve ultimate objective through sustained basking.

I went on acquiring benefits the more I went on basking under the heat of my roving. I realized the hermit's message of basking well to develop golden nest from sustained basking.

For, it is true that man doesn't achieve any incentive without sustained basking. He alone would achieve progress, he who makes his career bask, which is the ultimate Sadhana for achieving objective. So, I insist you folks to sustain basking of the career to achieve the objective. The interpretation has been enumerated in Taittariya Upanishad, as

*Manasashwa Indriyanaam cha ekagrayam paramaam tapah*

It calls such act as penance where we focus our mind and sense organs on some particular task. Man's career thereby sticks to such objective. The way how some stone or metal or clod of clay gets moulded to become an icon, similarly, personality development has transformed itself to an art.

Take the case of stone idol. A sculptor churns some beautiful icon out of irregular piece of stone. He shelves off the worthless portion of that piece of stone other than the very icon. Man assimilating virtues of that icon gets qualified to become a giant sculptor.

However, every man has got some pluses, as well as minuses, which shapes his overall and effective personality. The extent of vices alone from minuses inhibits the sprouting of his real personality.

**Failure is an ordeal that never stops. For, failures alone shall lead us to the path of reforms.**

One finds effective personality following the scooping out of vices from his aura akin to some sculptor etching unwanted portions from raw specimen of icon.

Celluloid actor Shahrukh Khan believes, 'I have my own modus operandi of setting flop stories into coherent hits. I always attempt the stories through the stages of—wake up, play the game and establish runs beyond 250. Go on batting the ball without fear, for scoring 150 runs won't make you secure. For, you have nothing to lose, except your personality, endorsing you to go ahead without fear.'

Shahrukh sent SMS message to the IPL team—the players of *Kolkata Knight Riders*, when the team was on the edge of losing after successive defeats. The motivation message of king Khan enthuse players in such manner scoring innings afresh for the loss of three wickets against Kings' Eleven.

Shahrukh Khan is one amongst those, who went on exploring how to win day through night. We could christen such thought as '*Law of Attraction.*' For, it has been such philosophy ushering effective role in your life. So, you ought to bid good bye for the hovering cloud of doubts before acknowledging such development.

You could realize voluntarily—the *Law of attraction,* manifesting in life, on expulsion of clouds of doubt.

Attempt to observe such experience. For, you would believe life to be replete with such moments, *'Oh, it happened through sheer accidence.'* It would make you believe that the *law of attraction* has been functioning through your career. It is also true that the law had been functioning every moment according to the vibrations of your mind. Your mental vibrations get transformed according to your thinking.

So, your dreams get fulfilled the lesser the extent of doubts. For, our negative thoughts get transformed into positive ones in the process. You could visualize such thoughts through fulfilled dreams. However, you need to venture ahead with hard work for achieving success.

The procedure doesn't have any *short cut,* unless the risks of failure knock during such non-performance in phased manner without hard work. For, reinforcing your efforts connotes stabilizing of the blend of outward thoughts with mental aptitudes. Your memory could condition the spectrum of your activities.

**Life is an ocean and you ought to encounter tides with certainty during sojourn. For, the input of tides beautify the ocean to look serene from natural challenges.**

You wouldn't find any delay in reaching at the zenith of success had there be regulation of your mind and memory in proper direction. However, regulating transitory mind remains the most difficult proposition. It calls for your training such condition on our prescribed formulae given below.

- **Ascertain the cause of failure:** An old adage advises us to proceed without vetoing the efforts of previous failure. Perhaps, you might have heard of the frequent attacks carried by Mohammad Gazni, who has been successful in reigning over the shrine of Somnath. Earlier, he had to face defeat for sixteen times. The incident justifies that courage and hard work alone could elevate us to success. Success ladder might justify in failure unless you ascertain about its cause despite making frequent attempts.

- **Facts are compulsorily needed:** Mother Nature has bestowed everybody with creative potential. It is such boon gifted through Nature without any offense. You ought to realize of the presence of facts before initiating any act of creativity. For, facts could work wonder like some fuel—a natural object influencing like magnet, attracting others to its core.
- **A positive concept:** Mother Nature has bestowed *'Tit for Tat,'* signifying you to have such company as you're so. It has also been said that you become so proportional to your thinking.

It is also true of everybody leaving his mark in life with earnest desire that he had secured appreciable prestige-regards, respect and esteem with respect to others. However, it is less said the better, for it is not even impossible. Positive thinking alone could influence effectively to become the person of importance in society.

**You never make future but your habits do. Such habits alone will shape your future. For, you couldn't rein in your mind without addicted to habits.**

However, the way you dress reflects in projecting your reflected personality. Now, the world of fashion has been sprouted with varieties of styled apparels. You ought to select the attire correlating with your personality, age and profession.

For, your first interaction has remarkable impact about your identity as permanent impression with the acquainted and strange personalities alike, while liaising with people of different strata. So, it is essential for becoming an effective personality to remain loyal and diligent towards your work. Do not regard any task as insignificant through its evading. For, none of the work could be insignificant or remarkable. Accept work as worship. For, destiny backs with him, who regards work as worship. Sage Tulsidas has interpreted this as,

*Jehi ke Jehi par Satya Sanehu,*
*so Tehi mile Na kachu sandehu*

Satya Sanchu means virtuous diligence and commitment. However, commitment comes under variegated forms. Generally, it means keeping the household folks well fed with adequate comforts. A few people have the desire to earn more money by hook or crook. The few always dream to build empires of business or industries. The latter variety avails the opportunities galore for millions of people to work sustainably after realising dreams.

Mr. Arun Sareen leads the latter category of dreamers. For, the entire world has been desirous of backing the ideals of Mr. Sareen. The credit of making Vodafone reach at the zenith of success goes to Mr. Sareen. His hard work upon diligence has made the company Vodafone, the universal brand in CDMA network telephony.

The year 2006 made the company's business suffer appreciably. The loss incurred by the company has been regarded as the worst in the annals of European corporate giants. The business echelon disbelieved at the outset of Sareen's capabilities. His business acumen has justified their disbelief without much ado. He led the performance of the company into unbelievable gains traversing through the path of mutual acquisition. Mr. Sareen has acquired success at the young age of 35, which has made network telephony access the portals of success.

You shall come across another giant Mr. P.L. Lamba, who has established ice cream vend outside Regal Cinema in Connaught Place, the heart of New Delhi. Subsequently, he opened the outlets in Lucknow, Kolkata and Mumbai, which reached London under the brand, *Gaylord*. Success smiled on the brand, which transformed the ice cream logo into *Quality Walls*. Today, *Quality Walls* has beyond forty outlets and workforce beyond some 1,600 with turnover outstretching some five billion rupee. However, Mr. Lamba credits his success to the blessings of lord Ganesh.

❑

**"Whatever you achieve in your life is the gist of your experience. You should always think from positive angle to achieve any objective."**

**—Tarun Engineer**

Everybody desires
eventually to become
**rich.**
**World War III**
couldn't be postponed if
**every second person**
couldn't become rich
**in another decade.**

# PRESSURIZE UPON BRAIN FOR THINKING BIG

The incident relates to the year 2005. I was getting felicitated from the print media in New Delhi, with the title 'Upanyas Guru.' I was amidst the guests on the dais, when a scribe met me from elsewhere queried, *'Mr. Engineer, so far some thirty novels have been published. Could you attribute the best title amongst them?'*

Suddenly, I responded, *'The forthcoming title.'*

'Does that mean your forthcoming title would be better than the previous titles?'

I answered smilingly, *'Without any doubt! For, the probabilities of writing better novels won't end up. The desire of forthcoming title to supersede previous titles would always sprout within me as the author.'*

For, wishing something to be splendid remains the first step towards big thought. One couldn't become splendid without such desire. Similarly, the president of Philippines Mr. Ramon Magsaysay was always thinking giant. One day, when he realized that pump didn't reach his capital from abroad, even then he found the chief engineer has decided to finish the construction of dam behind schedule. President Magsaysay reached the site of construction. He found the pace of construction activity proceeding briskly and the chief engineer is also actively involved in the work like an ordinary labourer, pushing his status aside.

The president was taken aback and went euphoric when the chief engineer was found placing US trucks in place of pump. He asked him, after summoning, 'Have you taken permission from anybody to use diesel trucks in place of pump?'

'No Sir, the construction work could have suffered, had I not used the truck in place of pump. The dam could have commissioned rather delayed,' answered the chief engineer without any hesitation.

The president said, on being bewildered out of chief engineer's tack, 'Please come to me immediately.'

The engineer reached the president on being frightened over the development. The president said smilingly, patting on his back, 'I have been pleased to appoint you as the public works department deputy secretary on being extremely delighted over your diligence in keeping the morale, etiquette, and responsibility.'

**Internal engineering is such faculty of science responsible for enhancing your consciousness and retention power so that you ought to accomplish your objective without much ado.**

This is an example of such big thinking. The US automobile giant Henry Ford also adopted similar thinking. Once, he sued *'Chicago Tribune'* on contempt petition against the management for labeling him as an idiot in one of its lead stories.

The solicitor appearing on behalf of the publication asked Ford, 'Who was Benedict Arnold? When did the industrial revolution flare up?'

Mr. Ford refused to reply for he had least formal education.

The solicitor reiterated, 'Answer Mr. Ford.'

Eventually, Ford was found much concerned and roared, 'I do not know the answer to your queries, but I could bring such personality within five minutes, who knows the answer to your questions.'

The solicitor was stunned on hearing Henry Ford's swift remarks. It has been evident from the argument that Henry Ford was least interested in useless data, which is the proper answer for his big thinking. However, he has extreme penchant over his ambition, which qualified him to become the giant.

Mr. Ford asked his son, on an occasion, '*Wait not for becoming big and get glorified, but be a glorified son.*'

A similar advice erupted from philosopher and British premier, Winston Churchill, while addressing a public meeting, *'You ought to merge deeply in the ocean of sentiments before being influenced. You ought to shed tears before making others cry. You ought to have self-confidence before making regaling others. For, unbelievable predicaments beget giants. So, whatever you do, think over them at superficial level despite the job relating to the scrubbing of streets.'*

Parle Agro Products director Ms. Shona Chouhan is a virgin of some 26-years. Her functioning as the director at such tender age for the multinational-level firm had been extremely laudable. Ms. Shona had been pretty mischievous during childhood. She was caring much for curricular activities, such as playing football or volley ball. She was admitted into boarding school at Kodaikanal (Tamil Nadu). Later, she took admission in Berne-Switzerland's Franklin College. She returned Mumbai after completing studies in the international management. She began taking training in marketing and production with Parle Agro Products. She undertook research in the production and management of pet bottles, besides caring for multipurpose projects undertaken with mineral water production, marketing and pharmaceuticals.

**A cricketer always plays with attachment and persistent efforts, but he could be knocked out even scoring zero runs. Inspite of that he plays another match with vigour and vitality.**

She began working as director, launching *'Enjoy.'* The beverage was some blend of milk and fruit juice afresh. The working women liked the drink.

Ms Shona Chouhan worked beyond the dictum *'Brain and beauty don't go together.'* Today, she has become the modicum director working swiftly with turnover of some six billion rupee.

The antecedents of Mr. Sanjay Singh resemble Ms Shona Chouhan. His father was an ordinary clerk in the Sasaram magistrate court. He completed the degree through distant education from *Indira Gandhi National Open University*. He left the job from the Indian Merchant Navy after earning some money at the rate of thirty six thousand dollar per annum. He joined a tutorial college in New Delhi and prepared for I.A.S examinations, now he became an IAS officer.

It has been found that firm will power would bestow immense power on beings. Perhaps, you might have observed the reaction of some bullock cart owner, when his wheels get trapped in the mire. He went on pressurizing to retrieve the wheels besides mobilizing the bullocks to pull through. He was pretty optimistic, which has made the passersby help the cart pull through the mire. Imagine another cart owner whose wheels couldn't roll out even on the plains. He was attempting equally to roll the cart out but in vain.

Swerve from getting disappointed. Learn to proceed by aligning with hopes. Think like Dhirubhai Ambani. For, neither he was an economist nor an MBA. He was just a matriculate. He became successful on abiding by the principles of conventional bazaar.

The giant industrialists were ascertaining about their capability in plunging to the profession through market dynamics. However, Dheerubhai drove past with enthusiasm and initiated his ultramodern plant with unbelievable capacity at Patalganga, installing *polyester filament* plant. The plant has initial production capacity of some 10,000 ton, when Indian requirements stood at 6,000 ton. Mr. Ambani blew his fellow giants upon this angle. He was being pleased on justifying the work to fellow giants through such competitive edge.

*Baaton mein hi bah gaya, nikal gaya din raat*
*Muhalat jab poori huyee, aan paree jam ghaat.*

Often, it endorses men spending entire life on thinking about frivolous issues. He zooms afar on returning to senses.

However, such personalities were pretty rare, who knew well howsoever, they proceed shall remain pretty incomplete on being illiterate. They keep abreast of themselves after such developments.

**You couldn't change somebody else. For, the access to any such change opens from within one's heart. The individual alone could unlock that with the key from self-analysis.**

Albert Einstein said in response to acknowledging public felicitation, *'My knowledge remains insignificant in front of others'* wisdom.

You would trail behind instead of proceeding ahead, when you find yourself proud. For, a radical thinker Joss Wildings says, *'How could we learn when our garage of memory remains shut?'*

So, you ought to focus on what Joss Wildings has stressed of doing nothing by mere shutting eyes. For, nowadays, you won't get moral education. You ought to ascertain about your attitude through the following questionnaire. Tick the appropriate answer in front of your personality and appropriate thinking.

1. I could solve many problems simultaneously and successfully. ☐ Yes ☐ No
2. Generally, I couldn't focus on my work, on being more concerned. ☐ Yes ☐ No
3. I am not habitual to explain comprehensively out of my negligence. ☐ Yes ☐ No
4. I have been pretty curious about the state of development. ☐ Yes ☐ No
5. I have been pretty curious to ascertain about the development around. ☐ Yes ☐ No
6. I ought to get money and fame at younger age. ☐ Yes ☐ No
7. I always dislike chatter-birds. ☐ Yes ☐ No
8. I could explain myself before others without much ado. ☐ Yes ☐ No
9. I dislike in blowing vehicle horn on roads when becoming eccentric. ☐ Yes ☐ No
10. I Switch to another work after accomplishing one job at a time. ☐ Yes ☐ No
11. I could take independent decisions swiftly. ☐ Yes ☐ No
12. I always remain contented on accepting whatever I often get. ☐ Yes ☐ No
13. I could work appreciably under pressure. ☐ Yes ☐ No
14. I remain more concerned under crisis. ☐ Yes ☐ No
15. I never get defeated during debate and argument. ☐ Yes ☐ No
16. I could hardly condition over my sentiments. ☐ Yes ☐ No
17. I don't worry about work, for I always work at ease. ☐ Yes ☐ No
18. I always infer after serious deliberation over issues. My point of view shall always remain analytical. ☐ Yes ☐ No
19. I always find myself wounded. ☐ Yes ☐ No
20. I am very much pleased to keep quiet and get involved in something. ☐ Yes ☐ No

Your test is over. You will know voluntarily about your attitude. You ought to add up the mark over the ticked answers. You could have medium attitude on scoring less than fifteen numbers. A score of less than ten could make you possessing least attitude. Your score above 18 could endorse you as an extraordinary skilled person. Your spirits are always on your sleeves.

I will share an incident that took place in my career for justifying the cause. I had been to Singapore discussing with a Japanese industrialist during mid 1999. He was the managing director of power semiconductor accessories. He was competent enough to sell his product across the continents.

He told me, 'I shall appoint you as the distributor for my company for selling our power semiconductor accessories across the country. You could earn more money at home.'

It was some probable thought, for anything is possible today. It doesn't mean that it could be probable thereafter. However, our objective shall always be based on this topic whether we could sell the good product in our country.

**Cleanse your brain off piled up dust, mire and grease to entertain splendid facts so that it could enable in becoming financially rich.**

Professor Irving H. Shell, a US specialist on leadership training, *'A correct decision is necessary to achieve some objective in life apart from aptitude and comforts. You could make use of your aptitudes to the optimum level provided you infer correctly. You shall reap good results in no time.'*

For, there would be absolute difference after taking right decision. He claimed, *'A salesman with correct inference could have crossed beyond his objective. Any student with such inference could get meritorious results through his examination. Couple with such inference could enjoy marital bliss. I believe you shall encounter slew of challenges without much ado. You could proceed ahead without any difficulties on proper thoughts.*

Give attention with utmost care on the following points and deliberate over them within yourself.

1. Expanding the meaning and role *about me being euphoric.*
2. Expanding the importance of *your decision altogether.*
3. Expanding the *decision arrived at services.*

You ought to possess some splendid power, will power, good public rapport, mood swing, and power of sufficient time (gestation period). For,

*Jitna Utsaah hoga, parinaam utane hee achche milenge.*
*Aur utsah ka matlab hai,*

**'I can do it.'**

I have arrived at such decision after studying in depth about the probable thinking—*You could not amplify the probabilities without creating problems. You couldn't become successful without creating struggles. Others could disown your ideas. However, rejection of opportunities is not in your favour.*

So, I took the distribution rights from that company for selling power semiconductor gadgets across the country, whose results were pretty astonishing. You ought to proceed on this philosophy. For, when the issue of becoming successful enters your inner core, some unconscious power could lure you in mobilizing towards such path.

❑

"An individual should sneak through the opportunities at definite periods to become successful facing hardships, else he will end up in failure."

—Tarun Engineer

Concentrate on
golden eggs alone
**if you wish to
become financially rich
without disregarding the hen
hatching such eggs.**

# NURTURE POSITIVE THOUGHTS ON YOUR HEALTH

You feel pretty relaxed and afresh when you wake up some morning. It signifies that you have had sound sleep overnight on enjoying life full of happiness. On the other hand, your observation of being exhausted subjected to stress, despite bathing and breakfast, could mean you're virtually under tension. However, none of your objectives often get fulfilled during such crisis.

Attempt to retrieve such crisis to become triumphant in life. How could we do? I am explaining this procedure through ten formulae given below. You ought to follow them in letter and spirits.

01. Eliminate the terms difficulty and problems from your lexicon, signifying hardly any solution for slew of problems. Adopting terms challenge and opportunity in memory could make you becoming triumphant when opportunities stay afloat in positive-oriented manner.

02. Work according to facts. Infer not on half baked ideas. Avoid in imbibing the principle of uttering earlier think later. Deliberate over the state of development for some time. Do not utter any such thing that could become the cause of your embarrassment.

03. Avoid using terms such as *'now,' nothing,' 'forever,'* during your negative thought-oriented interaction. The syntaxes like *'I shall remain unsuccessful in my life', 'All are enjoying life better than me,' 'Nobody finds me attractive,'* prune your self-confidence and ends up your capabilities.

04. Learn to acknowledge sentiments without rejecting them. Learn to cry during crisis. Express anger creatively rather than vulnerably. Express your sentiments with open mind. Think how far you could think about others.

05. Take the onus on yourself. Avoid thinking about your boss or colleagues hardly responsible for any ups and downs. Your thinking

alone owes to your success or failure. Explore not others' shoulders to cry for your follies. For, everybody should explore his own ways of shouldering responsibilities.

06. Avoid depending on unnecessary hopes. Think not that some wonder could swiftly change your life. You could steer your life swing in proper direction. You would be relieved of tension when you realize about this development.

07. Think about your problems through positive angle. It could swiftly redress your grievances. Focus on future plans and think what original steps you embrace in fulfilling dreams into reality.

08. Make your lifestyle simple and natural, but stay over-ambitious. Avoid becoming too ambitious in the era of competition that could drool you pretty aggrieved. Give up such discouraging works. Take only such jobs that give you happiness on completion.

09. Always spare yourself with nature. Walk bare foot on green grass (meadow). Affix portraits of flora and fauna on your walls and computer screen. Realize through imagination about such scenario.

10. Make up your mind with courage. For, every decision would make you realize more and more about life. You ought to observe life as a philosopher, for life is a laboratory.

Charlie Chaplin, the famous comedian believed, 'I have been secure from slew of physical disabilities derived from euphoria. However, you ought to remain hale and hearty for enjoying such happiness. So, it calls for resetting your diurnal routine.'

**Sorrow is part of one's life, which commutes between ends but saturates on being aggrieved.**

Quite often, many people are being frightened to remain happier. For, they knew about their failure on being subjected to others' evil eyes. You will have increased will power provided you're happier. You will soon achieve your objective.

For, your memory gets effect from your ideas and determination. Your sentiments remain more powerful than ideals and self-commitments. You should analyze about the cause of anger that needs to be conditioned. For, anger would flourish when you swerve from your fundamental nature or originality. You would drift apart from the prefix 'self,' when you become pensive, but anger is the symbol of your weakness.

The elites remain ever euphoric and stay aloof from anger. For, the words uttered in anger hit your rivals like an arrow shot from your bow at lightning speed.

Ms. Hansa, the managing director of *Yogoda Institute* says, 'The entire world is reeling under tension. The cells in our body have been frozen, which were aggravating us to reel under ailments.'

However, yogic feats could enliven our cells. So, yoga is essential to remain hale and hearty. For, one finds damn relieved from stress out of developments within physical, physiological, mental and spiritual core.

Man couldn't bring himself into senses on being subjected to stress and grief upon future thoughts. Yogic feats work like wonder, when he lynches towards the highest altitude through concentration. Concentration remains the forte for sustenance of beings. It could be so especially for students and business magnates galore.

**Success follows failures. For, its path has to traverse in between such failures.**

Yoga could enhance positive thoughts. The aura of enveloping positive energy could influence your personality. The integrity of sentiments gets charged when everybody could find solutions for slew of issues. A cleansed mind and mantra of will-power extend utmost support in character and image building. This would prove to be the successful formula from the scientific angle.

The team of astronauts from NASA have realized on reaching space of their ball pens ceasing to function from zero gravity. Perhaps, they might have spent some ten years to produce such fountain pen functioning at minus 300$^{\circ}$ Celsius and underneath water at colossal expense of some twelve billion dollars. Russian astronauts have used pencil in place of pens to arrive at the issue.

Perhaps, somebodv might insist of your failure to digest over the state of developments. Do you mean limericks yield any solution? Limericks are frequently used to subject you under euphoria. A quantitative experiment has justified beings enjoying sound health provided they remained under sustained laughter. You would look aesthetically appealing, the more you look healthy.

The laughter along with brain and physical body gets activated. Laughter would enhance heart beats and pulse thereby stabilizing your immune system.

You could report this as the science behind laughter. How could sense and humour be developed? There is no necessity of learning the art of laughter. It has been the direct testimony of comedy king Charlie Chaplin making everyone has boisterous laugh. Do you mean has he been trained to make you laugh boisterously?

**Personal victory precedes the real one. An individual ought to keep up promises done for others to have it.**

No.

For, comedian Chaplin making others laugh boisterously knew that life is another name for jolly looking man, to say, 'Take things in lighter vein. Take it easy.'

Ken Dad, the humour king of Britain believes, *'Laughter works like a safety valve. It belches out under the pressure of negative sentiments.'*

Everybody has been subjected to stressful life reeling under competitive atmosphere. Perhaps, it owes to the dwindling happiness among beings. Laughter is some universal behaviour, easily understood by one and all across continents.

It is absolutely true about the programme telecast to highlight about varieties of laughter, *'Laughter Challenge,'* has brought unique change across the world. Methinks, there could be acute competition in this sector, when everybody yearns to make out his career. One should know the behaviour of laughter is not confined to comedians alone.

However, we come across several phases of laughter, viz., laughter therapist, which highlights how laughter could stabilize immune system through stress busting techniques.

Any humour consultant would make you work at ease with happiness to keep you afresh and healthier. However, the laughter coach spells out in qualifying you as some comedian. The duo approach the behavioural instincts through the formula, laugh, make others laugh and carve out niche for life.

Science has justified that laughter without inhibition could act as panacea for millions of ailments. The rule of law in arithmetic has sustained the theory of laughter. A Japanese behavioural scientist Dr. Yaozee Kimuera has defined laughter as the expression of happiness through body language. He has devised a equipment to record laughter, with its magnitude and duration, expressed in AH units.

Dr. Kimuera believes, *'Laughter is such ammunition, whose appreciable magnitude could end up rift among rogue states.'* Children laugh at the rate of 10 AH per second, which is double the magnitude of laughter amongst adults. Adults were found restraining from laughing. The folks seldom laugh even availing the opportunity to laugh. Animation through simulating computers has put laughter on priority. *A boisterous laugh would be more significant for humankind.*

Dr. Kimuera and his companions have been exploring the theory behind laughter at Osaka, the Japanese epicentre for standing comedy in the world. He wonders, 'Why not we transform 21st century into an era of laughter and fun, when 19th century drooled under World Wars?'

**Think not about improvement of country's economy but keep on thinking about your financial condition improved.**

Laughter has been the divine remedy for stress busting. Laughter would pace up your heart. The lungs would get cleansed air. Sustained guffaw could increase blood circulation on your face and brain. The person would become extremely intelligent with blush on his face. Let those people drooling in negative thinking subject selves to some guffaw. William Shakespeare has advised, 'People subjected to instincts of laughter would have longer life.'

The adage *'A slew of worries equate with some corpse,'* has been in vogue. You won't find anyone free from worries. The matter of concern has been necessary to some extent, for it could keep you under vigil on duty and responsibility to some extent.

However, *such folks virtually free from worries could be triumphant, whereas those folks drooling under worries could remain aggrieved forever.* Behavioural analyst Zimmerman believes, *World would laugh when you laugh, and cry when you cry. 'The world evaluates anybody the manner in which he cognizes. The community responds according to the manner, in which you react.*

So, it is very essential for man to possess such knowledge facilitating mankind acquire such path for living real and good life, in order to achieve such objective. Man needs to tread this path of *Sarve Bhavantu Sukhinaha,* or to say everybody should live happily possessing such sentiments.

We often forget over the fact that the world survives on give and take relations. So the adage. *As you sow, so you reap,* makes us realize with certainty over life. *For, the building remains stable and tall so long as its foundation stone rests pretty shallow.*

The US philosopher Prof. Vandal Willkie has brought out his ideas in the form of a book. None of the modern thinkers have endorsed his view despite the demonstration after pretty long analysis. His dream of fulfilling such hypothesis remains incomplete. The dream doesn't belong to Prof. Willkie but of those spiritual giants such as Mahaveera, Buddha, Gandhi, and Acharya Tulsi. So, professor claimed, *'The happiest people alone would find their proliferating opulence.'*

**Do not worry on falling on the ground while walking, for you learn the art of better walking.**

Professor Wills asked Egypt's philosopher Arastu, during his meeting, 'I wish to meet with your guru.'

Arastu replied, 'You couldn't meet him.'

Professor Wills said, 'Is he not alive?'

Arastu said smilingly, 'The stupid people on earth are my gurus, but seldom would they die.'

Professor Wills was taken aback on Arastu's comments. He felt as Arastu might have gone mad. He wondered how great thinker's gurus could have turned stupid.

Even then, he ventured out, *'People take asylum between ashrams and maestros and erudite in their bid to explore wisdom. I haven't found anyone take asylum with some stupid people.'*

Arastu continued smilingly, 'You couldn't understand about this, for I always recapitulate of appreciating any stupid out of his characteristics. I always anticipate for the dawning spiritual aura to ascertain whether I had such vices. I shall try to dispel such vice that has been manifested within me.

However, it is also true that I couldn't have existed had there not been any stupid guys. Now tell me who could be my guru—any stupid guy or an erudite? What could the erudite impart me? His ego makes him crushed under the weight of his own erudition.

Arastu continued, *'There is no limit or age or the necessity of any guru to acquire knowledge anew. So, it calls for parameters such as self-deliberation and self-influencing.'*

George Santayana has claimed, *'Have confidence in such person who hesitates to describe about anything. He should be hardworking and diligent. Avoid from slew of arguers.'*

Everybody in the present universe lives on pseudo ideals. S/He tries to lure others to gain mileage. Why should we not try? For, it is the call of the time. But, there should be an aesthetic beauty in our body and mind to become victorious in life. An adage justifies this fact

*All that glitters is not gold.*

It doesn't mean that one should stop earning money. It connotes you to spend little of whatever money you earn for altruistic activities.

However, human mind has been subjected to vacillation. It is very difficult to assimilate the pace at which the mind functions. The erudite and the wise are finding themselves perplexed. Anyone among the laity also finds pretty difficult to regulate the mind.

The *Mahabharata* quotes some wise spirit (Yaksha) posing Yudhisthira, the lead Pandava, *'What is swiftest on earth than wind?'* Yudhisthira replied, *'Mind. It functions swifter than wind. For, the role of mind across the universe is splendid.'* The Scriptures have endorsed the dynamics of universe owes to mind.

*Jo Jaisi Sangati kare, so taise phal khayee.*

It describes—'the fruits enjoyed by human being is dependent upon the company of people s(he) has had in life. Happiness remains the sine qua non to keep his mind harmonizes. Today, man doesn't have such happiness in life. He chases behind money day and night on account of such unhappiness. He could hardly differentiate between the fair and unfair objects.'

For, the root cause of unhappiness remains latent in his desires, which remains unlimited without any end. So, the company he enjoys need to be taken care of for cleansing of mind. A good company could dispel negative thoughts arising within such mind. A bad company could usher him towards disaster and his end. Saint Tulsidas interprets about this position,

*Moorakh sang na keejiye, loha jali na tirayee*
*Kadali-seep-bhujang mukh ek boond tiham bhaiyee.*

The verse describes the company of stupid people could end up in vain, putting him to virtual loss. Does anybody cross the river Ganges onto shore by roving through metal boat?

Does the fall of rain drop on banana convert it to camphor? Does such raindrop falling within shell convert it to pearl? Does such raindrop entering snake transforms to venom? So, I wish to share with you keeping these facts in mind,

*Zindagi ke safar mein khush rahna ek mantra hain*
*Aur Khush rahne ke liye muskarana moolamantra hain*
*Aap khush hain to sansaar khushiyon se bhara hain*
*Khush rehnewale ke liye sansaar mein har mausam hara hain*
*Duniya mein kuch pane ke liye kuch khona padata hain*
*Parantu khushiyan pane ke liye sirf khush rehna padata hain*
*Kyonki khush rehanewala saare avagun tyaag deta hain*
*Aur Devatavon ke samaan swarg kee khushiyaan paa leta hain.*

The radical thinker Hume Fled believes, 'The custom of yore has accorded highest status for clowns in the durbar of princes, wherein the clown used to keep the audience enthralled with his nuggets of pun and limericks, making them subjected to constant guffaw.

King Likugas has hung the portrait of angel of humour in the banquet hall of Spartacus. For, he believed, *'There couldn't be any sauce other than boisterous laugh on the dining table during lunch or dinner.'*

Lord Chelmsford also believed, *'Realise that day as the worst during which you couldn't laugh.'*

> Your facts cross all obstacles and
> your brain fathoms all limitations
> when you are near the objective in life,
> **on being influenced from**
> **glorified personality.**

So, the wise believed to initiate the day over good mood, and hum slowly in the morning with the verses of the Sermon of the Lord.

*Too apanee raah banata chal, too geet karm ka gaata chal*
*Ambar ko chhoona sahaj nahin, dharati bhee simtee simtee hain*
*Too pag-pag paanv badhata chal, too apani raah banata chal*
*Sooraj nikalega nischit hain, andhiyara phir bhee garvit hain*
*Too snehil deep jalata chal, too apani raah banata chal.*
*Padhne kee koyee umar nahin, badhne kee koyee limit nahin*
*Too sabko yahee sikhata chal, too apani raah banata chal*
*Nadiya apana path chunati hain, har dhadhkan sapane buntee hain*
*Too sabko yahee sikhata chal, too apanee raah banata chal*
*Too lakshya saamne rakh apana, too guru pustak ko chun apana*
*Too apana dharm nibhata chal, too apanee raah banata chal.*

This number would never allow you to swerve from objective. It shall keep on reminding that the journey of success is still incomplete.

For, brain remains the memory of your computer. However, you ought to utilize in proper manner so that the disc doesn't crush. It is also true that people worth their words won't suffer from unsuccessful.

For, Goodier before inventing rubber plant on earth has merely imagined about such element. George Washington struggled for life so long as he emerged triumphant. *Buddha* became enlightened through the impetus and his inner voice.

The justification derives from the fact man would proceed ahead according to his ambitions. He would get such imaginary concept in mind. Success would smile on him on fulfilling of firm will power. *Success is not a stage but a phase in life.*

For, you'll face a new objective the moment you emerge triumphant in life.

❑

**"Do that act, which you hesitate to make fear extinguish by itself."**

**—Tarun Engineer**

# EXTEND YOUR INFLUENCE IN ABANDONING FEAR

Perhaps, you know the adage, *'First impression is the last impression.'* Anybody meeting the stranger would form the silhouette of the person at the first encounter. For, it shall sport at one stroke about your body language, mannerism, etiquette and attire. The image remains the final, making you recapitulate during the next encounter, and becomes difficult to erase. Such image alone owes to your future relation in the society.

So, think about this whether it relates to your career or social life–the first impression should be everlasting to hypnotize the onlooker.

For, the people would get influenced from such look, which they visualize during the first encounter. You might have visualized this aspect with your own kids. The kids will do only such things, ignoring what you direct them often, but imitate what the adults used to enact.

You could be the most influential gentleman unless you have behaved before them as some dependable and positive-oriented personality. You could be the most influential howsoever they knew about you.

I don't know how far you're effective on others, when you're reading this book. However, your work might influence thousands of people, or anyone might turn a deaf ear to your advice.

Mark Collins believed, *'You ought to do the work you're supposed to, when you would accomplish on such day, when you desire to do so.'*

Psychoanalyst and philosopher William James has expressed Collins' statement as, 'Everybody ought to work at least two jobs that brings him absolute happiness every day.'

However, management analyst Mr. Sangeet Verghese believes, 'At the outset, everything remains complicated. It is so, since the objective remains pretty difficult. We observe such objectives as though we were watching someone from his outward appearance. The stranger appears pretty frightened from his outward appearance. We also find ourselves frightened on observing him. It could be the cause for us remaining vigil in undertaking any risky job. We seldom know about the outcome that could land us on our destiny.' Sigmund Freud, the guru of behavioural psychology believes, 'People seek permission before doing any new job under conscious and semi-conscious level. It warrants them to stay aligned to the slew of available resources, diligence, time duration, and frequent attempts.'

**This is not the measure of success for your difficult problems seeking solution but the problem has already surfaced before you.**

You ought to complete two tasks to get the answers from your inner voice. You should remain optimistic and hone positive skills within your heart towards the job you wish to complete. You should visualize complete picture about accomplishment of such objective.

It would become complicated to keep your mind elated unless it harps on vicious thoughts. For, this is the only option left to accomplish your objective without much ado. So, you ought to think of the outcome before initiating into such objectives. Management guru Mr. Robin Sharma believes, 'I have already identified four prime causes from which it could be ascertained why people oppose inevitable changes at the cost of ignoring to improve their career despite availing such opportunity.'

I have labeled the four causes through 4F syndrome. You could make some better selection. Certainly, you would experience better outcome have you selected any of them. It is true that leadership drive shall commence through personality-oriented approach. For, how could you bring improvement without knowing about your weakness? I have been deliberating upon those four causes that repulse you through life.

Syndrome-**(i) Fear (the awesome):** Many of your colleagues wish to achieve something anew. For, it could be some burdensome task leading to your fear. The fear will chase you from which you're afraid of. The fear could embrace you out of your dislike. For, every fear has some precious treasure hidden behind its walls.

Syndrome-**(ii) Failure (Becoming unsuccessful):** Nobody desires to end up in failure. Majority of your colleagues seldom attempt. The failure manifesting in your memory is your failure to attempt. So, go for some swift smaller trial. For, sports superstar Michael Jordan once said, *'What is that if I couldn't give one shot? Failure is some significant part of the accomplishment of success.'*

Syndrome-**(iii) Forgetting (Losing memory):** You will be prepared to change the world after coming out of a workshop. You will forget everything on the following day when you enter the office. The basic formula of success is to keep your priorities ahead of everything in your psyche. Cultivate sensitivity around such thoughts. Do not forget about such promises, and make them lurk in between your slew of thoughts.

Syndrome-**(iv) Faith (keeping confidence):** Most of the people don't have faith. They suspect over the state of developments. Often they comment, *'I am not ready for change, for I have been pretty old. The suspected guys won't be successful in life for their failure owes to slew of doubts. Indeed, you become glorified in life, which calls for your desire to commence.'*

**Objective shall remain distant on erasure of desires when its base gets shocked.**

**Think beyond undesirable tasks:** The best available option to desist from undesirable tasks is to do your work according to an estimate. Try to accomplish the work in swift and constructive manner. Think beyond the slew of undesirable tasks. See whether you were left with any other option after disregarding such tasks.

**Get into action:** Psychoanalyst Stuart Wilde in his book, *'The beginning,'* claims *'Get into work and stop uttering nonsense.'* However, it wouldn't look nice to visualize such impetus mobilizing your reality. You were well versed with self-restrained personalities. Always reach the objective of desirable tasks through undesirable with soldierly temperament.

**Learn first and do later:** Seldom were you interested in doing any work, for you will realize somewhere that you're incompetent enough to accomplish such task. You don't know how to accomplish the task. You're hesitating to do that. So read more and pool up with necessary data.

**Why don't you ignore the matter?** This advice is not there to avoid the task. It could have made you desist from undesirable tasks. You'll orient towards the destination. Your withdrawal would influence you from backing out.

**Accomplish the task on being insisted:** Someone's love could motivate you in accomplishing such desisting task. For example, my daughter Vilsha proposed that seldom would she lick her fingers on my giving up of smoking. It was lovely proposal in between us. Now, the condition remains our weakness out of avarice that love of either could withhold from our habits.

**Do some desirable work initially:** Let the initiation be swift. You could reach the destination without much ado. Similarly, doing some undesirable work after desirable task could be an easy option. The success from such phase could keep you happier. You could do undesirable work at ease with that euphoria.

**Celebrate over success:** Imagine that objective could prune your weight. Appraise yourself to weigh some 20 kilogram by physical weight. Such figure couldn't have been the biggest objective, but it could take some time in disciplining yourself to regulate your weight.

**Aim should be petty afar when failures of short-distance disturb you.**

Celebrate through patting on your back after reducing the girth by five kilo. Gift yourself with such appraisal for proceeding with double elation in reaching the destination. You won't reach the mark unless you desist from doing such undesirable tasks.

For, Mark Twain has alarmed us, *'Keep away from such people who wish to prune your ambitions. However, giant also make you realize that you could become glorified sometime later.'*

So, you had to embrace the principle of positive thinking for achieving the goal. For, the folks will always visualize *impossible* proposition when subscribed to negative thoughts. Those banking on positive thinking will find the clue that I could accomplish the *impossible task* even *amidst impossible* occasions.

Please bear in mind that your talent alone would surface, when there is harmony in between your mind and the environment around you. Career counsellor Ms. Usha Albuquerque says, *'Let everything proceed as desired. The courage and positive thinking could transform you towards such shades of opinion on making you to align with such circumstances leading to disappointment.'*

**Dream precedes objective and craze ought to be created to become successful but self-confidence always comes into picture for creating such interest.**

So, give up on becoming jealous about others' virtuous deeds through worries and negative thinking. For, you would end up in failure unless you ascertain someone else has been doing or not. Such thinking could plunge you to become unsuccessful in your mission. But, the person with positive thinking explores the way to become successful.

I have come across some living example through an insignificant farmer of Punjab's tiny hamlet, Mr. Harnam Singh, who gets awarded every year for growing good yield of maize. He continues to experiment with techniques anew every year. He displays somewhat astonishing performance during such contest.

A correspondent of vernacular national daily *'Punjab Kesari'* reached his farm house to ascertain about the secret of his success. Mr. Singh was seriously involved in cleaning of his field in the light of approaching sowing season. So, he reached the fields disregarding the interviewing scribe. He began distributing the maize seeds to his neighbour on the occasion.

The scribe was taken aback on finding why the farmer has been distributing the seeds to his neighbour. How has he become the successful farmer? He could not understand over the development. Mr. Singh realized about the anxiety of the scribe through his body language. He said, introducing his neighbour to the scribe, 'He is my neighbouring friend. We cultivate our fields with seriousness. Our field of work is one at the same time. More or less, we have some unique feature amongst us.'

'My neighbour shares with me about the beneficial weather, or the splendid fertilizer useful for higher yield, akin to the manner in which I keep ascertaining about the good variety of seeds. We became successful in getting higher yields. We share our happiness mutually when I get rewarded on the occasion. The feeling of insecurity seldom arises amidst us.'

The complicated people are everywhere. They might be your life partner, business partner, or landlord, or children, or brother-sister, or relatives or any of your neighbours. Most of you people would not only encounter with complicated people but also ought to make them in your favour forever. For, quite often you could realize that they could trouble you through sentiments or assaults. They want to decimate you so that you would get crushed forever.

**You could win the entire universe provided you've a pen and some dream byte. These two objects are required for becoming triumphant.**

For, good sailor would usher the appropriate path for the followers. *'He is the leader who observes others seriously, foresees ahead and watches before others. However, packing off one's dreams could be to crush oneself in life, for, we have been the product of such dreams,'* claims Leroy Ames in his volume, *'Be the leader you were meant to be.'*

It remains some dream for you that you could reach your objective. For, it is very difficult to reach the objective without any tumultuous uproar. Perhaps, you might have heard of the adage,

*'Hit the iron while it is hot.'*

So, it means that you should work at an appropriate time. The adage belongs to 14th century, and related to blacksmiths of that era. They ought to hit the iron at correct temperature so that they could mould into the requisite shape.

It is also true that the triumphant would turn out to be supermen, but for becoming so, they should be super intellectual. Neither such triumph needs any miraculous power, nor does the destiny of such success have any relation. For, the successful people remain the laity, but there are also such people, who remain self-confident, with utmost faith on their capabilities and believe that they should emerge successful at all costs.

An old adage says about an old king renouncing from the world. He asked three of his princes and appraised them about his decision. He told them that he alone would inherit his throne who could utilize the time and powers well. Later, the king gave the trio some gold coins and said, 'This should get stuffed within the room by evening. Anyone accomplishing the task would find empowered to occupy my throne.'

The king reached to the eldest prince by evening and realized from the fragrance. He found the room was filled with fertilizers, sewerage and debris. He came out in haste and told him,' What is this stupidity?'

The first prince replied, 'You alone have told me to fill it in the room. So, in one gold coin whatever I could find I have filled that in this room.'

The king went to his second prince and found the room pretty empty. He asked him, 'What happened from that gold coin?'

The second prince replied, 'I couldn't understand what I could do from one gold coin. So, I went to gambling den and gambled out. Earlier, I won, but lost everything in the subsequent game.'

The king went out beating his forehead. He reached to the room of the third prince with heavy heart, where his anger took break. His room was lighted with lamps from within and the room was charged with incense from every corner.

For, the youngest prince bought incense from that gold coin. The king was delighted on observing him and crowned the youngest prince. The king persuaded the trio, *'One should have the capability and reasoning to utilize any object to the best possible level. Everybody gets time, resource and power in his life. However, everybody couldn't make use of them. But, he who makes use of them alone could reach the objective.'*

**Desire is the first shore of success. Weaker tides near the shore make it stink. Weaker desires yield weaker results.**

So psychoanalyst Prof Welford believes, *'Entrepreneurs ought to remain ever vigilant over their extent of self-confidence. They need to explore possible options before entering the market like celluloid super star Akshay Kumar.'*

For, Akshay Kumar was ought to buy the title available in the market—*'Amitabh Bachchan—A super star, A personality.* He ran short of one hundred rupee in his pocket. So, he went on reading the book, standing aside the book shop, where its jacket was written, *and 'One needs to become good human being before becoming super star.'*

The feature doesn't only apply to actors, but also with other professionals such as doctors, advocates, politicians, students, businessmen. For, the maiden Indian Police Service officer, Ms Kiran Bedi has observed elsewhere, *'I have mentioned in the UPSC application form—Humanity. For, I believed that humanity is the greatest religion on earth. However, some people have different values towards humanity. They long in making fool of others.'*

Similarly, someone joined the position of manager in a firm. However, his subordinate said, giving three envelopes, *'Open these envelopes in order, whenever you got trapped in some great problem.'*

**Man's spirit wakes up through self-confidence for blood circulates swiftly through limbs on becoming passionate.**

His position was at stake when the firm incurred appreciable loss after six months. He found the advice for himself, when he opened the first envelope, *'Throw all the defects on your predecessor.'*

The gentleman did accordingly. Six months rolled out through such mode. The proceeds of the firm through subsequent six months disappointed the management. He found the advice, on opening the second envelope, *'Accomplish mutual changes amongst subordinates.'* Accordingly, he replaced a few of them by axing the existing work force and mutually rearranged amongst others.'

Six months rolled out in phased manner. He found the eventual advice, on opening the third envelope, *'Prepare and present three more envelopes to your successor.'*

**Prayer**
is not only a part of your life,
but also works as some talisman during
**the hour of crisis.**

The gentleman manager began beating over his forehead on this predicament. Carl Menninger, the associate founder, author and psychoanalyst, reveals, *'You shall find some friend with whom you wish to while away, when he wins your heart. Everybody desires to have good number of listeners. He gets attracted to him. For, character develops from within, but the image from outside. The image is that on which you cash in on your character.'*

So, enhance your self-confidence. Prepare ten such achievements you confide as the secret of your success from your erstwhile life. *Perhaps, you might have bagged highest marks in an academic examination. You might have partaken as an ebullient leader in some significant team. You might have produced good sales at some stage.* It has warranted that you might have been at certain stage of progression, which has made you outperform in contrast with others.

Introspect yourself whither have you been at. Observe through your past achievements. Evaluate your potentialities according to the present state of development. Observe at your friends and analyze about their weaknesses and potentials. Think of such opportunities that could enhance your personality. Think for a while about your capabilities. Analyze which of the parameters is of paramount importance for you.

❑

"Imagination is the primary step of success. Arithmetic of risk alerts you to end up in failure followed by success after such risk."

—Tarun Engineer

# INVEST YOURSELF FOR FUTURE BENEFIT

Few days back, I along with my family was on a vacation trip to Shimla, when I moved through air-conditioned Volvo bus. I was sitting aside the bus window. My youngest daughter Vilsha was sitting left to me. 'We were compelled to watch an undesirable movie on the television.'

Meanwhile, I went on watching through the window pane. I found the outward natural scenario through the beaming moonlight.

Suddenly, my daughter inquired, *'Moon has been accompanying us like our trailing thoughts and rituals.'*

However, our desires seldom follow us. The mind accomplishes its mission, when we take the support of intelligence in making them trail us. I shall justify this fact through an anecdote.

A fisherman on some riverbank was catching fish everyday through sieve-net. He couldn't find any fish being trapped. He was getting disappointed when the sun used to set. He put the sieve-net on fishes galore, recollecting the name of lord, the Almighty on the following day. The fishes didn't find selves in his sieve-net. However, he found some bulky bundle being trapped in the sieve-net. He found many stone pebbles on opening the bundle. He wriggled out and got into the boat.

The boat was sailing past amidst chilly wind. His mind was preoccupied with thoughts anew. He began thinking, *'I shall throw the sieve-net aside another riverbank, which is inaccessible to anyone. I could catch more fishes from that bay.'*

His mind remained vacillating. How could he control himself? He went on throwing the pebbles one after another. The bundle got emptied. He was left with single pebble, which was on hand. Suddenly, he wondered, on gazing at that, 'Oh, this is diamond.'

The fisherman was left with nothing else other than utter disappointment. For, he went on cursing himself while roving amidst the river stream. Boman Irani, the film actor, 'My life is living book of performance, which was unknown to me. It set off during my childhood. My childhood was replete with exploring instincts and innocence.'

'I was an introvert and quiet child till I was four-year old. The subsequent period was full of commotion. I was pretty mischievous and nervous by nature. I never sat quietly at one spot. I never withdrew from the opportunity of harassing or making fun of anybody. I got admitted to Pune Wadia College after getting through formal education from St. Mary School. My family was running the small scale business of manufacturing salty snacks—Golden Wafers. My mother was managing through its production and marketing units.'

'My mother met with an accident in a couple of days. I got into the business when she was bedridden for sometime. My joining film industry was sheer accidental. I used to go on outing on Sundays shooting natural scenes, utilizing my camera. My neighbour Andrew Sequera running an advertising agency in Chennai, suggested me to adopt photography as my avocation.

**Scientists have christened the experiment done by Hadron Collider as Higgs Bozone signifying it as God's biggest experiment.**

However, my life took subsequent turn. I became the personality, Shyamak Davar. I replaced him when he was relaxing after photo-opp in some shooting locale. He often thought me to be on stage. He went on chasing me, ascribing during shooting, *'You are an actor. You ought to enact on some locale.'*

'I gave several alibis to make him abandon his obstinacy. It called for me accompanying the team to Shimla. However, Shyamak Davar insisted me over his version. He took me for an audition to Alaq Padamsee, the celebrity in ad-media.'

'I got an opportunity to enact in theatrical version of *Roshni.* The audience and critics accorded me with warm reception after the performance. Subsequently, I enacted in Family Ties, I am not repo part, I am not Beziro, Sixth degree of separation, Mahatma versus Gandhi, et al dramas.'

'A screen test took place for some ad-movie during those days. I reached the trial spot accompanying my friend. A model was expelled one day before the final shoot.'

'So, I was asked to undertake the test, where I got selected. I have worked in various ad-spot movies such as Fanta, Whirlpool, Bata, Tata Phone, Polo, Britannia Little Heart Biscuits, Smile Cough Syrup, Johnson and Nicholson Paints, Kinetic Honda, Safety Films, Laser shaving blades and Crackjack Biscuits. I got an opportunity to enact in the movie, *Munnabhai M.B.B.S.* from where people began glorifying me as an actor.'

Veteran celluloid actor Anupam Kher says, on being influenced from Boman Irani's success, 'Guard what you say. It would reflect about your opinion on life. For, the words you use would determine about your experience. The language you opt could glorify you in that manner through restructuring.'

'For, the success in any particular field owes to the vocabulary you experiment upon. Another gentleman Mr. Kinjal Singh chose this formula in life, when he secured 25th position despite being disqualified in civil service examinations. Mr. Kinjal Singh says, 'I have been successful due to the use of good vocabulary and positive thoughts. For, self-confidence always reflects on anybody's countenance through appearance and etiquette, showing him to be less self-confident.

**Model and beauty queen turned Hollywood actress Hailey began her career in some local departmental store.**

The person's body language articulates such weakness while appearing before the audience. Such people would turn down their head and shoulders, or keep their hands crossed upon the bosoms, or keep their hands into trouser pocket.

On the other hand, the man would justify being self-confident, when he walks straightforward, with head and shoulders held high, speak through eyes with another, and straighten his shoulders in ordinary way like some daredevil.

You might have observed people subjected to martial arts—karate, judo, and tek-van-doo. The guys attempt in knocking the opponent through such body language with firm will at one go. His (her) physical prowess comes into picture at later stage. The folks would be trained in such manner as though they won't appear pretty weaker for self-defence.

So, engage yourself in conversation. Keep conversing with anybody, equating eyes with eyes, at mall, coaching centre, college, or any other place of public entertainment during your next visits. Repeat this experiment with your people acquainted earlier.

**Sleep during night visualizing dreams with open eyes. For, dreams observed with shut eyes seldom proved true.**

It could be better to initiate discussion with concern over smile. Nobody could make out whether you're pressurizing your acquaintance.

For, direct conversation could bring you to the people straightaway from close quarters. A lyricist has uttered,

*Vasant kabhee alag hokar nahin aata,*
*Greeshm se milkar aaata hain.*
*Jhade huye phoolonki yaad,*
*shesh rah jati hain kopalon ke paas.*
*Phir nayee kopale phootate hain,*
*adrishya bhavishya ki tarah.*

It is evident from the above verse that dreams seldom appear alone, other than surfacing with self-confidence.

Someone inquired during Pune's conference, 'I couldn't find the cause of giving importance to words.'

I have persuaded him in detail. The words used in general could be understood as one's body language. The body could express such gestures which words could seldom speak out.

A line of an old number spells as,

*Tumhare honth mujhe na bolate hain,*
*lekin tumhari aankhen haan kahti hain.*

However, it is very essential at the outset to acquire its knowledge and utilize that for some gain.

This could be more effective tool during some interview or trade bargain, where these features won't find any necessity to go through. However, others were being influenced to perform and think so that it could give some definite result. Another lyricist has said,

*Aap muskurayenge to fiza mein bhi bahar aa jayenge.*

A mere smile with self-confidence could make the person sitting before you feel quite natural. However, please be attentive that your smile is poised, for more laughter could be counterproductive.

Always sport yourself afresh, for you could enthrall the people sitting before you from your condition. So, your condition could define many parameters. Meet him later, who had been in tension, bidding good bye for the moment.

Keep your body language fit. For, your body language spells out more clearly than what you have spoken earlier. So, keep your body language under control during maiden encounter. It should be so that your self-confidence gets controlled.

Stand erect during such encounter. Let there be smile on your face with your eyes equating the person concerned. Give a warm handshake, to make you extremely self-confident.

It is true that anybody could find himself (herself) pretty nervous on the first encounter. Keep cool by regulating your nervousness before such encounter. It might be possible that you are experiencing yourself under tension or subjected to basic formalities. Drink water and smile. Think again that the stranger is also meeting you afresh.

**You ought to light lamp of self-confidence to visualize happiness and achievements through its radiance.**

Always ascertain about their special features. Your discussion could be much easier had you been aware of requisite facts. Had the stranger been a lover of cricket, your dialogue need to be focused on that topic with that background. Your emulation of such procedure could facilitate you in becoming successful.

An analogous incident has taken place with 35-year old Reena Chopra. Reena had been serving in some private firm as the marketing executive for past five years. She got the news one day of her being

**Energy production within you reaches the ionization level when you went euphoric. Harnessing such energy could felicitate you in becoming extremely triumphant.**

axed from marketing department.

She was subjected to serious shock to tender her resignation before being axed for her managing director has behaved in unjust manner. For, she thought herself to be quite competent for the position. She has not only had the requisite experience but also adequate aptitude. However, she thought that she could face appreciable loss on being separated from the company.

She thought of submitting through proper channel before the managing director through argument without getting disheartened over the development. She prepared a report about various projects and tasks undertaken, besides those coevals for whom the company has extended training for various tasks. She told the managing director, on presenting the report, 'I shall endorse your decision about me on perusal of this report.'

The managing director reinstated her in the position of marketing manager after a few days. He told her subsequently, summoning her to his chamber, 'You are the most competent for this position.'

The development that took place with Reena Chopra justifies that self-confident folks seldom compare themselves with others. You could end up pretty disheartened on comparing yourself with others to be in better position.

Perhaps, you might be aware of the giants who've reached the zenith of success tumbled during their initial stages. Many of the managing directors of some companies were on errands without any destination before becoming so.

The folks never felt embarrassed in working selves in the least position. Their dreams eventually got fulfilled when they emerged triumphant on jobs. *Set off yourself at the lowest echelon for the journey extending some thousand kilometer sets off from smaller steps.*

The poet and philosopher Ralph Waldo Emerson says, '*I go on learning from whomsoever I have met during my career, for he remains splendid in his own field.*'

Always bear in mind the interaction of successful interaction would commence voluntarily. However, it could be more effective of making the business successful. Your becoming some giant at some stage would also be more significant in life.

For, the stepping stone of success could be moulded with several features like esteem, prestige and confidence. *Your becoming giant could be next to impossible had your foundation stone of honesty be pretty weak.*

Always think about the gains of honesty like you think about the foundation stone of your built home during dreadful tornado. Had the stepping stone be strong, the house could withstand firmly from dreadful storm. The house gets crushed under the pressure of the storm had the foundation stone be damn weak with divided layers.

It is true that anchors always hone skills on impeccable speech. The folks stick to the profession on being familiarized from 90 per cent of presentation with accent and style with five to ten per cent on blending of facts. The presentation of text shall remain divided between two such anchors, when the audience refuses one amongst them for his poor accent.

**You ought to eliminate scrap ideas for those surfacing without any effort reflects the experience of your past life.**

The effective anchor hypnotizes the audience from his digitalized voice despite possessing poorer facts.

The formulae seldom apply to anchors. It could equally apply on you. Former elite officer of Delhi Police cadre, Ms Kiran Bedi says, 'Any police officer could prove effective among the public totally on his (her) presenting style. At the outset, when I became the Indian Police Office-cadre officer, people were watching me inquisitively.

My interaction has hardly made any inroads on them. I kept watching my presentation seriously and have discussed it with linguistic experts. The experts have ascertained of my weakness of English pronunciation subjected to indiscreet style, while my vernacular Hindi accent was subjected to Punjabi overtones. Often, I rectified this defective accent, which I experienced during my interaction at later stages.

> You shouldn't disregard another opportunity through the phase of disappointment over failure, for success trails behind failures.

How is your image at office? Your presentation should remain exquisite. You should have intrinsic hold over the language through which you communicate, besides legible accent.

Perhaps, you shall endorse over the fact that interaction should be good, which could get felicitated everywhere. So, follow the formulae mentioned underneath to acquaint you with phonetics.

- You need not recapitulate the entire lexicon to enhance phonetic skills. You could be conversant with vocabulary anew through reading of newspapers, periodicals, and books.
- You could write in separate notebook about the words not conversant while reading newspapers, periodicals and books. Find their meanings through a good dictionary. Use the words during conversation keeping the meaning, incident and accent after learning their meaning by rote.
- Vouch yourself to recapitulate three new words every day. You could improve vocabulary through reading good novels.
- Open the dictionary. Jot down words you're not versed in some notebook or flash card. Browse those words from the note pad while standing near the bus bay or doing some work.
- Many researches have proved about people with good vocabulary to become triumphant in life through influencing others.

Your belief in spiritual texts could implant such powers in your sub-conscious sheath, mobilizing you to apply them during practical conversation.

The Sermon of the Lord, Upanishads and the Holy Bible interprets this fact,

*Mamaivamsho Jeevaloke jeevabhooto sanatanaha*

My differentiated power stays within the spirit on humankind. The saints who scripted Upanishads believe whatever manifests across the universe owe to lord, the Almighty, and remain embedded in His cosmos.

*Eeshavasyamidam sarvam yatkinchitjagatyaam jagat*

The Bhagavad-Gita proclaims that lord, the Almighty manifests in all the species alive (flora and fauna).

*Eeshwaraha sarvabhootanaam hridyerarjuna tisthathi.*

You will find hardly any difference in that eternal infinitesimal power, that is omnipotent, and remain without form.

**You ought to become crazy to produce the gadget of enthusiasm for objective loses senses in enthusiasm.**

A scribe queried Albert Einstein, when he was alive, 'What is your opinion on lord, the Almighty?'

Einstein replied, '*I never endorse the term God in the words we use in practice. However, I certainly acknowledge about the presence of some unseen force regulating the dynamics of our entire cosmos. The invisible force was guiding me often in solving some riddle, which I encountered during my scientific inventions. The solution obtained so was never contradictory.*'

Poet Kalidasa was certainly a poet of immense value. However, he was neither the devout nor any big seeker, but was extremely self-confident on his spiritual strength.

*Sataam hi sandehu padeshu vastushu*
*pramanaha antahakarana privruttayaha.*

It signifies that for enlightening, internal motivation or mission should be replete with virtuous thoughts. It is only possible when our heart remains aloof from negative thoughts such as enmity, jealousy, anger, desire and infatuation seldom intervenes within us.

The *Sermon of the Lord* justifies, '*Lynch your spirit achieving its destination keeping that away from distress and failure. For, there won't be any reliable friend or enemy other than that spirit.*

The Holy Bible says, '*Such people are fortunate whose inner conscience always remains sanctified. For, they're competent enough to become triumphant in life. So, thoughts sprouting within us have some importance for our facts seldom gets affected with doubts.*

'*Samshayaatma vinashyati*', spells that suspicious beings get certainly crushed forever. For, any suspicious folk *with double-mind* could never have any fair decision upon selves. He resembles ocean tides which finds subjected to wind disturbances. Disciplined *meditation* alone could reform them.

Observe the works of physicist Isaac Newton. He noticed an apple falling on earth, when he sat quietly in a garden. He often thought why the fruit fell only on earth? Why didn't that reach the sky? It made him subsequently pronounce the laws of gravity.

It is very necessary to quote that beings should have absolute confidence over their inner psyche beyond mind and intelligence.

**The probability of people doing business with you will be more when you appear financially rich.**

Similarly, some teenager was always interested observing space in New York. He was only twelve years of age. His father gifted the boy with an eight millimeter aperture camera. The boy produced fifteen documentary films by his sixteen years of age.

The young probable director relied upon his scientific imaginations, when he produced maiden scientific film, 'Fire light,' at subsidized budget of some 500 U.S. dollars. It was only his starting point.

The teenager was none other than *Steven Spielberg*. Spielberg's life gives us the impetus that merit doesn't beg for anybody. His subsequent movie "Jaa" hoisted the flag of success.

*It is evident from his mission that none of the works in life could be accomplished in one single day. One had to sow its seeds in the mind and nourish that through*

Do you know
**Bhagat Singh**
martyred for the cause was a
**positive thinker?**
He thought forever of India relieved
from colonialism,
attempting through day and night.
So, become positive thinker for
a lyricist nas advised
**"positive thinking is the first
letter of success".**

*the fertilizer of courage and irrigate through water of hard work. The plant would flourish as some tree yielding fruits after many years.* So, one should wait for the tree of success to yield fruits.

A few people say, *'The luck of my companion is fairly good. He got promoted or else we also do work equating his performance.'*

Most of the people evaluate their success and failure with their destiny. However, this is not a matter of fortune or misfortune but an issue of attitude.

Getting disenchanted or cursing oneself or thinking negatively could be much easier. However, many people are being less versed in conditioning their ambition under crisis. The folks pondering in positive manner will go on achieving success step-by-step. You need to be extremely cautious about conditioning.

❑

"Your honesty would make people believe in you. You won't become financially heavyweight without such confidence. For, confidence is the primary significant relation sought for professional relations."

—Tarun Engineer

# CULTIVATE THE HABIT OF BIG THINKING

The author of 'Success is easier than failure' E.W. Howe cites in his magnum opus, *'Some people end up their lives in cursing their hardships after passing through valleys of imagination, which remained non-existent.*

The citation applies equally on you, for the people who haven't tasted success in their lives couldn't ascertain about reaching the zenith of success under present circumstances. They find pretty engrossed in insignificant jobs and couldn't ascertain whether they opt for short circuit.

The philosophers have been advising us from several.centuries for self-realization. However, most of the people believe *to identify about one's negative aspect of life.* The folks subsequently make out a long list of errors, weaknesses, or negative aptitudes to back up the cause.

It is good of identifying about your weaknesses. For, you could find out on which sectors you need to amend. However, you could get encaged in such tension on identifying about your negative aspects alone. For, your estimation could be stymied verily under your own eyes.

You have been vested with the onus of breaking stones, with the mission to reach space. You are roving around impatiently to achieve your objective. For, you have been working hard to achieve your objective and successfully emulated *'Law of Attraction,'* but go on cursing your destiny despite completing the job.

You shall believe on reaching the destination after a few days that you're not attempting with correct procedure and you are lacking self-confidence. So, you ought to have absolute confidence (one hundred per cent) in accomplishing your objective, for even one per cent of doubt could spoil your mission. So, you need to have 101 per cent of self-confidence in place of 100 per cent. For, you ought to hasten of achieving the mission and visualize your wishers transforming according to their ambitions.

You shall find the signs of reaching the top the moment you race ahead towards achieving the mission, irrespective of their magnitude and pitch.

Your steps would tread ahead with certainty the moment your memory stabilizes on probability. The data stored in your mind gets automatically transform into probability, disallowing the sprouting of doubts with certainty at any cost.

Let me recollect an anecdote. Once upon a time there was siddha purusha. He was revered and extolled equally by the laity and the intelligentsia galore.

One of the devout was extremely anxious about him. He queried when he couldn't hold anymore, 'Guru Dev! People offer salutations or wish with folded hands to princes and kings, president and prime ministers. Nobody worship them. However, what is the secret of millions of people offering salutations, or worshipping or paying obeisance to you?'

Siddha purusha replied curtly, '*Self-restraint.*' The devout continued, 'When did you commence in your life following self-restraint?'

Siddha purusha replied, "I began emulating self-restraint when I was merely five-years old.' My father often advised me, 'My son, you'll be sent for studies in gurukul from the morrow. Neither your mother nor your brother nor shall I accompany you. Our orderly shall take you to gurukul on horse back after bathing and feeding. You ought to sit underneath a tree when your teacher shall ask you sit for an examination. You ought to present before him under *self-restraint* so long as he wouldn't ask you to enter his cottage.'

**The hero of Hollywood's controversial movie *Pirates of Caribbean*- Leander Blume started his career as clay trapper.**

I reached gurukul on my father's persuasion. Our orderly sought the permission from the teacher, mentioning the desire of a new disciple entering gurukul.

The teacher responded, 'Make him sit outside.'

The teacher came out of his cottage after a while, and told me, 'My son! Come and sit here with eyes shut. You need not open your eyes without hearing my voice so long as I won't come. For, I want to ascertain how much *self-restraint* shall be exhibited on your body, mind and your conscience. You will be admitted to gurukul on the extent of self-restraint you practice. You couldn't become the Siddha purusha when you lack such self-restraint.'

I have followed the teacher's advice. I came to know the practice of self-restraint is a must for qualifying his test. The teacher returned after some three hours. All the children fled to play in the open air. However, I hadn't opened my eyes. A mixture of sugar and jaggery was sprinkled around me after some time.

Ants swarmed around me. I recollected in following self-restraint. Another three hours rolled out. The teacher asked me with deep affection, 'My son, wake up. You got through my ordeal.'

**Your fearing over something makes fear overpower you. It would remain as guide provided you shall frighten very fear.**

Saying so, the teacher lifted me up through his hands. I got admitted into the gurukul. So, my advice shall be that *self-restraint* is the foundation stone in one's life. You couldn't concentrate on any issue so long as there won't be any *self-restraint* within you. We could classify the formula as, '*Self-restraint* alone is the formula for success. You could become a serious thinker on acquisition of *self-restraint.*

So, this book explains on how to practice *self-restraint* in your life. It is an exercise done with austerity to evaluate about your true format. I have assimilated this after undergoing intense training. It works wonders on beings.

| S.No. | Qualities | Names of acquaintances | Outcome |
|---|---|---|---|
| 1.. | Education | (1) | ☐ L ☐ H |
| | | (2) | ☐ L ☐ H |
| | | (3) | ☐ L ☐ H |
| 2. | Experience | (1) | ☐ L ☐ H |
| | | (2) | ☐ L ☐ H |
| | | (3) | ☐ L ☐ H |
| 3. | Technical Qualification | (1) | ☐ L ☐ H |

| No. | Parameter | | Low | High |
|---|---|---|---|---|
| | | (2) | ☐ L | ☐ H |
| | | (3) | ☐ L | ☐ H |
| 4. | Appearance | | | |
| | | (1) | ☐ L | ☐ H |
| | | (2) | ☐ L | ☐ H |
| | | (3) | ☐ L | ☐ H |
| 5. | Balanced Domestic Life | (1) | ☐ L | ☐ H |
| | | (2) | ☐ L | ☐ H |
| | | (3) | ☐ L | ☐ H |
| 6. | Behaviour | | | |
| | | (1) | ☐ L | ☐ H |
| | | (2) | ☐ L | ☐ H |
| | | (3) | ☐ L | ☐ H |
| 7. | Personality | | | |
| | | (1) | ☐ L | ☐ H |
| | | (2) | ☐ L | ☐ H |
| | | (3) | ☐ L | ☐ H |
| 8. | Leadership Aptitude | (1) | ☐ L | ☐ H |
| | | (2) | ☐ L | ☐ H |
| | | (3) | ☐ L | ☐ H |

Eight parameters were enumerated above in the tables. You ought to explore five of them inherited in you and highlight three acquaintances, which have excelled in respective fields. You will realize that you are ahead of them from those parameters.

You could arrive at the outcome honestly. Take a plunge into the original format. Think big about what you possess.

The person using the term *inaccessible* for *immobile* and *economy* for *savings* shall realize how far the vocabulary had been larger. Does he possess more vocabulary for the concerned? People experimenting with difficult terms look pretty arrogant and pretending. Such folks are least bothered about any development. One ought to go through the following content for greater concern.

*Kya is raah ne thaka diya hum ko*
*Lakshya ke itane paas laakar ladhkadha diya hum ko*
*Sochate hain hum kamee rah gayee hum se*

*Yaa apanon ne hee hara diya hum ko*
*Himmat to hum mein hai kya tut payee hai abhee*
*Sankalpa jo hum mein hai kya dhund payaenge kabhee*
*Uthana to padega sangram hai baaki*
*Is gaharayee ko paar kar saken taaki*
*Manzil to aakhir paani hai*
*Har raat ke baad ek nayee subah aani hai*
*Aaj hum khade hain us sthaan par*
*Raahen rook ke kahati hain yahaan vishraam kar*
*Par shaayad safar kuchh aur bhi hai*
*Kyonki manzil ab bas kuchh door hai baaki!!*

The above content disallows anyone from pursuing any of his objectives. Does it correlate with your desire? You shall find whether your adopting tack has been consistent?

A teenaged girl passing through similar condition explained, 'I have adopted all such tacks on becoming a lover, or some diligent better half or self-confident woman or some non-selfish friend. I have never tried to ascertain what others expect from me. I remain unhappy for I was little sentimental. I could have saved from being aggrieved had I known about my choice.

The *law of attraction* cites the good object you dislike has such unbecoming quality, which might appease or deject you. Attempt not to ascertain about your qualities from somebody else for s/he couldn't analyze properly about you. You ought to introspect about your state of psyche.

**It all depends on your psyche how you rate successful people in their or out of favour.**

On the contrary, your introspection on what appeases (offends) you without any effort by your quiet thinking whether it has appeasing effect shall determine your choice for the desired object.

You had to refract the brightness of the light on your path. This is the only mode available for your progress. You shall find such objects damn favourable in fulfilling objectives, endorsing your choice provided you emulate such tasks. For, Mother Nature has moulded life in such manner that would lure desirable objects towards it.

For, Gautama Buddha has asserted, *'Appo Deepo Bhavaba'* meaning, enlighten yourself.

For, you ought to decide upon your light within. This is the only option for proceeding ahead. Adopt this mode so that your life could get fulfilled about your ambitions. It would remain your ambition. For, nature has made our lives in this manner where our own ambitions would lure us towards them.

It equates with your position sometime in some condition, where you won't stop breathing nor the situation warrants you from doing so. Similarly, it doesn't warrant any exclusive technique to reach the practical object of choice.

Introspect yourself after acquiring chosen object where you could find yourself appeased. If you are a student, ask yourself *what was your ambition in life*, forgetting what others shall comment upon, viz., the choice of becoming a doctor, engineer, pilot, teacher, painter, businessman, which response ought to come from you.

**Madonna brought changes anew forever though she worked as some dancer for a musical group.**

The outward recommendation or co-operation could keep your mind pretty poised. You might encounter *'My subsequent choice of acquiring such objective after choosing the first option.'* The answer to this question should emerge from you.

You will begin swimming against tides on choosing such options. Swimming doesn't move your limbs for such regulation comes under the constant vigil of your brain. You will flow along with the tide of the vigil remains lackluster calling for utmost hardship to swim ashore. This formula applies equally on your objective for vigil remains the key to success.

I have kept some riddle before the group of women who were sharing about their experience—whether the computer is masculine or feminine in gender.

The women answered it as masculine in gender and also some of its masculine traits.

- The equipment carries unimaginable store of data.
- The data facilitates in arising at the solution, but majority of the information reflects the problems arising within the computer.

You shall realize that you could have found some better model following your choice done in haste. So, the women were justified in assessment as the computer equates with whimsical nature of man.

An anecdote report about a hermit bathed on the riverbanks of Ganges and giving ablution to the thronging devout aside. Someone said, on accepting the pail of water from the hermit, *'I have sinned more. Little water won't cleanse my sins. I need more Ganges water.'*

The hermit asked, *'How much Ganges water you need?'*

The stranger replied, *'Get me a glass of water.'*

The hermit offered him one glass of water. The aggrieved stranger said, on sipping water, *'I hope I won't be sinned anymore.'*

The moment he breathed his last, his vital force exploded through tenth hole in his body, signifying him to have reached the heavens.

**The formula of life and business is experience. You couldn't gain from others' experience so long as you share your experience with others.**

The anecdote justifies man gets the fruit of his action favourable to his sentiments. He attains that state at the moment, where he hangs on to such sentiment. Your sentiments attached to somebody, it will make you acquire such love. For, man's conscience desires to acquire that forever. Your choice of doing some virtuous deed will endorse you to do and fetches the fruit accordingly.

The morale justifies howsoever man possesses the objective, he shall attain favourable success. Desire should be stronger to achieve such success, which reports the brain about such mind power. You try to acquire that power in you. Often your conscience finds some aimless psychic power proportional to the very urge, which proves to be your objective.

You ought to possess such stronger mind power from which you would expand infinitesimal quantum of energy in fulfilling your objective. Urge is such invisible entity, which pools up your energy to harness such objective. It is such a magnet pooling up the particles around you in such manner so that you could materialize your objective.

The urge will put you *vacillating between the poles of magnet, either for success or for failure.* How your urge conditions you depends on your conscience at the eleventh hour.

Adage—*God helps those who help themselves*—is absolutely true at this juncture. Keeping idle won't make your urge materialistic. It calls for transforming yourself as an effective superior or controller. You would reach your path after successful expeditions.

Firmness of mind besides continuity of approach will stake your claim. It is not necessary that you would acquire such success at one go. Probably, it might make you attempt recurrently. The continuous approach is absolutely necessary. Success has the essential requirement of constant hardship. A child during yore has imagined of meeting with lord, the Almighty. He has heard about Him staying in some distant country. He prepared a journey to encounter with Him. He left home with a bottle of milk, and chips of cornflakes, both kept in his attaché. He reached a park aside on way to explore lord, the Almighty. He found an old woman caressing pigeon, sitting on a bench. He sat next to her and realized on becoming hungry. He went on munching chips on opening his suitcase. The old woman noticed him seriously. The child extended her the packet of snacks thinking her to be reeling under hunger. She beamed an attractive aura on munching chips. The child felt as though he has seen the beautiful smile on his childhood.

**Jennifer Aniston during her crisis has worked as tele-marketer and bike messenger.**

The child yearned to gaze her smile again. So, he extended the packet again towards her. The sequence went on passively till the afternoon. He returned home quietly on finding himself pretty exhausted. His mother asked him, on being surprised over his happiness when he knocked the door. The child replied, *'Today, your son has met with lord, the Almighty. His smile is the most beautiful smile across the world.*

The child's mother was taken aback on finding serenity writ on his face. Aside, the old woman also reached her home, when her son inquired about the delay in her return. The old woman said, *'Today, my meeting took place with God. He is younger in age to me, according to my expectation.'*

The anecdote reveals that those people who're triumphant shall reach the destination despite frequent efforts.

Avoid abandoning such efforts like children. For, you ought to fathom the distance in reaching Mt. Everest at each step. Your next pace might facilitate you in landing aside your objective. This remains the cause for the triumphant adapt the formulae given below in realizing the objective.

- The giants knew reaching the objective is next to impossible. To say, their choice is not any figment of imagination, but some concrete destination, the reaching of which is not so easy.
- They know the magnitude of hardships in reaching their path of objective. It signifies them to have arrived at the objective on the basis of reality without daydreaming.
- The giants are target-oriented. Not only they dream of its acquisition but also have taken the onus to work extremely hard.

**Success could be derived from some mania for the frenzy approach could get everything done from you, which you won't imagine.**

These are the three objects that could cherish the entrepreneur to undertake the onus of working hard. These are the three parameters, which reflect the difference in such reality between the cherished folks and set of dreamers.

Aside, the more your urge goes deep, your brain shall also be very active, for the intensity of urge would influence brain in such manner, as to expend complete energy and stamina in achieving the objective. You could never think effectively unless your urge is consistent for your brain doesn't have anything left to think or function.

Your working potential is also dependent on the acquisition of your urge. Your determination to fetch fruit afresh than you might

> Anger is not bad but man rears enmity
> after losing temperament.
> Stop not converging despite fighting,
> quarreling and assaulting well.
> For, the moment you stop conversing,
> **it would shut the doors of reconciliation.**

extend your hands till the branch of that tree else, you shall remain contented on taking the fruits fallen below. This issue has been related to urge and stay put through compromising nature.

Do not allow such tendency sneak amidst your urge, else repeat the following verses.

**Your idea could be secret power. Secret is the law of attraction through which you could explore hidden secret in such ideas.**

The content shall mobilize your urge and remind you every moment about the target objectives. Now let us reiterate about those lines

*Hamein jeevan ki raah par chalana hai, girna aur sambhalna hai.*
*Deepak jalte toophanon mei, andhiara door bhagaana hai.*
*Bekaar hain aise jeene mein, jab lagan hee na ho seene mein*
*jeevan ke path par chalna hai, yahan girna aur sambhalna hai*
*kabhi kaante hain, to kabhi kaliyan hain*
*kabhi gam hain, to kabhi khushiyaan hain*
*Hame jeevan ki rah par chalna hai , jahan girna aur sambhalna hai.*

These lines shall awaken you up with ambitions and remind you every moment about your objectives.

❑

"The bird perching on tree branch never gets frightened despite the latter shaking, as it confides through eyes, but not on the branch."

—Tarun Engineer

# HONE THE ENCOUNTERED ERRORS AS YOUR GUIDE

Everybody errs in life. However, radical thinker has been bestowed with the art of transforming things through positive, progressive and optimistic ideals. So, you should experiment such words for giant thinking, sporting positive sentiments. A few sentences have been displayed below which have been the cause of small, negative and pessimistic sentiments on the left hand side. The circumstances have been amplified with positive orientation on the right hands side. Introspect yourself through browsing—in what format have I been visualizing mental portrayal.

| Negative Thought | Positive Thought |
|---|---|
| 1. Nothing shall happen now as, I have lost. | I have been defeated. I shall keep on attempting continuously. For, in the race, I have new idea, from which I could become opulent in life. |
| 2. I ended up in failure when I initiated the business earlier. I won't venture this now. | I was certainly unsuccessful when I got into the deal. For, I have made mistakes, which I wouldn't repeat now. |

Please study the anecdote ahead to enhance your knowledge. A queen was letting her hairs dry on the terrace of the palace after bath. She kept her diamond necklace on the wedge and went on caring her damp hairs. Meanwhile, a crow fled on to the terrace and noticed something glittering. It fled towards the branch of a tree, picking the object and attempted to eat, but couldn't.

Its beak went on paining to break hard diamond. It left the tree after leaving the necklace hung on the branch. The queen began tracing her necklace after drying her hair and found that missing. She traced here and there but couldn't get through. She reported about it to the prince, through weeping, 'Your Excellency! My necklace got stolen. Get that traced out.'

The prince said, 'Why are you worried my dear. I shall get another produced.'

The queen relented, 'Now, I want the same necklace.'

The palatial entourage went on searching around the palace, but couldn't find.

The prince told his sergeant, 'Get me the missing necklace.'.

The sergeant was much concerned. His subordinates and the people of his state went on exploring the missing object, but in vain. Later, the prince proclaimed, 'I shall gift whosoever bringing the necklace back with half of my real estate.'

**We ought to shortlist important words from unimportant ones for words alone could shape man's personality.**

The people went into serious search with acute competition. Everybody began searching the necklace on being avaricious of getting half of his real estate. Someone traced the necklace along sewerage water flow. The necklace was noticed by everybody, but the water being effluent looked black and stinking. One of the soldiers dived into the drain with utmost courage. He began grabbing whatever came in hand, but couldn't find the necklace. He doesn't know where it vanished.

The sergeant also dived into the drain, on observing the necklace, followed by a venturesome youth and the minister.

So, the sewerage drain got swarmed with divers. They noticed the necklace before diving, but were untraceable on swimming across the stream.

The prince was also frightened. He thought why not he try his luck without losing half of his real estate. He dived into the sewer water stream.

Meanwhile, a hermit passed through the drain. He said, amidst laughter, 'What fun is on? The prince, people, minister, soldier and sergeant got mired up. Why are you diving into the sewerage water stream?'

The people replied, in unison, 'Sir, the fact is that the queen found her necklace to have been stolen. We have been observing it in the sewerage water stream. We find that missing, without anybody securing the moment we dive in.'

The hermit laughed at them, 'Brother, has anyone looked up? Look up the necklace been hanging from the branch of the tree? You folks are looking down in water. You're finding its shadow on water.'

**The brain hides the power of transforming any objective into reality. You ought to explore the tact of accomplishing such task.**

The anecdote gives us the impetus that the object we desire to have looks through its shadow, but serious thinking would bring it near, when the shadow transforms into the reality.'

We ought to introspect what we speak, irrespective of our profession. However, we ought to select proper words while interacting with the public, for,

| | | |
|---|---|---|
| The most important term | : | **I** |
| The most important plural.term | : | **We** |
| The most important two terms | : | **Thank You** |
| The most important four terms | : | **What is your opinion?** |
| The most important five terms | : | **You have done a good job.** |
| The most important six terms | : | **I wish to understand you correctly.** |

However, man has three original qualities—fact, statement and business. He is capable of discussing that he doesn't belong to any other species. Man's statement has such power, unfound among other species.

None of the species have that capability of his business. He has three qualities, which isolates man from other species forever. So, none of the species has developed that potential, which he has developed through deliberation.

Lord Mahaveera has preached, 'We should weigh facts, statement and business before speaking at the outset. So, bear in mind,

1. *Your facts shouldn't have any appeal.*
2. *Your statement shouldn't have any argument.*
3. *Your behaviour shouldn't be unbalanced.*

For, one whose facts don't have any appeal, his thinking sprouts every day with ideas anew. He could achieve the objective without ado, has he had any intention to accomplish.

Harinder Sikka belongs to that group of personalities. He has written the title, *'Calling Sehmat,'* with a Kashmiri lady co-author, based on the real incidents. Today, he had been the director of *Nicholas Piramal Health Care Limited.* So, *don't see what is there, but what could happen,* for greatest thinkers seldom observe about things but see whether anything could be derived.

**This is not an accidence but reality. One per cent of population earns about 96 per cent of money. This secret, when they make up their minds but nobody could hold them for doing so.**

A biological research has propounded *an ordinary person listens twice what he speaks, and five times what he reads or writes for any day.* We expend 80 per cent of our time in conversation. We spend 46 per cent of the overall time in mere listening.

However, majority of people seldom use such opportunity other than abusing their time. It seldom favours anybody, but results in appreciable loss. The articulation capacity of the people subjected to harsh speaking gets pruned to some 20 per cent. We have some formulae to save ourselves. The call for the hour is to articulate correctly with simple terms. Saint Kabeer has explained through his duet, as

*Aisi vaani boliye, man kaa aapa khoy*
*Auronko sheetal Karen aapahun sheelat hoy.*

So, you ought to draft out what you wish to speak with others, as to how you're going to present it. As such, you could express yourself in effective manner.

The erudites believe that 80 per cent of your articulation depends on how you articulate with people, 20 per cent on your presentation conditions, your compilation of facts. To say, success is squarely dependent upon diction as pizza upon potpourri.

Success would knock at your doorsteps provided you appear polite, using sweet language with certainty. For, God will also help those who help themselves.

The Sermon of the Lord says, *'The act done by man through hard work and courage would yield successful output. Any impediments, hardships or obstacles won't withhold such success.'*

People say that scarcity of words could annihilate the characteristic feature of the speaker. However, many saints have testified that scarcity of words alone would give the impetus for getting him isolated.

Ishwar Chandra Vidyasagar is the perfect example of such personality, for him being born from poor family. He didn't have even the facility of wick lamp to study at night. So, he studied underneath the shades of lamppost, and became such wise man, bewildering his coevals and other wishers. For, Ishwar Chandra was responsible for generating vernacular Hindi alphabets.

Today, we have acclaimed Vidyasagar as a giant personality: Similarly, Dr. Bheemarao Ambedkar took birth amidst scarce-hit lineage. He had to depend on princes in the pre-partition period for meeting expenses to study. He didn't get dishearten over the state of development, but became the draftsman of Indian Constitution treading successfully through slew of grievances and obstacles. He became an international personality known for esteem and prestige. So, many giants have taken birth from the womb of scarcity in this manner.

**The biggest thinkers ought to achieve objective when they make up their minds, but nobody could hold them from doing so.**

However, the giants couldn't become so, on being born out of scarce hit poor families, but because of firm determination, firm-self-confidence, firm will-power, and extreme hardship, which they have accrued for they're not entitled.

Now, I am sharing with you about such youth, who remain absolutely without any resource, but undertook training in smithy at the tender age.

The youth was to hang over near the kiln for the day and work under the shade of candle light. He was sparing sometime for studies before taking food. He used to read books during leisure, keeping one or the other book in his pocket. He made proper arrangement for studies, during the crisis subjected to scarce conditions, inconveniences and hardships. He became the successful orator in almost all languages communicated impeccably across European continents by the age of thirty.

You might be curious to know about this gentleman. *Yes, he is, Iyobret.* You ought to keep yourself under self-restraint on your becoming triumphant under extreme hardships.

The founder of Boston University Isaac Reich had only four US dollar in his pocket for eking out his livelihood when he landed there from his county Cape code. He established Boston University on the basis of utter self-confidence.

**Confidence builds up through biggest thinking, yielding some attachment. The effect of both works like some staircase to reach the objective, when man makes up his mind to work hard.**

Majority of people don't set any business through with zero bank balance. For, they had to abandon the hopes of commencing such business. They keep on waiting for the destiny to smile on them, but it shapes the man from hard work. Sage Asaram Bapu preaches, *'Destiny owes to father-hard work and mother-perseverance.'*

One doesn't know how many giants became triumphant through wonderful tacks and reached the zenith of success through business. George Washington was one amongst them, who was the son of a widow, born out of some farming shanty.

Washington didn't have studied through any university, but he had been bestowed with three degrees. He was confident of reading, writing and counting, which qualified him to become the first citizen

The path of
**determination**
is replete with strange obstacles and difficult terrains.
Fathoming them
**requires extra courage and attachment**
when probabilities galore shall transform into reality,
achievements and
**dreams.**

It became evident from old class teacher that happiness doesn't sprout suddenly without uneasiness, but it has to be acquired under sustained efforts. One ought to make habitual to remain happier.

Imagine how the old class teacher has embraced such easier tact to remain happier. Could you accomplish such task without ado?

You ought to get such delight at such place, which is practically impossible. You wish to sustain on borrowed happiness. Perhaps, what others narrate might serve as sops for your happiness. Whether shall you attain such cozy comfort and happiness? You ought to get that for others' comfort.

Similarly, you shall become aggrieved on such pattern. For, seldom could you simulate others. Neither have you become the ideal personality on the yardsticks of others. You ought to explore such happiness from within.

**Your imagination to acquire something sprouts from within with ideas and sentiments of acquisition. Law of attraction transmits that object to you in reality.**

You shall realize somewhat different world on accessing the interior of any issue. Appreciable part of your future sustains upon slew of impediments. It is pretty uncertain whether it was yesterday rolled out or the morrow rolled in. Either you might have been concerned about any past incident or worried about the future.

Acharya Rajneesh, advised us, *'Spare self from the concern of morrow and live for the present.' Buddha, the enlightened advised, 'There is no necessity to meditate if you live for the day. For, staying for the day is analogous to such meditation.'*

However, it is pretty difficult to hang over for the day. For, you could get aligned to the fantasy of the morrow had you been lost in events rolled by. For, your physical presence could endorse your day, without any heart.

The practical aspect of this presence appears—your presence at home might remind your heart at the office while your stay in office would make you recapitulate about your home. Similarly, your heart shall remain at studies, when you are playing in the field. Studies would keep your mind drooling in play. It means you're spoiling that precious time, for staying delighted calls for living in the present circumstance. You ought to bring your heart in laughter.

However, the condition of laughter is marvellous. Keeping your heart pretty agitated puts you under laughter, thereby laughter conditioning your personality. For, humour seeps into your heart straightaway, subjecting you to guffaw. Quite often, you will get into boisterous laugh out of your mischief. Similarly, the etiquette of people and social intercourse could confine you to such laughter.

Charlie Chaplin, the universal clown defends life subjected to humour as, *'The day on which you restrain from laughing would make it worthless.'*

**A tree seldom grows without seed, but requires water and fertilizers every day and the seed also needs to be sown into the soil.**

Most of our scientists of the present generation have attempted to sift through the dominant role of laughter interacting with people of various temperaments. Earlier, it was believed that laughter would be good for health, but a recent invention has justified the thought of laughter could be more lucrative than the very act of laughter. So, for one's splendid health, physicians began injecting the dose of laughter along with medicines to their patients.

The research done on those miserly folks could be more beneficial, who keep them frequently under restraint even to laugh on formality.

The radical thinker Khalil Gibran believes, 'Could you explore laughter elsewhere for it manifests already within you'.

Indeed, laughter is not an object of exploration, but ought to be experienced from within. For, Mother Nature joins you in your attempt to laugh. It echoes around justifying life as most trustworthy. Believe that your confidence has been overtaking you on attempting to laugh, when everything goes as desired. Seldom has any grief overpowers you provided the laughter is being sustained in the aftermath. None of the objects in the tangible universe could be precious than such laughter.

Look at small kids. Even the laughter of six-month old baby makes him thrilled and hopping, for his laughter never sprouts through lips but from individual veins, which we label as intelligence. Such laughter would result out of innocence, real sense without hesitation.

The reason remains our stage of delight during our play. Acharya Rajneesh believes, *'Life is a play. Play with utmost aesthetics. Get delighted from life. Think not about success or failure on your desire to ascertain about your happiness.'*

For, you shall get delighted from life when you explore seriously. Your life transforms into positive outlook when your exploration is through. So, you ought to cash in on absolute truth, whereas majority of people believe death as absolute truth. The Holy Gurubani (the Scripture of the Sikhs) of Sikhs illustrates this as

*Sahaj subah jo hoye so ho.*

The hymn remains wonderful. For, everything in the world is not under our control. One should not even attempt to take them under one's virtual control. So, it calls for an individual to explore natural path to retrieve from tension and stress.

Spiritual seeker Swamy Narayana Murthy says, 'Keeping delighted is absolutely essential. You could perform well when you're delighted. You could think well and arrive at the inference without ado. Negative thoughts could hardly haunt someone remaining euphoric. For, the efficiency of such people could multiply. It has been testified an aggrieved individual finds everything wallowing within negative thoughts. So, any individual remaining delighted and contented could keep him devout forever.

**Laughter is the tonic for becoming big. For, the laughing people have good longevity and proceed ahead piercing through their objective.**

Devotion appears as—(a) the enlightening factor, and (b) the laughter making life pretty contented. The humour afloat on real aspect is nothing but some serious sentiment for unarmed people. It keeps one desperate subjecting him to laughter with marvellous potential to bond people of different temperaments.

It resembles some game. You could play when you are versed well and abide by those rules in letter and spirit.

Ludwig Wittgenstein believes, *'Humour simulates him tossing the ball towards his opponent anticipating to intercept it. He also desires the man opposite throw the ball unto him. However, some people keep the ball in their trouser pockets instead of throwing.'*

Philosopher and comedian Andrei Watts believes, 'A real comedian resembles some daring guy. He ventures out to interpret and visualize, which his audience gets frightened on being embarrassed to express. The blend of circumstances, the fear and difficulties finds befitting slot in his honest depiction. However, natural humour and pun could not only de-stress but also emancipate will-power forever.

Spiritual seeker Swamy Ananda Murthy believes, 'The universal game owes to mind. It subjects often either to elation or humiliation. Sometimes, it gets into unbelievable phase which puts you aggrieved. You ought to make up your mind in how to tackle with and experience the environs.'

Concentrate on such foci where you ought to reach but not where you stay on. It should be the manner in which Noida's (Extended eastern city of New Delhi) Salim Choudhary has displayed during his studies. He was always carving positive thoughts during his engineering studies. He affixed such logo in his study room, which has justified him to become triumphant.

His logo spelt, *'My lexicon doesn't have the term impossible. The peak of the valley remains vacant, for it is being earmarked for my sojourn.'* He has affixed similar inquisitive logo on the walls of his bathroom.

He was always listening to motivating audio cassettes. He was working pretty hard, which qualified him to score the highest possible marks in the examination.

**Losing occasions means depriving the opportunity to become successful. For the field of occasions alone could yield the crop of success plants.**

Let us verify an anecdote about the influence of miserly nature of people.

A miser businessman undertook pilgrimage on foot to breathe his last. However, each of his footsteps got haunted by attachment and illusion. He was pondering over the fact that family folks might have been spending extravagantly in irresponsible manner. He was concerned with his sprouting thought.

Meanwhile, he suspected whether he has put the electric bulb on in the verandah before leaving home. Had he not switched off, he ought to pay the supply bill voluntarily after returning from month-long pilgrimage. The businessman might have fathomed some four or five kilo meter, he made up his mind to have the pilgrimage later, which made him return home for switching the verandah light off.

His son asked, on finding him back, 'Papa, why have you returned?'

'Oh my son, I left the verandah light on.'

'But, I have switched that off the moment you left home. You have unnecessarily made your slippers worn out.'

'Do you mean my slippers were worn? Have you thought me to be a fool? See, I have returned home barefoot keeping the pair of slippers under my armpit?' Saying so, the businessman showed him the pair of slippers.

It is evident from their behaviour that man doesn't only have beautiful and affectionate sentiments but also every individual will have some negative thoughts.

**Have self-confidence that you're the most important person on earth, while away through laughter without turning back. For, the foundation of success falls through vastness of heart.**

However, one who has constructive thoughts, he knows how to express them thoroughly through the medium of constructive deeds.

A psychiatrist, Dr. Anshul Gupta observes, *'The people of constructive disposition in contrast with the laity shall remain extremely intelligent with certainty.'* Their personality shall become so from the outset that they have more potential to withstand in their lives under negative tendencies and will explore some mode to express their positive sentiments, which is acceptable under the norms of society.

If any painter uses fading colour in his specimen, it means his unconscious sheath might have hidden his anger somewhere while presenting his specimen.

Sigmund Freud has expressed the art of exhibiting negative thoughts in the form of sublimation. He has propounded his theory in defense of human psyche.

Accordingly, man has been experiencing through different modes of mental struggles in his life. His brain shall explore voluntarily the way to successfully emerge out of such struggle. Sublimation is also such procedure of defense mechanism through which the person shall express his negative sentiments in positive manner but will do so often negligently or consciously.

The incident resembles some grocer disposing groom on the occasion of Indian festival of colours (Holi), offering special discount of sixty per cent for the bride buying a flat in the six-storey apartment. The discount would be subjected to some terms. Every floor in the apartment has different varieties of boys (would-be grooms). Any girl after reaching the room in the floor was not allowed to return. She was allowed only once to buy the flat. After reaching the final storey, there was separate way to get out of the building. A girl, on trial, reached the first floor of shopping centre to hunt her would-be groom. The sign board displayed that *the boys were employed.*

**Good experience brings happiness while the bad ones glorify man. For, sacrifice, faith and honesty are the sine qua non for his acquisition of objectives.**

The girl read the sign board and thought these boys were better than her earlier boy-friend. What is the harm in looking ahead? She advanced towards the second floor. The sign board displayed *the employed boys were extremely fond of kids.* She liked the deal, but proceeded ahead, for wider choice.

However, she got into the third floor. The sign board mentioned those boys as *employed, looking handsome and exquisite in appearance.*

The girl thought of advancing ahead towards the fourth floor. *The employed boys were fond of kids, look impeccably well and are willing to extend cooperation in household choirs.*

The girl thought to ascend one more floor and try her luck. The signboard on the fifth floor displayed, *'The employed boys look handsome and appreciably well, love kids extremely well, cooperate with household choirs, and obey what the wife directs.'*

The girl was pretty impatient to visit the sixth floor. She found the signboard mentioning, *'You're the 26th girl reaching this floor. You won't find any mate. It is impossible to satisfy you.'*

However, it is necessary to transform the dreams into reality that one had to identify the probabilities. The girl couldn't identify suitable groom, which made her thoughts vacillate in vacuum, reaching the sixth floor, and return disappointed.

The *Ramayana's* Sundara Kanda claims, lord Hanuman finding himself pretty bewildered in identifying his unbelievable potential. It was Jamvanta, one of his kins, who made him realize the potential. Subsequently, Hanuman accomplished the impossible task into possible. He fathomed the ocean by inflating his physique to giant size, one hundred times the dimension of ordinary physique. He encountered successfully many demons, which came on his way, and accomplished the feat without ado, in no time.

**The display of happiness is laughter. Success and delight surface where there is laughter. For, laughter enlivens our internal happiness.**

The above incident justifies *every individual being is badly in need of some guru, for ushering him the path of rectitude. He should be the one who guides with absolute confidence how to proceed ahead, and vanquish the vicious personalities coming on the way.*

The great poet and philosopher of Lebanon Khalil Gibran claims, *'The meaning of guru is to align the individual with the tangible universe by sharing his experience with the disciple.'*

A few people believe in the debut of karma (actions), but remain successful despite making efforts to acquire the resultant. Eventually, they cherish the life on the hands of destiny and lord, the Almighty. The individual, whose will-power is firm and strong, depends squarely on his karma.

A lyricist has explained, *'Some people got relieved from the tornado on their own efforts, but other got drowned in anticipation of oarsmen for rescue.'* This was the cause that Sikander, the Great vanquished Indian peninsula out of his own actions, for getting triumph out of destiny was beyond his apprehension.

So, I pray during the early hour everyday, and solicit you also pray. *'Oh my lord, everyday across the universe, you'll find someone born, who has the strong will-power of lord Mahaveera, the esteem of lords Rama and Krishna, mission of saint Kabeer, simplicity of Gandhi and Vivekananda and capable of getting death like Mahaveera, so that his demise could be celebrated among the mankind as Mahaveera Nirvana Mahotsav.'*

So, I believe that you long to learn the art of living. The Sermon of the lord is before you. However, if you want to die, learn that from Mahaveera.

You believe that ant is tiny insect. Its day rolls out by carrying the load from house to verandah and back. How many days it could take for it to traverse from Delhi to Mumbai? You could imagine about its horrible journey, but if the tiniest ant catches hold of someone's edge of sari (suit)or clothes, and if he boards the train leaving for Mumbai, then it could reach Mumbai without much ado on the following day.

Similarly, if you undertake horrible journey of life holding the edge of guru's apron, obviously, you could fathom your life without much ado.

However, keeping always delighted and smiling could be the biggest prayer to lord, the Almighty. For, you could realize yourself juxtaposed to lord, the Almighty in lieu of all such prayers.

**A lovely smile could win anybody's heart when the estimate of your sustenance could change altogether. For, the smile plays dominant role in the acquisition of success.**

Similarly, man is instinctively prone to laugh. Seldom could you find any other species of cosmic creation subjected to sustained laughter, in the form of guffaw. It is also true that *moths and butterflies would sit on blossomed flowers, but not on withered flowers.* The smiling human face, consequently, gets special aura about his (her) personality.

It is also true that any smiling person could seldom sport sentiments of anger, jealousy, and violence. So, smile alone is the antidote for anybody in anger for pacification. However, the other phase of laughter, giggle making the facial muscles contorted. The bard, William Shakespeare has claimed, *'Thy can conquer the world through giggle.'*

Jolly looking guys would keep pace with the world by adapting to the nature's whims. However, you should live under the present circumstances of living happily, whereas you could shape the future by streamlining your present life with some discipline. *For, man is his own friend and foe, but none from outside. However positive thinking could stabilize our mind forever.*

We could recapitulate how the war between the virtuous and the vice on earth took place. Let us preview over the *Ramayana,* where lord Rama fought with demon Ravana from the underworld. Neither had you any chariot nor any arms for safeguarding your physical body and sandals for his feet. How could you vanquish the demon armed with multiple missiles astride horse-driven chariot?

Lord Rama says, *'One who triumphs finds his chariot under unique mode.'* Explaining such chariot, lord Rama continues,

*'Amal achal man tron samaana.*
*Sam jam niyama silimukha nana'.*

The stable mind resembles some bow to vanquish against the tangible universe in the battlefront. So, you will find varieties of bows, to condition your unsteady mind.

Mr. P.S. Rathore, author of *'Fun best and Experimental Learning,'* believes that 'Modern lifestyle remains absolutely stressful without any corollaries. The circumstances couldn't be held responsible, but our miscomprehensions could play vital role. Once we realized how to counteract with such forces, then we won't find any such object that could be counterproductive in the path of success.

> **Your success depends upon your comforts. For, how long you feel comfortable, success will smile on you in the same proportion.**

For, we shall find the necessity of somebody mobilizing us whether we are doing correctly or not. Subsequently, the inherent self-confidence shall remain as the forte to proceed ahead. However, every individual ought to subject himself to some ordeal with some determination.

We could say something about such determination then the idea would arise in your mind, which transforms us with some desire. It will be called as the determination when the urge transforms into firm decision.

Great men have only determination, but the miserable men have only desires.

The giants emerged in the universe become so, for they have determined to achieve something in their lives.

*The wonders of such determination has made prince Siddhartha to become Buddha, the enlightened, Vardhaman to become Mahaveera, Mohandas Karmachand to become Gandhi, son of shepherd to become Jesus Christ and child Nathu to become philosopher Mahaprajna.*

American scholar Victor Mary Hugo claims, *'Man doesn't find short of energy, except will power. For, many giant tasks have been accomplished on firm determinations. Pyramids have been built on Egypt's planes. China has built tallest and longest wall on earth. Many provinces have been carved after felling trees and wild flora. Firm will alone owes to the exploration of the most developed country in the world, United States.'*

So, it is not impossible for achieving objectives. You had to make up your mind with will-power that everything is possible. However, if you concentrate and sift through such term, *impossible*, then it could be read as I am possible, meaning that I could do the job, or to say, nothing is *impossible*, and everything is possible. So, fructify your dreams with firm will power.

**Anyone fixing highest objective in life, certainly he would be successful in accomplishing that some day ahead.**

1. **Do some deed for gaining something:** You have to accomplish the mission with firm determination and will-power, irrespective of scores of odds and counterproductive measures. Nobody could change his decision if the individual had been cherished for his mission.

2. **Synchronize performance with promise:** You ought to define life in different format and emulate in practical life. You need to synchronize your performance with promise made earlier. Do not become so, who say something and does something else. An adage justifies as wolf in sheep's clothing.

So, adopt parity in what you say and perform in deed. You could prosper with utter self-confidence with enthusiasm anew.

3. **How to shortlist determination?** The determination comes under varieties—personal, domestic and social. However, it depends on the individual whether he is making up his mind at the personal level, or at the levels of the family, or the society, or the reforming of the nation. Browse through your career, whether you're comfortable or not, if you wish to make up your mind at the personal level.

Try to ascertain the cause of your discontentment. You could be the cause and make up your mind to glorify your future. Bear in mind that none of the wishers could make you triumphant, and you ought to work hard to make your life rosy.

4. **How to sustain determination?** Induce thyself after making such swift determination whether you could work without much ado. Keep a diary and write on its leaves every day without fail how nearer you had been for the mission.

**Keep gazing on the progress of your objective and think positively. You will attain everything for which you have dreamt so far.**

5. **Do something for sustaining your mission:** Do one determination on each occasion. Finish one before taking another. Mix them not in haste, which could get you perplexed. Avoid them abandoning at the middle level. For, leaving them in the lurch could put you off the gain. It could make you lose all the benefits accrued. Saint Kabeer has believed that,

*Dheere-dheere re mana, dheere sab kuch hoy*
*Maali seenche sou ghara, ritu aaye phal hoy.*

To say, try to laugh boisterously at least once, as a diurnal custom. It could become habitual for you to laugh boisterously like waking up from bed, taking food or sipping water (beverage), it shall remain part of your routine. Scientist Robertson has said, 'Laughing could be natural and make your blood circulate without ado. Your body shall sport youthful vigour, attractive and aesthetically appealing.'

Similarly, imagine somebody to have reached hell after his demise, he was told that every country has its own hell, and any individual has been given the option to select the hell of which country he has selected.

**Camel scares to go under mountain.**
**Vice scares to go to the saint.**
**Truth scares to go to the leader.**
**Snake scares to go to the robber.**
**But, the goddess of wealth**
**never scares to go to anyone.**
**She rests where she gets honoured.**

At the outset, the individual was shown the hell of Germany. Everybody was offered electric shock by making him sit on an electric chair. He was subsequently made to lie on mattress studded with nails, where the noose man used to whip him. However, that hell had lesser number of occupants, and he was also shown similar punishments meted out in hells of other countries.

Indian hell also meted its victims with similar punishment, whereas it was overcrowded. The individual inquired with the orderly of god of death, Yama, 'The punishments remain equal at every place. How then Indian hell is being overcrowded?'

The orderly replied, 'The difference remains that the country suffers from frequent load shutdown, when the electric chairs seldom will function, and people have stolen the nails from the mattress of nails, and noose man remains the government employee. He countersigns the official attendance register everyday, but won't work for the day. So, Indian hells remain overcrowded anticipating for his turnover. The victims enjoy the day with fun and frolicking.'

For, your mind shall be dispelled of sorrows during laughter depleting your negative thoughts through pruned reasoning skills.

Acharya Rajneesh says, 'I want you to accept the prayer to laugh. For, you shall remain in the present state of circumstances during such laughter. For, you could have laughed in the past nor do so in the future. The people who have begotten human beings have sapped out the sentiment of humour from their offspring.'

**6. Don't worry, be happy:** You always insist that seldom could you find happier. A psychiatrist says, 'Happiness is the phase of one's sentiment for physical health. Your efficiency and creativity would multiply proportional to the extent of your happiness. You could solve any riddle without much ado in no time.'

For, humour doesn't have any particular vocabulary. However, everybody knows how to read that provided outside environs stay extremely delighted, and brings that through positive approach. So, Bertrand Russell has advised us, 'Amplify your value system for remaining delightful. Befriend whosoever interacting with you.'

❑

**"Happiness seldom comes voluntarily. You ought to attempt continuously in its acquisition. Happiness beams through your face on achieving your objective."**

**—Tarun Engineer**

# CONCENTRATE MORE ON YOUR BODY LANGUAGE

I had been to Mumbai on some business trip. It was pretty evening. I was returning to the hotel on Juhu road, after strolling on Chowpatty beach. I got into some bye lane, on forgetting the way out. I came across sign board, after passing through the lane, *'The road ahead is closed.'*

Suddenly, I stopped there. I went on exploring the correct path leading to King Hotel. One of the boys from their bevy asked, *'So hero, have you come to select your heroine in this closed lane?'*

I avoided replying him, when I went irritated on his invective. The boy left with his bevy. I went on thinking for pretty long time, why did the boy address me as hero. Am I really looking hero alike?

A voice blared from a loudspeaker aside during such thought, *'There is only one road ahead to reach your destination. Abandon your anger and proceed ahead. For, your destination is little ahead of you.'*

Often I muttered, when my anger got vaporized from such advice, *'What is this lane? Is there only one road for my reach? Won't there be any other lane?'*

Meanwhile, I found the bevy of boys returning to me, when I was lost in thought. I observed the boy who addressed me with an invective. He told me, when I summoned, *'Why have you addressed me as hero? Do I look alike some hero?'*

The boy replied, on being frightened, *'Your body language reveals that you have landed in Mumbai to become a hero.'*

My anger got evaporated on hearing his reply. I replied over smile, *'Tell me the truth. Do I look alike some hero?'*

The boy reiterated, *'Yes, you resemble Amitabh Bachchan. That has made me address you as hero.'*

Saying so, the boy proceeded ahead. I went on consoling myself for some time, thinking about the significance of body language in our life. The people could identify you through your body language.

For, your slipshod acts would qualify you as a stupid, lazy and vagabond. People could find you as hectic busy person, if your body reflects the language of some swift businessman in action. So, you ought to learn some of the definite modes of your body postures.

Your focusing on the body language at your office or work place, your sagacity would obviously isolate from others hovering around you. Similarly, your resilience to study body language of others, it shall qualify you to have landed on the mines of McKenna's Gold.

The meaning of someone speaking to you equating his eyes with yours endorses how deep he was being interested in your dialogue. A multitude of such gestures could convey that you ought to change your body gestures in no time.

Studying the body language could enlighten you on being approached the boss, about his answer. The language could help you to explore something anew when the person's language is indifferent with his performance. The body language of any prospective customer inquiring about your product could decide whether he is interested in buying it or not.

**Have faith on destiny but without dependence. For, destiny never shimmers without hard work.**

Focus on your body language whether you're on work desk or coordinating with your colleagues. Try to improve yourself before the mirror, if your gestures are not up to the mark.

Always bear in mind to synchronize your gestures with body language. The matter of importance remains how you present yourself. What you're uttering? Whether your gesture chimes with presentation? It is such appearance that could synchronize our movements, postures and voice in totem.

Our memory could appreciate whatever gestures are being derived from our movements. You ought to go through for complete appreciation of body language, the anecdote given below.

Let us think about some prince. He believed that none has resembled or would resemble him in future. He used to plan afresh for the day and change over on the following day. He used to condemn on the morrow, what he had appreciated for the day. Most of his courtiers were offended of his behaviour, who always thought for the welfare of his province. However, his durbar had such personalities, who used to extol him on whatever he addresses them.

Once, the prince stood on the terrace of his palace. It overlooked the cliff of a valley. He thought to observe his stretched empire from overlooking valley cliff. So, he hurried towards the valley cliff accompanied by unscrupulous followers. The guys were always extolling his attire, movements and chivalry. The prince was lost in the shallow deep ocean of ego and finding himself next to the monarch of heavens.

Suddenly, the prince thought the approach road to the valley could have been straight instead of curved and less wide track. He shared his sentiments with the followers, who dittoed his proposal. He attempted to reach the cliff straight leaving the made-up curved path.

**Anxiety will swerve you away from life's main track. Speed barriers will subsequently happen through the path of success.**

He used to slip away swiftly with the efforts he took to ascend upon rocks. The dittoing unscrupulous followers went on saving selves from hardship.

Suddenly, the prince observed the deep ravine filled with water. He thought none could save him had he fallen into deep ravine. He shivered for a while. He reached the curved track with great difficulty, avoiding himself from falling.

He made up his mind not to repeat such mistake, which could make him die.

You ought to make up your mind to acquaint with the skills of body language. For, it has got many curved and congested paths. So, it calls for you to spare at least fifteen minutes in ascertaining the gestures of other people. The only spot where you accomplish the task could be the place of people frequenting and deliberating over issues of importance. The national capital-New Delhi's metro train is the perfect place, where you could dissect through the human body gestures. For, people express themselves with anger, curiosity. delight, misery and other gestures.

Any social get together, professional meetings and parties are spots of subsequent importance. You could also visit any club or inn to ascertain gestures of unacquainted and friends under or without influence of liquor. You could enjoy the fun derived from such gestures of other people.

Television is the next good source to acquaint with involuntary conversation. Attempt to observe the visual bytes under reduced volume of audio version through involuntary movement about the rolling events. Verify your involuntary movement's contrast after enhancing the volume of audio output.

**A thinker believing the world is replete with sorrows is the most stupid person. The option of selecting sorrow or happiness lies in man.**

You could see the entire programme without audio output on some day like other people, and ascertain what the characters are expressing during such intercourse.

*Kwachit prithvishayyaha kvachidapi cha paryakashyanaha*
*Kwachichchakahaaraha kwachidapi cha shalyodrucibi*
*Kwachit kandhadhari kwachidapi cha divayambaradharoh*
*Manasvi karyarthi na ganapati dukham nacha sukham.*

The quotation interprets the individual seeking to acquaint with the body language remains immaterial whether he is happy or unhappy. For, such appearance need to be mastered at every opportunity like ten men and a woman folks are hanging through some chopper to save their skin. The chopper finds it impossible to ferry them despite the rope tying them remaining weak. It was desirable for at least one person to leave the rope, else the lives of others could have been at peril.

Who shall bell the cat during such task? A serious discussion went on for some time. The lonely woman cried out, on being sentimental, 'I am ready to leave the rope through passive gestures, for a woman alone could cherish for the cause. She would renounce everything diurnally for the cause of her home, husband and children.'

Each of the men folks clapped hands out on hearing about the woman's statement. The rope made way for the ten folks die in harness out of stupidity, the moment they clapped hands. However, the woman saved her life out of sentiments of her sagacity.

Such was the unique technique adopted for ascertaining about body language, which should not have been followed in practice. However, our society has been the splendid place of ordeal. It goes on alerting about others and your movements simultaneously as mute witness. So, you could understand body language through improvised versions.

The adage, *See eye to eye, when speaking to stranger* makes us interpret how you ought to practice in noticing other person's retina while conversing or dealing with some business. *Ascertain about the reality of his sentiments from his retina movements.*

For, straight communication could be possible between him and you, when you converse through looking at his retina. You could also remain relaxed while conversing with some people, for others could make you uncomfortable and some others might prove damn unscrupulous.

**Accustom to speak, for speech generates self-confidence. Measure the words in the balance of creative ideas before speaking.**

We could realize only when such person in front of us either deliberately avoids himself (herself) in equating his (her) retina movements or sustains those movements. You might be more attractive or creative or s(he) might be treating you upon animosity, as evident from his (her) opinion, challenging you through passive gestures. For, you could have noticed his (her) flopped retina.

The creative aspect of the secret remains passive gestures galore could sprout from beings. However, people disregard this during practical exposure. Your proper understanding could make you learn from the power of such hand gestures.

Watch one's palms whether one is telling the truth. Man uses his palms to express his sentiments like some defeated dog shows its neck to its triumphant rival, as a matter of surrender or servility.

For example, people generally remaining honest could claim displaying either one or both palms, *'I wish to speak with you openly.'*

Anybody uttering truth would expose his full palm(s) in front of another. This is an unconscious gesture like appreciable body languages, which symbolizes that the other person is uttering truth.

However, an individual shaking hands with another like fish out of water, he could be regarded as weak-minded personality. For, his palms might have been subjected to arthritis, or experiencing acute pain for doing so.

The manager of a firm said, when his employee served him for a few weeks, *'You have written in your resume that you have been experienced in the line for five years. However, I came to know that this is your maiden job.'*

The employee replied, *'But, Sir, you have sought through your advertisement of those folks having reasoning skills are welcome, besides he could lie successfully.'*

But, the difficulty with liars is that unconscious memory reacts independently against your lies. The people who utter less lies get caught while deceiving somebody else, irrespective of the truth latent in their statement.

Their bodies began gesturing opposition when deceiving others through slew of lies, justifying them avoiding truth. His unconscious mind transmits nervous energy appearing in some format, countering the very statement of such person.

**Ascertain whether you're better than others when observing through a mirror.**

A few people accustomed to utter lies include politician, pleader, actor and television announcer, through amended gestures where body gestures were impossible, making people believe what s/he asserts as true.

However, the matter is dependent on the factor how long the other person equates his gaze with the person through body language.

The gazes of Bihar people sustain for pretty longer time, whereas from other states could be objectionable. However, the people from Punjab observe others appreciably through their necks. So, you ought to observe through the body language before initiating. Have you ever thought of your position after five years? Do you know the main objective of whatever you do now? Do you know the objective for the day?

You ought to explore the solution for the questions posed or about to be posed. It could be good provided your answers are in the affirmation; else, it doesn't need you to remain disciplined.

Mr. Anil Jain was not taken aback when his firm Venus Garments got felicitated with *'Supplier of the Year'* award last year from Wall Mart Group (People's Republic of China). For, he dreamt of such felicitation when he ran an outlet of drapers in congested lanes of Ludhiana.

Today, Mr. Jain's company Venus Garments has been functioning across the country through eight factories with an area beyond six hundred thousand square feet. He was to stitch garments of neighbours on losing his father at tender age of twelve. Since then, the needle, thread and garments made their impact on his sub-conscious mind.

A very few people could disbelieve how somebody working from rags could raise the biggest company? The same gentleman plunged into the business of exporting garments. Now, his firm had been working day and night to open retail outlets across the country

Mr. Anil Jain shares his secret as, 'I had only one issue in mind, i.e. to bring some poised time management and the garments with utmost finesse. I began producing underwear banyans through rags left-over after stitching army uniforms. I was selling such under garments for mere three rupee per piece. I had two assistants with old tailoring machines, when I commenced the firm. My mother was also working on them overnight. Today, Venus Garments has employed some 6, 000 people, fetching indirect employment for more people.'

**Equip in advance for becoming successful. For, success is little afar from you, which needs to be acquired through self-control.**

It is evident from this development that people could reach the zenith of success from any avocation, provided their views remain splendid. They would also work extremely hard. So, you ought to adopt two formulae, keeping in mind about your objectives,

1. Observe someone who had been fortunate seriously. You shall realize him to be the fortunate at the outset, s(he) has attained such outcome after adequate preparation, plan and success point of view.
2. Observe another whom you find as unfortunate. You shall find the cause. He learns from the successful person on hearing about his sudden loss. A man, who happens to be financially unsound seldom learns through such failures but subjects himself into pretension.

> **Focus on powerful ideas rather than empowering weak ideas to become successful.**

So, don't rely upon your destiny whether it relates to career incentive, success, and good things of life. You ought to develop such virtues that would make you triumphant, but you need to focus on some good points.

- Think what could transform in the ensuing year for experiencing yourself as happy.
- Try to understand such obstacles hindering your childhood, which might throttle your future.
- Imagine whether the present set of challenges won't destabilize and knock you off.

You ought to develop your thinking to tide over from great predicament. For, the author David J. Schwartz in his title, *'The magic of think big,'* claims someone expanding his thinking could equate to his activities.

So, he has adduced an easiest approach to expand thought from which you could think alike giants,

**As I think**

Does any opulent person think like me?

**As I have been worried**

Does any opulent person remains concerned like me?

**As I wear the dresses**

Does any opulent person wear dresses like me?

**As I speak**

Does any opulent person speak like me?

**As I laugh**

Does any opulent person laugh like me?

Preoccupy your mind whether any opulent giant follows your tact. Go ahead with the anecdote below.

Mahatma Gandhi was boarding a train. He got one of his pair of shoes lost in between the platform and train upon the track. He boarded the train throwing other shoe also on the track.

The commuters thronging the platform were taken aback on his behaviour. One of them couldn't hold himself anymore. He asked Gandhi the cause behind his action, *'Any poor man fetching one of the shoes won't gain. For, shoes could make you comfortable in pairs. Now, any poor man could make use of my pair of shoes.'*

Such is the product of biggest thinking. For, it reflects your personality in absentia. How do you appear? What image does it sport upon you?

For, your attire says something, while it articulates something else with others. The developments could ensure what others think about you. It certainly looks appreciable that onlookers should gaze at his personality but not on his attire. Do not get deceived, for the public could evaluate on your outward appearance. Your outward appearance alone could be the maiden yardstick from the public. It remains forever in public mind irrespective of the developments within you.

I always emphasize during my training sessions over the participant's attire. The folks always endorse my opinion about the significance of their attire. Often, they wonder, why should I buy such expensive clothes, when the work could be expedited at cheaper costumes?

The question has kept many of the executives rather worried. It has annoyed me too for pretty long time. The solution could be, *'Sasta roye baar-baar, mahanga roye ek baar.'* Fit this formula within your subconscious sheath. Quality always remains significant than quantity as far as your appearance is concerned.

**Advising unsuccessful people resembles quacks treating the patients of AIDS.**

You shall find on emulation of such hypothesis that not only you shall get felicitated in the eyes of public, but also your esteem gets multiplied on similar grounds. You remain extremely beneficial on wearing pretty expensive wear, for you shall become so, whatever you think earlier.

On the other hand, if you feel you are stymied wearing poor wear, you become so. Similarly, your belief that you are insignificant, you shall become so subsequently. So, attempt to look as though you are financially a rich man. You could read the importance of such stage when you would voluntarily transform to such personality.

Practically, enhancing one's significance doesn't mean that you're trying to get attention from the public. Get such attention, but only for good deeds and such behaviour.

Appreciate the sentiments of others as and when you perform good deeds in life. Apperceive about yourself by imposing your personality in them. Make it certain that the bond between other person and you have cemented well, when s(he) thinks you're always backing him in every act. How far you could assimilate about others? So, this needs, you to study others' body language, when you shall realize whether other person is really taking interest in you or not.

**Befriend with your experience when you could read the person's face overlooking you.**

Perhaps, you could realize later about other person slowly losing interest in you, especially when s(he) is withdrawing from discussion after showing interest through eye contacts at the earliest phase.

The symptom has made you vigil for keeping your tack changed. You will also understand about your boss during discussion through his body language, when he becomes inattentive on your posing questions.

Disapprove such body language of someone with dissimilarity arising from his utterance and body language.

Engage in discussion through eye contacts, for, open fingers of palms sport seriousness and receptivity. Speaking very nearer or taking interest and isolating justifies the discussion as fragile. Such relaxed posture indicates you're ready for instant communication.

Standing in front of someone with crossed shoulders disqualifies your image. Your discussion following mere handshake indicates of your seriousness in such debut. Keeping hands on your forehead or cheeks does sport negative body language. Care should be taken not to speak with anyone in harsh temperament or aloud. You are supposed to lose your personality.

**Happiness**
cannot be borrowed from outside world.
You ought to identify
**the source inherent in you.**

It is true that your density of hair shall reflect your personality. For, positive thinking would strengthen the density of hairs. The famous coiffure Javed Habeeb believes, *'Human hair becomes stronger and dense proportional to the intensity of positive thinking. So, improve the density of your hairs for good thinking.'*

However, Dheerubhai Ambani has justified that hair density is unaccountable when someone becomes giant. He believes forever, *'Success doesn't bestow on people having dense hairs, but one needs to think positively for achieving success through constructive manner.'*

Avoid concentrating on hair density theory. For, every success in the universe density of hair is insignificant, other than stabilizing of one specific issue. Importing polyester garments into the country and producing design ware was prominent issue. Dheerubhai Ambani worked hard for materializing this issue. *So, think anew, think big, think quick and become giants like Dhirubhai Ambani.*

❑

"You ought to have somebody to coordinate in acquiring biggest triumph. You could have that coordination provided you have inherent leadership potential."

—Tarun Engineer

# ADAPT YOURSELF TO LEAD THE TEAM

*Manzil ki zuftazoo mein kyon apne dil ko haare*
*Itana Azeem ban jaa ki manzil tujhe pukaare.*

It applies for everybody, who forgets the objective in anticipation of reaching at the pinnacle.

However, getting into objective is very easier. You ought to develop the instinct in becoming leader and enhance drive for publicity. Let each of your decision for becoming triumphant hoist the flag of success endorsing you becoming leader unopposed. Follow the tips given below, which were quite significant in becoming leader forever.

1. **What is leadership?** Generally, leader signifies someone possessing the capacity to lead others through issuance of directives and distribute visiting cards to whosoever approaching the person. The man on vigil shall realize how one could be made competent enough for invitation.
2. **Do not become prince:** Any leader by sheer accidence couldn't hang on forever. For, his personality remains shallow, and attempts to emerge as the paramount persona introducing several blockades. Leader is one who directs others with responsibility on work load, on ushering the correct path for unity, integrity and communal harmony with absolute confidence.
3. **Explore new options:** An irresponsible folk would hang on to daily routine. His working tact resembles mutilated cracker that couldn't blast on lighting. Blast signifies here his facts seldom remain anew.
4. **Versatility on job:** Any business transcending limits needs something anew everyday, so that market and work place get new impetus. Such work culture needs badly variety of ideas. An idealistic leader always thinks of something best beyond his capability. He ought to keep his clear vision and focus himself to become successful on every ordeal.

You ought to be cherished in the work if you feel yourself to be the splendid role model. For, in the real sense, leader signifies accomplishment of task irrespective of its complexity and odds, with complete finesse under all circumstances. He ought to explore how he could deploy his subordinates on the task.

5. **Crushing out of job:** Many leaders seldom speak of finishing jobs. The folks get involved with other tasks before finishing the assigned task. The leader, in the real sense, usually makes some chart to finish the task before deadline.
6. **Learn to appreciate followers:** Thoughtful leaders' decision remains fiery and strong. The folks utilize such tacts to motivate their followers simultaneously vanquishing their opponents.

For, those folk selves get stronger, with strong followers on the principle of commitment.

**Leader should be competent enough to deliberate. Go on commenting in between whatever you've heard. Let the critic realize whether you have heard his sarcastic remark seriously.**

Leader, consequently, shall understand the requirements of the future, and keeps on motivating his following members.

It calls for him holding mutual discussion of members, extending incentives for good work, bonus, or reward, so that they could support him with renewed vigour and forte.

Leadership specialist Freud Smith believes, *'I always try to expand the horizon for my subordinates on the manner in which I became successful. I endorse him as the real leader on meeting failure despite doing glorious deeds. So, such leaders need not be afraid of intermittent failures.'*

A few such leaders have been classified in the title, *'You can become the person you want to be,'* as Failure means you're unsuccessful.

**It connotes you're still unsuccessful.**

Failure doesn't mean you haven't achieved anything.

**It signifies you having utmost loyalty on the system.**

Failure doesn't mean that you've been humiliated.

**It signifies that you're desirous to attempt.**

Failure doesn't mean that you're incapable of doing something.

**It means that you should approach the work in some other manner.**

Failure doesn't mean that you've spoiled your life.

**It means that you have a reason to commence work anew.**

Failure doesn't mean that you should acknowledge your defeat.

**It means that you ought to attempt with utmost hard work.**

Failure doesn't mean that you won't be successful ahead.

**It means that it requires some more time.**

For, failure resembles that wind known to everybody, but nobody could imprison at any cost. However, the people leading others always become successful. The important bye-law of such leadership makes one explore such delight so that one could enhance one's potential.

This is the cause that leader always carries *'Learner'* signboard. The guys always make use of their brain. They went on learning things. For, they believe that exploration of meaningful objective doesn't entertain *'Time Out.'* So, they attempt continuously to acquire something anew.

**Believe on your dreams disowning predicaments. For, your disappointment could mar your future.**

It means that the folks experiment with their brain even when they fall asleep, without holding selves. For, innovations have justified that working nonstop without any obstacles is better than sustained reading for four to five hours.

The novel describing the success of spies in *Sherlock Holmes* was their brain revolving around problems forever, whereas Sherlock was an imaginary character. You ought to learn lessons from this novel for, it would impart you with leadership traits.

Novelist David Ambrose advises *'Small opportunities facilitate in initiating splendid deeds, provided some leader shadows the individual.'*

The author James M.Cruise of the title 'The leadership challenge' advises, 'Leader remains guide. He always steps without knowledge and goes on guiding towards strange portals.'

A scribe queried former president of Indian Democratic Republic, Dr. APJ Abdul Kalam, to which he replied, 'Could you share with me how a leader could cope with slew of failures?'

The president replied, 'My objective during the launch of Indian Satellite Launching Programme–ASLV-III in 1973 was to put satellite *Roshni* into the space. However, the condition imposed by the grants commission was to make the satellite land in space by 1980. A team of some thousand scientists and technocrats got into the mission of completing the job by 1979. I believe that it was the month of August. We were prepared for the job. I reached the control centre, on being the project director. The computer verified the check list four minutes after the count down of the satellite. The computer program held back the launch after one minute of count down. My team of some five engineers and technocrats assured me not to worry, for the computer has erred in accounting for fuel discharge. So, we launched the rocket using manual mode. Everything went on well under the first phase. However, the problem arose during the second phase. The satellite instead of getting into the orbit fell in the Bay of Bengal, which was our major failure. Later, the chairman of ISRO Professor Satish Dhawan took the failure on himself while briefing the media representatives on that day, whereas I was squarely responsible for the major failure, on being the project director.'

**Success never curtains down but begets new problems. But, leader would certainly arrive at the solution.**

Dr. Kalam continued, 'My team did extremely hard work, but we were badly in need of appreciable technical support. So, we thought our team could be successful in its mission in the year ahead. We launched the same satellite during July 1980, and we emerged successful in our mission. Professor Satish Dhawan gave the credit of successful mission to the entire team, while addressing the media representatives. I have learnt the lesson that leader should take the onus on himself (herself) when becoming unsuccessful. I have learnt about the splendid management during crisis, which I couldn't gain from any book till such period.

Authors *Dr. Coingel* and *Dr. Deir* in their book, *'Climbing the executive Leader'* have described, 'The gain from appreciating about the time taken and hardship faced from unsuccessful people practically could be got from very few objects. For, your height couldn't be increased by any other object and no other object could make you contented or secure comfort.'

My sane advice for you is to mobilize such leadership traits within you and follow the tips for developing progressive opinion.

- *Always think of reforms whatever job you do.*
- *Always keep your status above whatever job you do.*

The maiden Republican US President Abraham Lincoln was believed to be an expert in making ebullient and competent leaders across the world. He sent a message to General Ulysses S.Grant on him being appointed as the chief commander of armed forces, 'I dislike in knowing or inquiring about the strategy you've adopted. You should take the whole responsibility and speak to me in case you need my coordination.'

You ought to follow similar shades of opinion. For, empower others with such responsibility and extend cooperation, if the situation warrants.

**Any objective seldom possesses any future. However, future has certain objective. For, anybody's future is dependent upon objective. Man fixing up his objective ought to depend upon his future.**

For, Indian industrial giant Krishna Kumar Birla told a gathering, 'The person responsible for satisfactory outcome would not only be the industrious but also the one responsible for splendidly maneuvering the brain and merit of his colleagues.'

So, follow the experimental tips mentioned below, to coordinate and keep appreciable rapport with your colleagues.

- *Establish an open and friendly rapport and greet the team members every morning.*
- *Always speak to them with correct accent and mode experiment with motivational communication skills.*
- *Take the initiative for team work. Ask your colleagues whether you could help them in completing the assignment before deadline making their job damn easier.*
- *Don't leave any of them in lurch. Let them realise of working for an organization under team spirit.*

- *Always keep yourself cheerful bearing in mind that one such virtue could make your mission successful.*
- *Show your coordinates how you emerge successful despite slew of critical moments.*

Think about the inherent secret prevalent amongst struggling folks mobilizing them to emerge successful. How do they encounter tooth and nail during the hour of crisis when others vanish from the scene? For, they visualize about the problems galore with different perspective. It could preferably be through some reality and practical mind and progress during crisis without much ado.

**Man without ambition shuns from problems but puts forth problems anew from his own arguments. However, leader evaluates others' potentials and makes him reach the condition of becoming successful.**

I being the author of this book have some personal experience on becoming successful in my business mission. Successful entrepreneur encounters host of problems in comparison with ambitious person. You could be vested with the onus of giving optimum results provided you were a leader for the firm with scores of work force.

So, be dynamic in your role. Become a performer of positive actions without anticipating for the crisis returning to normalcy. Let us remember what French essayist Guan La Fontaine has believed, "God has made man in such manner to accomplish anything impossible. For, his vocabulary doesn't entertain the term 'impossible' at any cost."

I have addressed a recent seminar on *Resource Management,* where the corporate executives took part, *'Women are the best resource managers.'* I wanted to explain that none in the world could manage the resources better and optimum level than a woman. For, the women's brain are balanced, whereas men folks remain specialized in particular field. Women advance in the field of management damn well and deliberate on any issue from various angles in unison. Experimentally, you could find any woman chief executive, manager, secretary, nurse or teacher, they remain extremely creative in talents, but in the fields of art, architecture and engineering men folks find instant results without much ado.

I have also found most of our men folks involved in maintenance of vehicles such as motorbike, cars, or mailing or chatting through internet or watching stock market or playing games, whereas women folks involve in gossiping with family folks or friends, watch films or serials on the television.

Mr. Ralf J. Gardner, the chairman of General Electric Company has recently observed in a leadership conference, *'Anybody aspiring to be a leader ought to make up his mind with firmness and chalk out some development strategy. For, none could advise you about your progress in particular profession. Moreover, who went past or trailed behind depends on whether he had extreme concern for his development or not.'*

**The great secret of success in life is to traverse through the silhouette of the individual who seldom gets split from severe exhaustion and remains ever energetic.**

An incident that shook Albert Einstein could be recollected on the occasion here. Einstein was discouraged by the management of Munich Institute of Technology that he couldn't emerge worthwhile, when he applied for admission into the institute. He seldom accepted defeat and propounded the theory of gravitation during his spare moments that has endorsed him to be successful scientist of the era.

Bear in mind you have the capability to emerge successful. You ought to explore what commodity has been scarce in you.

For, Greek philosopher, Plutarch has said, *'Nothing could grow other than weeds on the irrigable land unless it gets properly cultivated.'* So, it is essential to team up with like minded people. It could prove to be more useful if you motivate them with positive thoughts. We could bring an analogy with some running train as far as the people of various potentials are considered. Imagine a goods train carrying precious commodities transported elsewhere, which needs to be joined with the engine, is being parked on the railway track. At the outset, the engine comes on the track, which had to drag many coaches attached from behind. It began coming and going back towards the coaches due to magnetic flux. It attaches and detaches in succession.

*they're responsible folks and any negative approach could affect the success of the company.*

Perhaps, Dheerubhai Ambani might have spelt on this ground, *'This is not the clue of highest evaluation on man about his function during work and relaxation. The matter of importance could be how he reacts during crisis and arguments.'*

Your objective should be in making them stay put during crisis. For, writer and corporate leader Joseph Sugarman has claimed, 'Your justification as honest with such quality before others could shove you towards extreme success.'

❑

"The importance of life is not in the length of the day but in our success, which we acquire with attachment in few days."

—Tarun Engineer

# RECAST YOUR THOUGHTS TO UNIMAGINABLE LEVEL

Perhaps, there might be some Indian unheard of the grandeur of lord Ram. He might not have heard or remembered about lord's manifestation, like his preceptor Valmiki couldn't recollect, when he said,

*Ulta naam japat jag jaana*
*Valmiki bhaye brahma samaana*

Now the question arises why not we attain salvation when Valmiki attained it from taking lord's name. For, there is nothing left for comments while deliberating about the splendor of lord. The subject came to my mind, why not reciting Ram naam will benefit us, when doing in reverse manner benefited Valmiki. I have adopted the technique as the philosophy of motivation. It could be spelt irreversibly as MAR. Now, the same has burdened immensely on our affairs. The first generation old folks commented the fear of MAR has even dispelled the bevy of ghosts.

*Jab-jab maar padhi bhagatan par*
*Ram naam ne kiya bhagaton ka Beda paar.*

So, you could also emerge through this principle, but how. I shall let you know make it as principle guru formula, MAR-RAM, as it signifies like—

**M** (methods), **A** (adoption), **R** (repetition), /**R** (robust), **A** (accountability), and **M** (means).

You shall find the inherent weakness through the above key. You have been repeating to get crushed out. You've been embracing frequently to get such outcome, which you have secured so far.

Now, transform this to straight form through a firm and justified manner, giving importance to answerable facts. Investigate about the complementary resources before adopting the technique. It could appear as your guru mantra, for we have said about Ram naam.

Reciting in reversible manner has changed the thinking format of beings. We shall come across the unique qualities of lord Ram as exquisite practical principles, qualifying him to be the colossal management guru in the world forever.

For, His prominent qualities—credit, motivation, strategy, values and vision—were infallibly superb, from which the present day business management has emulated his very characteristics in letter and spirit around the world.

**A few people allege you couldn't do this work. It could be the splendid successful debut in your life if you complete that work without much ado.**

Professor Ashraf Khan of Indian Institute of Management, Indore, says most of our country's management institutes highlight about the virtuous characteristics of lord Ram about His unique personality and pluses of leadership drive and management instincts, citing epic Ramayana, every now and then, endorsing management studies as worthwhile. We shall find on analysis.

**Motivation:** The unique virtues of Lord Ram were to encourage others, which he has inherited from childhood. He went on supporting brothers, friends and whosoever He has met from time to time. The bear, monkeys and other domesticated animals played special role while ascending Sri Lanka from his encouragement. It was the lonely reason behind of Lord Ram appreciating the utility of such animal species, when even a tiny squirrel also contributed its might while making the bridge on Pacific Ocean.

**Strategy:** Lord Ram's was uniquely effective. He could have killed demon Ravana within a day had he desired. He wanted to mobilize public opinion in favour of encountering the demon with might without fear.

So, he availed the accompanying army to testify every participating being with his might. Everybody was significant in His army, whose motto was, Unity is strength.

**Credit:** Lord Ram extended the credit for others for accomplishing virtuous deeds. He acknowledged for Himself whatever erroneous acts have recurred. He seldom acknowledged the credit for slaying demon Ravana and triumph over Lanka for self, other than for His army, as

*Guru Vasishtha kul pujya hamaare,*
*inki kripa danuj rana mare*
*Ek sab sakha sunahu muni mere,*
*bhaye samara saagar kah bere*
*Mamahita laagi janma inha baare,*
*bharatahu tehi mohi adhik piaare*

It explained how lord Ram credited guru Vasishtha, and the army of bears and monkeys, by loving the species beyond His own youngest brother Bharata.

**Values:** The entire saga of lord Ram had been replete with values and ideals. Obeying the orders of parents and preceptor, serving the citizens, amelioration of downtrodden, etc endorse his value system in its whole. He regarded demon Ravana on his deathbed from wise message through brother Lakshmana.

**Vision**: Lord Ram was a visionary. He knew well to annihilate demon species for community welfare. He desired to hoist the flag of truth, by destroying untruth. He accomplished His province to remain Utopia where fellow citizens seldom faced any hardship, as per wish. The habitats of his people remain without being locked. Sheep and lion used to drink water together on the same river bank. He used to say, the king remains the ruler of hell, if his fellow citizens were aggrieved.

*Jasu ram priya praja dukhari*
*So nripa avasi narakadhikari*

The above virtues have endorsed lord Rama as the present era's management guru. A philosophical write up in the December 1982 issue of British edition of Readers' Digest endorsed lord Ram's philosophy, under the slug, **Anyway**.

Had the people be subjected to terror and self-centric

***Love them anyway.***

If the people accuse you as being selfish despite your doing good.

***Do well for them anyway.***

If you have been unsuccessful and people turn as false friend and children enemies.

***Let them be successful anyway.***

Had there been some criticism despite being honest and idealistic,

*Always be honest and idealistic anyway.*

If people forget on your doing good deeds.

*Do virtuous deeds anyway.*

If your people disown your giant issues owing to abhorrent ideals.

*Always remain big anyway.*

If the people follow the triumphant despite favouring fallen victims.

*Always fight for fallen victims anyway.*

If your foe guts down your home overnight despite your many year-long efforts to rise.

*Build your house anew anyway.*

If you rely on hearsay instead of them eulogizing you as paramount.

*Extend such prominence for the world anyway.*

It explains how you could be attentive in amplifying your thought under every circumstance and what altruistic services you could do for the society or the country.

**Appreciating the person concerned remains the only procedure for the job got done. For, human weakness is to hear such appreciation.**

At the outset, identify your latent talents and imagine what virtuous deed you could accomplish under any circumstances. Care for your strengths and weaknesses, for, Acharya Rajneesh has said

*Fear makes man coward*
*Greed makes him backbiter*
*Aversion makes him devil*
*Biggest thought will mould him glorified.*

An ideal example could be the budding writer Chetan Bhagat. It could be an unbelievable wonder when his title was printed some 500,000 copies, in the world of books where one couldn't sell one's produce as hotcake.

We could adduce that as vocabulary were enslaved under Chetan Bhagat. For, he has used the vocabulary as the source of making money. You could also claim that his writing world has been transformed into the world of idioms. He has adopted the opulence of words as his guru mantra.

Let me go through an anecdote of a youth, whose birth happened in a poor family, which qualified him to stay back from studies. However, he dreamt of becoming some financially rich person whereas he didn't have even single penny to initiate in business. He reached Delhi, the national capital of the country in search of pastures anew. He went on roving without job in the city unknown. He made up his mind to return Hapur, home town, and hang on to the bus bay near I.T.O. waiting for a bus.

**You could become euphoric provided you've clear picture of the dream, for brain blindly duplicates the content of such vision.**

Suddenly, the season took umbrage with swift breeze across. A few bites of an important paper kissed around his feet. A swift current induced in his eyes as though he got some vista anew. He swoop to act and went on grabbing bites of scraps, paper, lying around streets. He used to sell them when the bag filled and stayed on for some time. Many folks were influenced by his idea. He took over, the job on saving money, and began supplying to contractors after buying them hawkers. After a couple of years, he began supplying the stock on being relieved from contractors, when he became the rich fellow from rags.

Yes, I advise you to adopt similar approach. For, a scribe asked Rockefeller, 'What is your secret of success?'

Rockefeller replied, 'I study through jobs before undertaking. I won't do anything in haste nor undertake any risky job.'

Observe what Rockefeller has interpreted as to sift through work before undertaking. Study the business if you wish to work that under limited capital. Undertake the work after identifying set of probabilities of such business.

**Go for measurable objective:** The objective should be such whose time, place etc could have been kept to confide yourself to have reached the objective. Find out the distance away from and the time required to reach the portals.

**Opt for easily affordable objective:** You should have the objective that could be easily acquired. See the practicality of such objective. Do not go for such impossible objective unattainable and find yourself humiliated. However, find out your aptitude and feasibility in selecting such objective.

**Let that be timely objective:** It could be stupidity on the individual had that been selected without being timely. For, our life had been circumstance-oriented and we should synchronize according to winds of change. A scientific technique could be to fix up certain time in accomplishing the objective.

**Let the objective chime in:** It could be somewhat stupidity if the objective chimed out with time. For, our life has been bound by time, so it should chime with times. Scientifically, to achieve some objective, some time needs to be apportioned.

**The fear of fall prevents from jumping. Think before making a long jump. Shut your eyes but keep the window of your brain open.**

You shall find some craze to end up with the objective over a particular time-frame. You shall go on evading from completing the task had you not been eclipsed with certain craze, making you pretty lousy in keeping the objective hang on.

Celluloid hero Shahrukh Khan observed, keeping this fact in mind, '*Initially, any individual remains pretty ambiguous in getting into the job, which makes him to hang on without any particular decision. For, such people alone gets through, who initiates particular job at certain stage, and proceed without treading on to accomplish the objective.*'

No doubt, your brain works like a computer, but it works according to its preset specifications, excelling with extraordinary skills. However, it could make you unsuccessful working on the tacts of other personalities.

For, our body knows very well which sort of food we have to take. Similarly, our brain also doesn't find any packaged meal, nor it could be bought from particular departmental store. For, the environment around itself would fix up its meal. Scores of objects find classified for that brain meal under conscious and unconscious levels. Your habits, etiquette and personality get moulded up according to the meal fed to your brain. However, the dominant path for success rests on such sentiments beyond the reach. Such thoughts could be diabolic suppressing the brain dynamism through virus, keeping our thoughts pretty inferior. Find out whether you're under such cluster of thoughts, which could damage your personality.

You shall come across many obstacles at work place. Moreover, every group has such inferior personalities, who are misfits and stay as obstacle for your progression. It is also true that ambitious personalities were subjected to utter humiliation with repetitive threats that they would become triumphant with least efforts.

You have to appreciate the depth of your actions. A few would like to downcast with ulterior motives, restraining you from reaching the portals of success. The few reach the portals disowning others' comments irrespective of the winds of change. One amongst such personalities had been the proprietor of Delhi Cloth Mills establishment Mr. Shri Ram.

**Your happiness depends on elements of delight, attachment and appropriateness. Check swiftly whether the three elements are fairly blended in life.**

Mr. Shri Ram initiated his business somewhere around 1905, through a small establishment in the walled city of Delhi, at Chandni Chowk. He established the textile mills at Bara Hindurao, joined by a few people in the network. He was the first person to establish textile mills during Imperialist regime in the country. Mr. Shri Ram has extended social service and established few educational institutions across the country. Lady Shriram College had been one of the institutions affiliated to his family.

Subsequently, the company got into the tyre industry, with a unit in Dubai. Today, SRF has made its mark in the industry around the world. Mr. Arun Bharat Ram, his son, believes, *'Lord Krishna has advised mankind to do work, converting sorrow in happiness and cowardice in chivalry. For, the individual working hard would reach heavens by heroic death. A coward shall die hundreds of time everyday. So, do the work intelligently and according to preset planned procedures.'*

Lyricist Mir Kasim might have believed accordingly, *'Moments have scripted, while eons got imprisoned.'*

It is absolutely true that our thoughts mirror our personality. For, *Chotu* alias Alka Tomar has shown her debut in freestyle wrestling, belonging to Meerut's small village Sisouli. She recollects what her grandma Shanti D'evi has dreamt that her grand daughter should show some debut in Indian wrestling.

Alka's father, a wrestler Nain Singh desired to make his daughter an athlete like P T Usha, but suddenly, the coach Jabar Singh Som some day expressed his desire to make Alka, a prominent wrestler. The women wrestlers assembled in the stadium were unaware of Alka's debut when the coach took her there. Nobody has even dreamt of some rustic lass hailing from traditional western Uttar Pradesh could excel in her performance. For, Alka didn't have any excellent coevals but found the company of trendy boys for practice. Who thought of her small foray some day after four decades could bring laurels to the country in the world wrestling championship? Our wrestler would stand on the victory stand and sing national anthem amidst loud applause.

**Triumphant zoom ahead without craving for dangers piercing through the crowd. For, they won't find the crowd, which had been eclipsing their vision.**

Alka's career took u-turn after winning the title in World Wrestling Championship held at Beijing Olympics. Her debut gave us an impetus for begetting self-confidence from within in achieving our objective. For, faith is such wonderful power, resembling some seed, whose imagination is beyond comprehension. It is true that attachment seldom leaves any individual behind, but your failure could make you divorce from such attachment. You couldn't get fruit without sowing particular seed. It will hardly sprout without watering on time. Sprouting comes to the second phase. The development commences the moment you feed water after sowing the seed. The plant also requires proper nourishment.

Attachment will come of its age when you cash in on scores of ideas, transmitted from lord, the Almighty. However, your glorification seldom depends on you, other than watching how far you respect positive thoughts in tandem, which makes their presence through imaginary powers.

Acharya Rajneesh says, *'Mother Nature is summoning you. However, you're lost in your selfish issues turning you pretty deaf for reasoning skills. So, focus on them and hear what those ideas share with you.'*

People often claim that their objective is to achieve success, but when they opt for such objective in their portal, perhaps, they would end up in disappointment. That is the reason why, Jurisprudence specialist John Kennedy claims in his autobiography, *'I was meeting the expenses of my studies in law through polishing pairs of shoes on pavement. The expenditure on my food and clothes were borne from giving tuition. I got qualified in the final examination that made me the judge of local court of law.'*

Could Stephens prove as judge of local court, unless polishing shoes believing the job as pretty shameful? For, happiness and success hide behind every sorrow and failure resembling some resplendent nights trailing behind full moon darker nights. So, man should not kneel down before slew of accidental grief or misery. Whatever happens shall always be there for one's good. So, one should be dynamic in achieving objective through hard work after learning lessons from antecedents. A few people are quite strong and sturdy, which qualifies them decimate any host of difficulties sprouting from time to time without much ado. For, the path of success is not rosy, but tumultuous and harsh with ups and downs. Our ambition gets transmitted through waves from pockets of energy and its fulfilment commences when the procedure unveils functioning. Lord, the Almighty bestows our share of fruits reciprocating the manner in which we have thought of. So,. for optimum results, we should remain ever vigilant and *smart* for good positive thoughts.

**Shaving of the objective could be worthless unless your dream-razor is not sharp.**

The word *smart* has hidden meaning, as

**S : Specific**
**M : Measurable**
**A : Attainable**
**R : Relevant**
**T : Time-bound**

Select such objective, which could guide you in subsequent stages. For, industrial giant Dhirubhai Ambani has believed, *'Adopt scientific techniques before lord Ganesh, while selecting objectives. For, his elephant head symbolizes the power to dispel obstacles. Anyone shouldering the onus of giant responsibility through determination, he has to stabilize his mind (head) like an elephant's head, when his burden won't get transformed into other, irrespective of getting others' support in their presence or absentia.'*

**Development of qualities takes place in solitude but that of character shall always take place in terrific upheaval.**

For, lord Ganesh, imparts such knowledge through his limbs. The individual interested in dispelling such obstacles should change his perspective through entreaty for powers hidden in elephants' eyes. The tinier eyes of massive elephant body reflects every object pretty magnified, making the pachyderm crush every obstacle as abhorrent weed on becoming proud over its immense might.

The idioms such as keeping one's nose above, or twisting one's nose, etc reflect the prestige of everybody pretty higher. Here, lord Ganesh's elephantine nose reflects such personality accomplishing the task successful as pretty inevitable. The elephant seldom forgets in keeping its prestige in mind.

## IMPORTANCE OF TIME

- Ask a student **who has been detained in a class on poor performance to ascertain the importance of one year in life.**
- Ask a mother **who has delivered child one month before actual period to ascertain the importance of such period in life.**
- Ask a bride **whose husband has left to jail after honeymoon night to ascertain the importance of one week in life.**
- Ask a labourer **who ekes out livelihood on daily wages how much he earned for that day from job to ascertain the importance of such period in life.**
- Ask him (her) in **whose presence the train has chugged off over a furlong to ascertain the importance of a minute in life.**
- Ask that athlete **who couldn't return home from recently held Beijing Olympics with gold medal to ascertain the importance of a second in life.**
- Ask him (her) **who couldn't have read this book between the pages to ascertain the importance of a microsecond in life. Perhaps, had s(he) went through this book, she could have been financially well off by now.**

Any individual imperfect in his task instantly believes by treating the real friend as foe and vice-versa. Lord Ganesh's big ears symbolize the hidden meaning—that he had been perfect in time management, ignoring insignificant and baseless issues through one of his ears at the cost of entertaining host of infinitesimal ideas.

The adage of elephantine teeth for display and performance through some other outlet endorses the fact that lord Ganesh's teeth symbolize some good outcome in reigning over obstacles through bullying tactics.

**A fakir's purse seldom fills up but that of rich man shall never go empty.**

Lord Ganesh having vertical belly symbolizes (lambodara) one who is acquainted with digesting every idea shall ever remain free from obstacles, without becoming victim of disasters. For, ambition is significant from selfish point of view. So, adopting the qualities of belly is extremely important from this consideration.

An individual anticipating of finishing the task without any obstacles calls for his involvement in sustained conversation. Lord Ganesh's human body influences us in accommodating humanity at heart through adoption of some immortal personality. His four arms symbolize man to focus sustainably upon machismos for — duty, riches, desire and salvation.

Lord Ganesh has elephantine forehead and has used rodent as his vehicle. The secret reveals us of having the capability to shoulder the onus for the success of any task. It also calls for such common sense extolling the support of giants in decimating frivolous forces from abhorrent personalities. We should accompany and avail them an opportunity with the belief that our desired objective shall remain unfulfilled without their support.

The Industrial giant Dhirubhai Ambani has adopted this scientific technique completely in his mission, which made him accomplish every objective in life.

❑

**"Intelligentsia learn from discretion, laity from experience and idiots upon the potential."**

**—Tarun Engineer**

# LET IMAGINATIONS CALIBRATE IN YOUR CONSCIENCE

Any being could have sustained happiness, youth and riches through virtues. *Why not labourer has them if they be availed through hard work? Why not wrestlers could have had* that acquired by pundits through intelligence? So, do two virtuous acts every day to make your mind orient towards actions. Your mind could accomplish that task had that be oriented towards actions. How to acquire them? Lord Krishna advises, *'Do your work. You shall get fruits on doing work. For, human beings are dependent upon mind. The beings' mind is three-folded, physical, mental and spiritual, but you have to arrive upon them and proceed accordingly.*

You might have been aware that unity has solidarity. It substantiates that some wooden stub could be broken easily, but it could be difficult in breaking the bundle of aligned ten stubs. What is the base of unity? You shall find on serious thought that when you come out voluntarily, you ought to have the support of others. It deals with others' support. Coordination is mankind's lonesome parameter through which millions of activities could be accomplished.

You might have heard people uttering selves as independent in every aspect, uttering—the individual to have accomplished the task voluntarily on his (her) own might without anybody's support. *'I am a self-made man (woman).* I don't need anybody's help.' Such folks remain misapprehended and forget that they require hundred people in reaching to a particular destination. Had those hundred people rebut through non-cooperation, the logo of *self-made man (woman)* couldn't have been achieved by the individual. You believe often how such development took place. How come one hundred people support for an individual's progress? You could also fall under that category had you been thinking on such terms.

We could divide the history into two phases—struggle and coordination. The term struggle cognizes as some war, a destructive procedure, which couldn't have taken place without the element of coordination. To say, war is also a type of coordination, for it falls under negative-oriented thought system. It assumes the form of coordination when umpteen individuals join to accomplish some objective through specific drive. Such cooperation could liberate the country from the shackles of tyranny. It could develop human culture and extends support in tiding over the crisis. The union of such elements leads to the number eleven, juxtaposing number one with another, when man accomplishes extraordinary pursuits with unlimited capabilities.

**Intelligence and stupidity differ on one condition, for intelligence has some limits while stupidity is not.**

British politician William Gladstone, keeping this theory in mind, propounded, 'He is pretty intelligent, and who never expends his precious energy, for which he has not been authorized. Moreover, he also is extremely intelligent who selects the splendid duties and emulates them in practice amongst host of other duties.'

Such experience could be adapted to parachuter Sheetal Mahajan, the first Indian girl, who has dived from North Pole through helicopter without anybody's assistance. Her life was surcharged with such euphoria after accomplishing something unbelievable that she forgot to encounter death under such circumstances. She dived through the chopper ignoring of such predicament where the temperature averages around minus 30$^{\circ}$ Centigrade where one could see beyond three meter of irregularly piled up ice across the plateau. Nobody could predict when the climate could change. Scientific exploration has justified the region could lose ice within a decade due to the effect of green house gases.

Ms Mahajan has turned the pages of history after accomplishing the unbelievable task for her age and sex. Perhaps. she might have been influenced by scientist Albert Einstein. Dr. Einstein was pretty daring during his times without acknowledging defeat at any cost. A scribe queried on one day, 'You're damn old. Why are you working?'

The scientist replied, 'you're wrong my dear'. Could anyone go infirm on graying of hairs and wrinkles on skin? I am pretty young to you.'

My sane advice for you is to plunge into the universal arena like Einstein. For, philosopher Edgar A Guest believed, *'Believe upon clouds gathering across space except sun's shimmering rays. Fix up through the light of compass streak except galaxies'. 'Believe on sun except shadows. Believe upon your dreams except cluster of doubts. Believe in your hopes except shocks.'* Certainly, you could reach the zenith of success on emulating the above advice in practical life.

Accordingly, table tennis wizard Anuradha Paul has entered the portals of success. Her maiden performance took place when she was pretty young, eleven years of age. Her brother backed her singing classical music through playing table tennis. Often, she was concentrating more on table tennis rather than her voice. Everybody advised her to keep away from playing table tennis as it was men's art. Not only was she acclaimed at home but abroad, when she played with excellence, turning the deaf ear to elders' advice. She believes that learning any faculty is like some worship. Psychologist Roy Disney believes, 'Taking any decision won't be difficult on finding individual's life pretty precious.'

**It is insignificant what you think about others but is significant what you think about yourself.**

The incident relates to the year gone by. I have intercepted an SMS on my mobile phone, *'The errors of the day would surface as bouquet of experiences morrow.'* Another message appeared after a couple of days, *'You shall identify scores of errors so that you couldn't commit them again.'* The messages surfacing frequently on mobile phones air real facts. Once, the message read, *'You shouldn't curse any correct or false decisions, for correct decisions bestow with triumph and delight. However, false decisions won't go astray, but address some experience on us. Either of such messages have prominent role in our lives.'*

Observe any flute little seriously. It is shallow, but has an array of holes. It wins one's heart through sonorous voice. Its smaller holes resemble the tiniest errors made in our lives. Similarly, the former US Democratic president Bill Clinton once shared with few of his friends, *'Errors are being conditioned reflexes for one playing longer innings in life.'*

The adage is true, 'Err is human and forgive is divine.' It is better to err without sitting idle. Every human being has the freedom to do something on his (her) wish, but the freedom could be useful when we learn from slew of errors, so that we shouldn't hesitate in doing this way or that. The chances of success and failure remain 50:50 in every sector. However, your victory could scrape through half of your age on your hanging through passively.

Mohandas Gandhi erred during childhood. However, the world has acknowledged him through his experiments with truth through trial and errors. For, he proceeded ahead continuously amending the errors committed during childhood. The human character is to err under the influence of nature, but one shouldn't be afraid of them. It is true that successful person errs and falls at the outset, and rises to the altar of success. However, dispelling of errors is hidden through some mantra of courage. So, analyze yourself in seclusion about the errors. For, bard William Shakespeare has said, *'Explore the slew of objectives hidden within the pile of husk like needles so long as you won't access them. Their access eventually could transform you into some significant personality.'*

**The manner in which a big stone upon falling shall create ripples similarly a biggest thought could make men sit on the throne of success.**

Methinks teens of Israel were imparted self-defense training in Army on being inspired by William Shakespeare. Anybody becoming an engineer finds himself to land in a village. The chairperson of PepsiCo, Ms. Indra Nooyi says, *'You couldn't proceed in your business without working through the support of others, howsoever attractive might be your personality and how far you work.'*

I recollect an anecdote at the moment. A man was always finding hanging through the tree branch upside down. Some day, a passerby asked him, *'Why are you hanging upside down under the tree branch?'* He replied, *'One needs to hang upside down to observe the topsy-turvy world.'*

Similarly, you would have to monitor sole objective on becoming upside down, or to say, you ought to survey through turning about the mission's progress, outcome and requirements. You ought to observe whether you've prepared the blueprint of such objective;

the actual cost in contrast with your estimation; your re-evaluation in case of any hike to ascertain the lacunae in that blueprint. For, a Scotch author and thinker Thomas Chapman says, 'any life seldom avails another opportunity. So, go on repeating that you ought to meet the objective. Every year, I shall reach the portals of success, without failure.'

Let us recollect another anecdote for justification. A lion and another man together were on the journey. The man went on blowing his own trumpet on his way. The beast-man duo observed some portrait in a corner, where man fighting with lion excelled in his might in comparison with the beast. The man cried out with proud, 'Have you seen? Man is fighting with lion. So, man is mightier than the beast.' The lion replied, 'I know that this picture was not portrayed by lion, but some stupid fellow. Had the lion portrayed it could have mounted itself on man.'

**Man standing on the foothill couldn't see the cliff of valley but continues reaching the altitude, for reaching the valley shall remain his objective.**

The anecdote explains one shouldn't blow his own trumpet but focus on work. The world will extol you had your performance be glorified. For, Alfred Ormond Montaparte has said, *'Majority of people witness obstacles. A few observe through objective. For, the annals of history record the triumphs of people, but forget the people who have performed earlier.'*

Similarly, the emperor Bharata, the younger brother of lord Rama believed him to be the maiden emperor, who could access the valley of Vrishabhanchal. He desired to carve his name on its cliff so that people across the world could find his immortality. However, someone's name was already carved on the valley cliff without leaving any space behind. Bharata was peeved over this and asked him to stamp his name on erasure. The royal priest uttered on his return, *'Your Excellency! You've spoiled the base of immortalizing one's name. You have initiated the tradition of carving your name on erasure of earlier record name. Who knows who shall eliminate your name?'*

The story justifies us through the fact that one ought to proceed continuously, keep one's mind always open, and get one's name recorded in the annals of history, but not like emperor Bharata, but like Dheerubhai Ambani. For, Ambani when he was pretty young, he was selling hot samosa and savory in front of a temple. He has stockpiled many of unbelievable dreams. He left to Aden in 1949, accompanying his elder brother Ramniklal Ambani, when he was seventeen, for selling inflammable fuel, with the dream of becoming a giant. He had monthly salary of some three hundred Indian Rupees. He didn't have even one hundred rupee to buy garments anew. He borrowed money from some restaurant man so that he could get the garments stitched for moving abroad. He was to stay outside the cabin of purchase officer and cash chest for hours to get bills encashed at Aden. He got into the list of Forbes 50 fortune seekers of the world.

**Your ideas work like a magnet, shaking other person influenced. The same person stops paying attention to your ideas when that thought loses its magnetic flux.**

My advice is of imagining about earning money, hoping, planning and making blueprint for achievement is necessary. For, it prepares our mind and brain to become such giant. One who dreams to become peer shall also think of the ways and means to fulfill them. He shall cash in on his efficiency, dexterity, and dynamism. The world gets stunned when he transforms voluntarily in his own efforts.

Anyone buying available books shall find this book with feeling. Dreams shall appear
but nothing gets achieved.
The same person reading this book shall sprout with a unique power. It could make him pretty confident so that every dream witnessed hither
**to could get neutralized.**

A firm decision in transforming to the portals of success has dominant role in one's life. The peers of the entire world shall acknowledge his position. So, mobilize yourself to accomplish such mission with absolute might when the success would kiss at your feet. ❑

**"Any firm determination endorses, man to reach his objective for nobody on earth became giant till today without determination."**

**—Tarun Engineer**

# WORK ON THE OBJECTIVE FOR BECOMING SUCCESSFUL

I wish to ask before you undertake some work towards the objective; do you mean the hero shall give up acting when his movie flops? If any candidate loses election to Indian state legislative assembly or Lok Sabha constituency, she/he should quit politics? If any player gets with zero score, should he quit the game? If any publisher stops bringing any author's manuscript, does that mean the author should give up writing? If any old man falls while moving on the road, should he stop leaving away from home?

Perhaps, you people answer in the negative. You know very well to reach the objective, the role of strategy, evaluation of one's aptitudes; ideas, discipline and courage do contribute appreciably in achieving the objective. For, the manner in which chemical dyes leave impact on spilling either over the floor or walls of some building, similarly man learns after experiencing failures in life. Please keep the following tips in mind, while selecting your objective.

- *The objective should make you realize about him.*
- *The objective could take care of your character.*
- *The objective should make your associates contented.*
- *The objective should be accomplished pretty easily.*
- *The objective should appease even to lord, the Almighty.*
- *The objective should make you glorified.*
- *The objective should keep your future secure.*
- *The objective should not keep you frequently disturbed.*

So, you ought to feel crazy about such objective. Scriptures have highlighted *the sapling will sprout according to seed and action do surface according to ideas.*

Man accomplishes duty on being conditioned by ideas at random. For, ideas have their importance in life, which puts your life on checks and balance.

Ideas owe to mind. You ought to recondition mind so that bad ideas couldn't surface any more at the cost of good thoughts or ideas. Kalidas, the prime poet character in Kumara Sambhavam and Raghuvansha, the magnum opus of Sanskrit verses, says—

*Nastya gatirmanorathana,*

means nothing is impossible for hard worker. Urges alone shall influence you to proceed ahead. So, your urges should be positive and harmonized. People say that touchstone shall turn iron into gold. Nobody has seen touchstone but have heard some anecdotes related to their wonders. Some business men would reap immense benefits whatever he seeks for others, it could doom their career.

However, man's mind resembles touchstone. It calls for some positive thought like iron to touch the mind touchstone, when it gets cleansed like pure gold. So, mind needs to be stuffed with warp and woof of positive thoughts. Wipro company chief executive Azeem Premji believes, *'A correct objective needed for achieving some objective through extremely hard efforts like the mall needs some dexterous architect.'*

**Nobody could guide in the universe other than books. For, they would share with you about the secret of success of glorified personalities and usher directions for your mind.**

Nothing takes place in life so swiftly. One ought to have one's objective voluntarily. Perhaps, you might have realized about your coeval businessman might have been benefited instantaneously through ascension leaving few others behind in the business arena.

Have your thought of professionals hopping so quickly? What is the reason? Now, look into the anecdote of MNC industrial giant Mr. Ratan Tata. Mr. Tata flew to the US before setting up his automobile plant at Singur (West Bengal) to discuss ways and means with US automobile giant Ford. The tet-e-tete between the duos got fixed up for the evening, as Mr. Ford was pretty busy in the work hours for the day.

Mr. Tata reached Mr. Ford's house by six p.m. in the evening, where he found an old man scrubbing crockery in the ante-room wash basin.

He told him, *'I have to meet Mr. Henry'*

He made Mr. Tata sit in the dining hall and returned. Later, the old man introduced himself, by saying, *'People call me as Henry Ford.'*

*'What are you asserting?'* wondered Mr. Tata.

Mr. Tata was rather perplexed, when he resisted, *'Methinks, I have been finding myself to suspect about you as Mr. Henry Ford.'*

*'Yes my dear, anybody could find confused on noticing you scrubbing crockery on being the boss of World's automobile giant,'* said Mr. Tata inquisitively.

Mr. Ford said, *'Earlier, I was an ordinary folk. I was doing everything myself. It is the fruit of work done from my own hardship that I became the overall boss of world's automobile giant, FORD. I shouldn't forget about my antecedents that people should believe me as the automobile giant's boss. I do everything with my own hands. I won't feel myself hesitating.'*

Mr. Tata said while being on his feet, *'Now, I shall move. For, I got my objective within a few minutes, for which I came to you. Now, I have realized that the key to success seldom rests on others trust, but one should fulfill the objective on one's own trust.'*

**The competition alone shall guide when you select the career befitting your capability and taste.**

The analogy could be found in Stephen R. Covey's book, *'The Seven Habits of Highly Effective People,'* where he has been beautifully articulated,

- *Be successful at home, and later at business.*
- *Seek help from lord, the Almighty, and get qualified for His grace.*
- *Never compromise on honesty.*
- *Remember those verily involved in your experiment.*
- *Hear the pros and cons of the issue before taking decisions.*
- *Take the advice of others.*
- *Safeguard those without any means.*
- *Remain unbiased arbitrator.*
- *Learn some aptitude anew every year.*
- *Plan today what is necessary for the morrow.*
- *Always proceed ahead while waiting.*
- *Always carve out positive-oriented thoughts.*
- *Align with your job and about yourself.*
- *Be not afraid of errors.*

- *Make way for subordinates achieve success.*
- *Speak less but listen more.*
- *Focus thyself on your work.*
- *Worry not about your subsequent job or promotional vistas.*
- *Initiate every job focusing on its outcome.*

For, initiation of any job focusing on its outcome would interpret your successful reaching the portals after ascertaining the journey, so that the future could proceed in proper manner.

**Time and tide waits for no man. For, time is such an arrow, which shot once never returns to its receptacle. People shall seldom pay attention to this aspect that makes them swerve from objective forever.**

A few people however ascend the portals of success pretty fast. One of such giants is the chief executive and president of Airtel's India operation, Mr. Manoj Kohli, whose saga of success was through hard work.

Mr. Manoj Kohli, born to a middle class family believes, 'I was a bad student up to eighth standard, but my subsequent class has proved to be some turning point. I began achieving top rank that fetched me scholarship. My ambition was to become an Indian civil servant (IAS officer) or an airline pilot. But, I never thought that I would be away from this profession. The subject of economics was pretty ticklish from the start, but I achieved pretty good marks. Often, I decided to study through Shri Ram College of Commerce, which had ample scope for my future. My career commenced with posting at Deorala Sugar Works (DCM) when I felt of trailing behind unless I complete my educational studies. I completed three year degree in Law, had one year diploma and completed three-year degree in MBA from an evening college, working simultaneously.'

Mr. Kohli continued, 'Initially, I was associated with DCM in their Human Resources Department. I was attending regular business meetings. Later, I looked after the marketing, finance and purchase divisions of DCM that qualified me to become the head of Human Resources Unit after nine years of service. I took it matter of seriousness to learn motivation, team building and associating with teams, as the forte of my profession. DCM trained me what to do and what not. Any professional could immolate himself (herself) unless (he) had some strong vision to reach some target in life. At the tenth year of my services, DCM appointed me as the general manager of their factory at Kolkata. I went through the professional ups and downs when I was just 29 years of age. I took over Shriram Refrigeration at Hyderabad after a year, which has some three billion rupee turnover. The unit in dire straits called for some structural reforms, through launching of AWQ compressor anew from silent model. The company has proved to be market leader within a year.'

**The thoughts of MacDonald's to Ford, Reliance to Coca Cola and Pepsi to become financially rich were sown as the seeds of glorified people in their dream plateau sometime earlier.**

Mr Kohli wonders, 'Often I felt three parameters were important for any company—vision, strong values and strong execution. I associated myself later as Indian representative for the US company Allied Signals, which was Fortune 50 companies. I raised an industrial software park in Gurgaon. Unfortunately, Allied Signals couldn't make base in India, as we believed, which I abandoned later. I stayed on my maiden job for sixteen years and eighteen months in the subsequent one. But, during my stay I kept versed with mix sigma (Business Management related strategy), quality processor techniques that made me join telecom sector.'

Mr. Kohli recapitulated, 'I have worked for seventeen years in the manufacturing sector and sought for some change. I wished to have experience for India has experimented liberation drive under third phase of its economy. I got some break with Escorts Ltd. The establishment made me as the chief executive of Escotel, which unit was my cup of tea. One could avail good opportunity in learning anew as and when one joins some establishment anew. I ought to learn how some business anew remains afloat and what experience one could have. I learnt how MNC technologies were adopted in our country, how the resources were mobilized, how credit gets waived, how marketing organizations were stabilized, besides how distribution and retail showroom were franchised. These were the strategies to be learnt for anyone from ab initio.'

Mr. Kohli heaved over a sigh of relief, 'I have left the job in 2001, for the telecom sectors didn't have experienced people in India. My love for the sector, made me join Airtel's India Operation and worked for pretty long time with chief executive Sunil Mittal. This was my life's most ambitious, exciting and energizing round.'

Mr. Kohli continued, with a pause, 'I advise entrepreneurs anew—Keep your character clean if you want to become some giant in your field. For, any professional remains confident and cashes in on your strong character. Let the energy of positive thoughts seep through you. Liberal attitude, buoyant and positive brain alone is the essential requirements for any professional beyond the academic qualifications of MBA or Ph.Ds. Always keep bigger objective. Have the aspirations about your association with the company as the world's giant. Learn the strategies of analysis as how the stages could be. Any problem could be differentiated into small heads. However, balance between your work and life. Think like such punter who wins five games at one stroke in air. The first four games are, viz., family, health, friends and split, which are products of glass, while the fifth one made out of rubber related to your work. The first four products would break on mere fall, but the fifth one falls and bumps out, on being elastic. Everyone chases behind rubber ball. A glass ball seldom remains alive, but rubber one could last long and enliven life forever.'

**Please go coolly through the array of difficulties if the situation warrants you. For, iron could be shaped only when it is hot.**

So, you ought to think like Mr. Manoj Kohli. For, life is some pastime, a marathon race, a competition, which you ought to win every year.

However, you will find success in business comes in two ways, horizontal and vertical.

The horizontal business makes you proceed for the company, while vertical would make you land in another company to exhibit your earlier skills. You will see any serial entrepreneurs hopping from one job to another with volition for multiple jobs, ascertaining how much success S(he) had in the previous job and the gestation period. Your confidence level ascends as and when you achieve success in any project. The entrepreneur enjoys taking multiple risks at his own confidence. The person ought to have such risks in individual businesses, else, could always end up in failures.

Mr. Anil Ambani advises, *'High risk, High gain,'* or in other words, the more risk you undertake, the more you shall get benefited.'

Practically, there are some professionals around the world, who like to encounter calculated risks. The company plays chess, I win you loose. However, the entrepreneurs of such companies have good idea with craze for undertaking risks. These would be successful in quashing the rival companies.

One finds entering the portals of success simulates ascending the cliff of some valley. The trekkers often find themselves slip out many steps down during their efforts to ascend the cliff. For, they are quite crazy to undertake risks at their own cost. However, seldom they find disturbed while slipping away. They relax selves on reaching the portals after pretty long time.

**The grace from some stranger could play prominent role in your objective for some whip is necessary to wake up an animal lost in deep slumber.**

Let us revert to the saga of Mr. Jitendra Chouhan. The 49-year old entrepreneur established garment stitching unit at 250 square feet space in Ahmadabad, at an estimated capital of some Rs. 80,000 rupee. Does anyone believe *Supremo Clothing Men's Wear* could emerge some day as Gujarat's prime brand *JW*? Today, the brand *JW* has shook brands like Louis Philips, Wills in the south-western Indian state of Gujarat. Mr. Chouhan says, 'People find themselves glorified on wearing my garments. For, my brand garments were always available at one-third the price of other brands in the market.'

Mr. Chouhan has been felicitated by state chief minister Mr. Narendra Modi, for designing his apron. Besides, Adani Group's Gautam Adani, Lloyds Candle's Pankaj Patel, Nirma's Karsen Bhai Patel, and Torrent Group's Sudheer Mehta are some of the customers for Mr. Chouhan.

Most of the NRIs visiting India between December and February of the subsequent year find Chouhan's JW brand very attractive. Today, Chouhan's enterprise is worth some 400 million rupees, with the business sustaining forever.

Mr. Chouhan says, 'My present existence owes to my mother and brother. For, I have gone through such hardships during childhood, when my mother used to stitch the garments of neighbour for our livelihood. I was supporting my mother in her work overnight on my return from school. But, I was always dreaming to become a giant one day. So, I ventured into the business, after my graduation. I became triumphant after much perseverance.'

**Courage and decision are required to manouvre some giant business rather might and money.**

So, do not get discouraged so long as you couldn't enter the pedestals of success. For, merit won't be somebody's begging bowl. Mr. Ratnakar Gutte could be some ideal example to understand about the nitty-gritty of merit. You might have seen many chocolate heroes after completing MBA or IIM from abroad, but have you ever heard any daily wage labourer raising some company worth three billion rupee in the country without having even formal education? The M.D. of Sunil Hi-tech Engineers Ratnar Gutter is such a man.

Mr. Gutte was sent as senior foreman in some foundry to Madhya Pradesh after one year, where he was to monitor work force of 40 people. Sooner, he got some job in BIW at Bhusawal, which was being outsourced by the area's thermoelectric plant. Mr. Gutte was getting Rs.1200/- as salary every month. Some night, success knocked at his doorsteps when he went to watch the movie in local theatre with his wife.

Mr. Gutte recollects about his past, 'I still remember of watching Shratughna Sinha starred movie *Vishwanath*. The screen was empty when the dialogue of the movie went on, when someone cried out my name. I was taken aback, for the proprietor of the firm, Mr. Vinod Jain, where I worked came to meet me. Mr. Jain kept some proposal, which I couldn't turn back. He expected me to become the contractor of the plant with assurance of shouldering the burden, if I encounter any loss. For, it was my premier contract with the thermoelectric plant, followed by mini contracts ahead, when my income reached around Rs. 3,000. I established a small enterprise, *Sunil Engineering Works,* accepting minor contracts, which later became *Sunil Hightech Engineers,* when the turnover touched ten million rupee at the outset. Subsequently, senior executive of BHEL contracted me to prepare blueprint for some 285 million rupee plant, from where I haven't looked back.'

You will come across some people desiring to become successful by sheer hard work. Let me recapitulate with an old anecdote.

The foursome travelled together. The folks came across some deserted haunt piled up with bones of animal corpses. One wise man wondered, 'These are beast lion's bones. I shall assemble them to get some skeleton of lion.'

**Chase not behind an objective, but work damn hard continuously.**

The trio replied, 'OK man, prepare the skeleton.'

The first one chanted some mantra, which made the skeleton of lion to surface.

The second one said, 'I could fill it with flesh and tissues.'

He also filled the skeleton with flesh, tissue wrapped in skin sac, by chanting some other mantra.

The third cried out, 'Now, I could blow this product with live spirit through the success of my mantra.'

The trio intervened, on being frightened, experiencing the presence of the beast alive, 'No, No. Don't do this. Spare us alive.'

The trio fled from the scene, but the fourth one was desperate to try their patience. His mantras brought lion alive, which had its sumptuous meal by devouring him.

Now, the trio fled from the scene on finding the bones of the fourth guy, responsible for fusing living spirit into the beast's skeleton.

The anecdote interprets how, when, why and where, a wise man should experiment his knowledge. For, acquainted with principle is something, but putting them in practice is something else. For, experimenting of such wisdom for reality could have been some easier proposition.

*Jahan log pahunchte hain chhalaang lagaakar*
*Wahaan aapko pahunchna hai dheere-dheere.*

For, ascending the portals of success at one stroke won't keep you encountering risks. For, *Sahajam Karma Kounteya Sadoshamapi tyajet,* meaning the real action being natural could be unfit to abandon. Proceed with natural pace without amplifying such action in the light of inevitable errors quite frequently.

**Imagine if you're on with some objective, you shall equally come across oceans of isolation to fathom across.**

Let us remember the incident with the epic Mahabharata, when Pandavas are in the wild forest with polyandric consort Draupadi. They come across the fragrance of some wonderful flowers. It was a wild forest. She asked, *'Bhima, will you bring that flower?'* Mightiest Bhima was making way by destroying rocks and trees of the jungle. He was also slaying domesticated animals and birds. Meanwhile, monkey-god Hanuman, the product of wind was flying aerially. He realized on finding Bhima's craziness to have turned arrogant out of his prowess. Had he not shed his ego, not only the forest cover could get dwindled but animals would perish forever. Hanuman assumed the form of a giant ape and slept across the forest, on coming down. Bhima cried out, on finding an old ape, *'Oh old monkey, you don't know who am I? Flee from here and make way for us. Else, I shall send you to the heavens by my mace's single stroke.'*

Lord Hanuman replied on his arrogant plea, *'You might be whosoever, but I am pretty agile and infirm. I couldn't wake up my dear. Either you turn back or jump over me, or else, shift my tail aside on your unwillingness.'*

Bhima attempted to lynch Hanuman's tail through his mace. The tail stayed unmoved. Bhima attempted all his might, but the mace couldn't move tail from its place.

Bhima realized him to be some glorified deity, but not an ordinary monkey. He went on tendering apologies with folded palms. Lord Hanuman made his presence through natural form, on waking up. He persuaded Bhima, *'It made me to fly down on finding your arrogance. Now, use your prowess only to achieve the objective. Shed your ego to achieve some objective. One ought to align with failures to reach the pedestals of success. Failures alone steer one to reach the path of success. However, success doesn't have any corrupt knowledge.'*

Indian Army always prioritizes with such candidates who remain unmoved from minor issues or obstacles. He should be competent enough to command during training or on the battle front. For, army doesn't call for any wisdom. People might have lesser information about the rejection of celluloid veteran Amitabh Bachchan or former president APJ Abdul Kalam into the Indian Army.

**Accustom to some natural instincts for, habits simulate stranded rope that couldn't be easily broken.**

The top echelon officers were selected after serious deliberation in the Defence Institute of Psychological Research (DIPR). Apart from this, the officer gets scrutinized from the group testing officer, and the interviewing authority. The trio had their own shades of opinion on the selection of senior incumbent. She/he will be rejected had there be any weaker personality of expression, or poor physique, poor tolerance or suffering from poor internal aptitude or coordination.

Let me recollect an old anecdote. An old cat reached another enclave hunting for its night meal. It encountered with youthful cat, which was desperately perambulating in a sphere to catch hold of its tail. The old cat objected the youthful cat, *'What are you doing my kitten?'*

The youthful cat whispered, *'Someone told me that success, fortune and happiness were sitting on my tail. I ought to touch the edge of my tail, which could bring me utter happiness forever.'*

The old cat wondered, *'I am elder to you by age. I also knew that success, fortune, and happiness lay coolly on the topmost edge of my tail. However, I seldom attempt to touch it.'*

*'Why! Don't you dream of living life with utmost comfort and fortune?' asked the youthful cat, curiously.*

*'Certainly, I ought to possess, but I work at my level with utmost hardship. I get life with utmost comfort wherever I go,'* replied the old cat.

*'How come you get?'* asked the youthful cat.

*'My tail stays in its place, wherever I go. It is not necessary for me to catch,'* confiding so, the old cat proceeded ahead.

The anecdote lays store the mantra of success. It says 'Chase not success from behind, but do your work. For, the action alone would reach you towards its pedestal.'

**Life looks beautiful with pluses and minuses galore but the important aspect that should be accounted for how to reach the objective voluntarily.**

You could understand this justification from the saga of M.K. Gandhi. The opponents were busy in criticising him through various state legislative assemblies across the country. For, he was not backing the British Imperialism that colonised India. He was moving through paddy fields to share with farmers and farming labourers about his hardships, in hiding. The entire country expressed its confidence through endorsement, when he didn't have any political power to eke out his livelihood. He compelled the British to kneel down before his qualities of showing empathy, courage, through frequent fasting and upholding morality.

Dr Thomas Cohen in his title, *'The structure of scientific revolution,'* claimed that *Gandhi was triumphant in transforming his success into traditional concepts.*

India's ace trekker Ms Parul has become triumphant in her career, following the principles of Gandhi. She desires to hoist Indian tricolor on the cliff of every mountain, which could glorify the country forever. For, her objective was to transform some failure into success under extreme hardship. She voluntarily claims, 'Our trekking team has ten members, nine Indians and one African woman. Two of them lay unconscious on scaling an altitude of some 18,000 feet, due to the exhaustion of oxygen cylinder. I went on suspecting similar condition for myself, but dared to hoist tricolour on the cliff of Mt. Kilimanjaro. Now, I dream to hoist the tricolour after scaling Mt. Everest.'

Now, you will come across Ms. Neha Aggarwal. She has glorified India on being qualified at recently held Beijing Olympics, at the tender age of 18. Ms Neha Aggarwal and Mr Sharat Kamal are table tennis players who have emerged as top seeds for India. Ms. Neha has given equal attention to studies and games at tender age.

Last year, I had been to Beijing when I visualized three monks, but nobody knew from where they have landed. Local Chinese were finding them pretty ugly.

I asked them, *'Who are you?'*

The trio laughed at one another on observing me. They went into guffaw on my reiteration, when I joined their laughter. Slowly, our laughter sustained when I realized them to have been glorified as monks.

I ventured again, *'Why are you laughing at my question?'*

One of the monks, replied, *'You're asking us seriously about any of our answers could prove vulnerable for us ahead. For, you would be serious about each of our answers.'*

The second monk replied, *'We folk's seldom take life seriously. For, seriousness means that the tangible universe has some sop. We find the universe pretty insipid and some fun. However, we face obstacles from people like you, who take life seriously. So, we are laughing about you as damn innocent, accounting life so seriously.'*

**No glorified person has rolled out on earth without the caliper of hopes for none could glorify without dip in the ocean of hopes.**

The third monk intervened, *'We are laughing so because some enthusiasm has freaked in our veins endorsing us to take any decision ahead without much ado.'*

The assertion of third monk was somewhat significant, for he has justified anyone to accomplish any task under laughter easily.

The anecdote makes us to sift through the principle of laughter with founder and chair person of Jet Airways, Mr. Naresh Goyal. You would disbelieve on meeting with jolly-looking personality to have flown in some jungle above hilly terrains. He was to fathom pretty long to reach his primary school before shimmering on the runway of aviation.

Mr. Goyal used to get some three hundred rupee salary, when he was selling airline tickets. However, the same job made him take off through vision, which got transformed into the establishment of domestic airlines anew. He christened his dream, Jet Airways.

Mr Naresh Goyal, the maiden private airliner boss has not only taken off on domestic runways but abroad. During his interview, Mr. Goyal admits about the secret of his success, *'Happiness is somebody's personal capital, which is inherent with everybody. It calls for the concentration of mind but not money to mobilize capital. The account could be initiated on zero balance, but it requires the capital of sentiments. This is the secret of my success.'*

**The quantum of energy amasses unbelievable when you go extremely elated, steering of which you could have success beyond your comprehension.**

'Altruistic opinion, real confidence, trusting on goodness, affection, love, friendship and decent business could get you unbelievable happiness. Happiness could be less exhaustive if one extends cooperation and behave politely in place of road rage. It is also true that most of the airliners take off on definite routes at definite intervals, eventually reaching the destination safe,' adds Goyal.

So, fulfill your dreams what Mr. Naresh Goyal asserts with us. You could be triumphant quicker, for it is the boon of Nature, for every individual on earth.

So, Cecil B Mellow producing his historic movie, *The Ten Commandments* has said, *'Breaking laws is not so easy for us. For, we shall break if we break the laws.'*

Always attempt to stay aloof from others while reading this book. Ponder for a while over the enumerated facts ascertain the manner in which your brain has functioned. Is it swift and vigilant? Do you feel your brain to have been divided into two halves? It has been functioning mentally aside wondering whether mere browsing could make one financially rich on earth. On the other hand, it is justifying what have you achieved by mere reading?

However, you should duplicate those guru mantras into your memory and appreciate them through natural instincts.

It should resemble *some good engineer realizing about the scores of pressures and strengths effecting in bringing the blue print out.*

*A good teacher does evaluate the entire class room before getting into teach.*

*A good guardian understands about the habits a child had been acquainted with.*

Appreciating something unbelievable is part of nature's principle, whose reality gets reflected in every field of one's life. It is general principle; which is pretty comprehensive, but more powerful as far as mutual relations are concerned.

I wish to let you know about my personal experience, before finishing my dissertation. Nature has got intrinsic principles. It remains the virtual source of lord, the Almighty, caring for flora and fauna across continents. It owes to one's own conscience.

The principles I have enumerated in my book were experimented by the world's corporate giants, as their personalized experiences. I have deeply studied their autobiographies and infused the gist of what they have had in life in this book. I have drafted sequentially through scientific justifications so that you could understand and imbibe those individual principles in your life.

**Sit with confidence on some rock or aside pond-bank during spare moments, for you could visualize without aberration about your objective.**

I believe you could have been obsessed from the scores of anecdotes and quotations I have borrowed from epics and Scriptures at random. I understand that you could apply them as incidental corollaries in your practical life and emerge triumphant in the days ahead. For, millions of successful people have already emerged triumphant through mere reading of autobiographies of giants.

Now, it is your turn. So, sharpen your hacksaw blade. You need sharpest blades for felling giant trees and cut their timber for practical use. I understand that sharpening the blade of your hacksaw blade means honing the skills of your brain through serious reading. You could emulate them later in life as enshrined in my earliest chapters. So, read them quite frequently so long as you endorse most of those principles alive in practice.

Once, sage Narada queried lord Shiva, *'Oh my lord! You're fulfilling the ambitions of human beings since millions of years. Why Indians are still poor in comparison with Americans?'*

Lord Shiva replied, *'Go to planet earth. Ask Indians what they want in life so that they could become opulent like fellow Americans.'*

Sage Narada obeyed lord Shiva. He reached most of Indian cities and verified by interviewing one after another, what she / he wants in life. Someone sought money, some one desired for begetting child, somebody else desired to build a house, another businessman sought success, and yet another desired to get his daughter married, but the rest wished to become successful.'

**Embrace slew of failures with regards but without destruction. For, they alone shall usher you the path of success.**

Sage Narada approached lord Shiva again, after compiling those requests, *'Oh my lord! I have traversed across Indian townships. I met with thousands of individuals. I have come to this conclusion that everyone is desirous of enjoying mundane comforts without any effort. Nobody sought me the formula to win over slew of predicaments through systematic regulation of mind.'*

Lord Shiva replied smilingly, *'I wish to emphasize that Indians are pretty poor for they are desirous of getting everything on earth without working hard. They always find selves infatuated with attachment and illusion. I reiterate that Indians shall remain forever miserable unless and until they work hard to fulfil their ambitions on earth.'*

Meanwhile, lord Vishnu intervened aptly, 'The people establish rapport with desires galore in mind, the moment they beget such thoughts. The more they make efforts in fulfilling them through firm will power, the more it would make them poorer.

However, I believe, one needs to be optimistic and have full faith in meeting with desires begotten. The entire universe sustains on such faith. Americans subsist on principles of hope, and so is India. Let me recollect a bit of history at this juncture.

Someone asked, when Sikander, the great was on his voyage across Asia Minor, *'Why have you opted for this drive under whose courtesy?'*

Sikander replied smilingly, *'Under the courtesy of my hopes, for they hang on to me till I breathe my last.'*

We find French emperor Napoleon Bonaparte was not let down under dire consequences when one of his trusted friends queried, *'The work you've undertaken would be impossible to accomplish.'*

Napoleon often replied, *'The term impossible could be found in the vocabulary of cowards, but not with me. I am virtually confident on the strength of my hopes.'*

We also find Indian warrior Maharana Pratap, whose cord of hope seldom broke. He sustained his warfare activities despite hiding in the bushes across the jungle.

You shall find the biography of Joan of Arc, in the title, *'Hot Thinking,'* wherein it was mentioned, *'Abandon everything, but leave not your hope. For, hope alone would bestow happiness, opulence and success forever.'*

So, hope extends the biggest support for mankind. One day, you will certainly get that for which you longed through hope. For, the issues of opulence, objective and success beget from your own mind. The ideas enlivened through hope shall have unique characteristics.

**Assimilating the ideas incorporated in this book after serious reading could influence you with the harmonised ocean replete with infinite ideas. You could believe the book as other epic versions of Bhagavad-Gita and the Ramayana from ordinary point of view.**

Try to have their support once in your life. You could realise how much support have they been lending. Make up your firm objective and find how your hope could get fulfilled.

Every triumphant giant in the world has accomplished each of his objectives through these principles. Now, you ought to accomplish such objectives in your life by emulating those principles.

I wish to end up my thesis on this note that you always think big, become big and fulfil your dreams. For, this is a unique book that could transform your overall life.

*Log kahte hain ki yah ek kitaab hain.*
*Lekin main kahta hun ki yah ek khwab hai.*

• The End •

Good thoughts
flash voluntarily
while doing
**evil acts.**
Thoughts are magnetic and
every thought
vibrates at particular
**frequency**.
The moment you feel bad,
they will hit the
**cosmos**
and bounce back
**at the same frequency.**

www.ingramcontent.com/pod-product-compliance
Lightning Source LLC
Chambersburg PA
CBHW031321230926
51848CB00001B/44
* 9 7 8 8 1 2 8 8 2 2 9 7 1 *